Off the
Beaten Path®

ohio

Help Us Keep This Guide Up to Date

Every effort has been made by the authors and editors to make this guide as accurate and useful as possible. However, many changes can occur after a guide is published—establishments close, phone numbers change, hiking trails are rerouted, facilities come under new management, etc.

We would love to hear from you concerning your experiences with this guide and how you feel it could be improved and be kept up to date. While we may not be able to respond to all comments and suggestions, we'll take them to heart, and we'll make certain to share them with the authors. Please send your comments and suggestions to the following address:

The Globe Pequot Press
Reader Response/Editorial Department
P.O. Box 480
Guilford, CT 06437

Or you may e-mail us at: editorial@GlobePequot.com

Thanks for your input, and happy travels!

INSIDERS' GUIDE®

OFF THE BEATEN PATH® SERIES

Off the Beaten Path®

ELEVENTH EDITION

ohio

A GUIDE TO UNIQUE PLACES

GEORGE AND
CAROL ZIMMERMANN

INSIDERS' GUIDE®

GUILFORD, CONNECTICUT
AN IMPRINT OF THE GLOBE PEQUOT PRESS

The prices, rates, and hours listed in this guidebook
were confirmed at press time. We recommend,
however, that you call establishments to obtain
current information before traveling.

To buy books in quantity for corporate use
or incentives, call **(800) 962–0973**
or e-mail **premiums@GlobePequot.com.**

INSIDERS' GUIDE®

Text design by Linda R. Loiewski
Maps by Equator Graphics © Morris Book Publishing, LLC
Illustrations on pages 78, 119, 188, 214, and 228 by Carole Drong. All other
illustrations by Keith Knore.
Spot photography throughout © Pyramid Hill Sculpture Park & Museum, Hamilton,
Ohio

ISSN 1539-8196
ISBN 978-0-7627-4427-5

Manufactured in the United States of America
Eleventh Edition/First Printing

To Brian, America's best son.

NORTHWEST OHIO

Toledo

Cleveland

NORTHEAST OHIO

Akron

Lima

Mansfield

Canton

WEST CENTRAL OHIO

EAST CENTRAL OHIO

Newark

Columbus

Dayton

Lancaster

SOUTHWEST OHIO

SOUTHEAST OHIO

Cincinnati

Contents

Acknowledgments

Our thanks to the Ohio Department of Natural Resources and the Ohio Historical Society for providing supplemental information and materials about many of the places described in this book. Their cooperation made researching *Ohio Off the Beaten Path* a productive and enjoyable endeavor.

Introduction

Ohio is an excellent state to explore—it has breathtaking natural beauty, a rich historical heritage, countless fine restaurants, and varied and unique overnight lodging. *Ohio Off the Beaten Path* exposes the reader to Ohio's best—from rolling pastoral farmland to rugged wooded cliffs and gorges, from restored canal towns and gristmills to country inns and working historical farms. After years of researching and traveling the state, we can only conclude that Ohio offers a wealth of opportunities for recreation, for appreciating the history that shaped its present and future, and for pleasurable excursions to suit any tastes or interests.

Most of the destinations described in this book, be they historical, culinary, or recreational, are located away from interstate highways and major metropolitan areas—an indication of our preference for scenic roads and picturesque towns and villages (traveling by interstate highway just does not provide the enjoyment of winding through forests and cresting hills on a narrow, two-lane country road). To take full advantage of *Ohio Off the Beaten Path,* you will need an Ohio highway map. The Ohio Division of Travel and Tourism will mail you a map at no charge if you call (800) BUCKEYE. The Division of Travel and Tourism can also provide another valuable service—confirmation of specific information on thousands of sites and attractions around the state. Although every effort has been made to ensure that addresses, phone numbers, rates, hours, and seasons of the places described in this book are accurate at the time of publication, establishments do change owners or hours of operation, relocate, and even close. For this reason, we advise taking advantage of the state's toll-free service to verify important information before making that two- or three-hour drive. Another excellent resource is the Division of Travel and Tourism's Web site, www.discoverohio.com, which includes links to hundreds of other Ohio tourism Web sites.

Whether spending a week, a weekend, or just an afternoon traveling to a new destination, you will probably find as we did that Ohio's friendly people and splendid countryside make any trip that much more rewarding. And if you have yet to experience the state's historic and recreational opportunities, we believe you will be impressed and amazed by all Ohio has to offer.

Ohio Facts

- **Nickname:** Buckeye State
- **Capital:** Columbus
- **Population:** 11,464,042

- **Admitted to Union:** Ohio became the seventeenth state when it was admitted on February 19, 1803.
- **Major Cities and Populations:** Columbus, 711,470; Cleveland, 478,403; Cincinnati, 331,285; Toledo, 313,619; Akron, 217,074; Dayton, 166,179
- **Famous Residents:** William Henry Harrison, Ulysses S. Grant, Rutherford B. Hayes, James Garfield, Benjamin Harrison, William McKinley, William Howard Taft, Warren G. Harding, Harriet Beecher Stowe, James Thurber, George A. Custer, Johnny Appleseed, Wilbur and Orville Wright, Neil Armstrong, John Glenn, Charles Goodyear, John D. Rockefeller, Thomas Edison, Clark Gable, Bob Hope
- **Travel Information:** Contact the Ohio Division of Travel and Tourism at (800) BUCKEYE or www.discoverohio.com.
- **State Parks:** Contact Ohio State Parks at (614) 265–6561, (877) 678–3337, (800) AT–A–PARK, or www.ohiodnr.com.
- **State Song:** "Beautiful Ohio"
- **State Rock Song:** "Hang on Sloopy"
- **State Wildflower:** White trillium
- **State Flower:** Red carnation
- **State Bird:** The cardinal
- **State Tree:** The buckeye
- **State Animal:** White-tailed deer
- **State Motto:** "With God All Things Are Possible"

Northeast Ohio

Cuyahoga Valley

Tranquil, stream-fed Chippewa Lake provides the setting for an outstanding country dining establishment, the *Oaks Lakeside.* Eight acres of tall trees surround this rambling former estate, which rests a stone's throw from the water. Railroad industrialist J.F. Townsend remodeled this former farmhouse in 1914, using it to entertain such captains of industry as J. Pierpont Morgan. Townsend dubbed the place Five Oaks for the semicircle of oak trees that graced the front of the home at the time.

Don Casper and Al Hitchins purchased the Medina County property in 1961 and earned a reputation for an innovative menu and an impressive kitchen. Today, Don's niece, Bonnie Casper Drushal, maintains the family's tradition of gracious elegance and outstanding cuisine. Each of the four dining areas has its own distinct character, and the large windows allow a view of the spacious patio—a perfect spot for a cocktail or after-dinner drink—and the gazebo at water's edge.

Dinner at the Oaks Lakeside includes dishes such as rack of lamb, roast prime rib (Friday and Saturday only), several cuts of steak, and veal gesina, which is veal sautéed in wine, butter, and mushrooms. Seafood fans can choose from Alaskan king

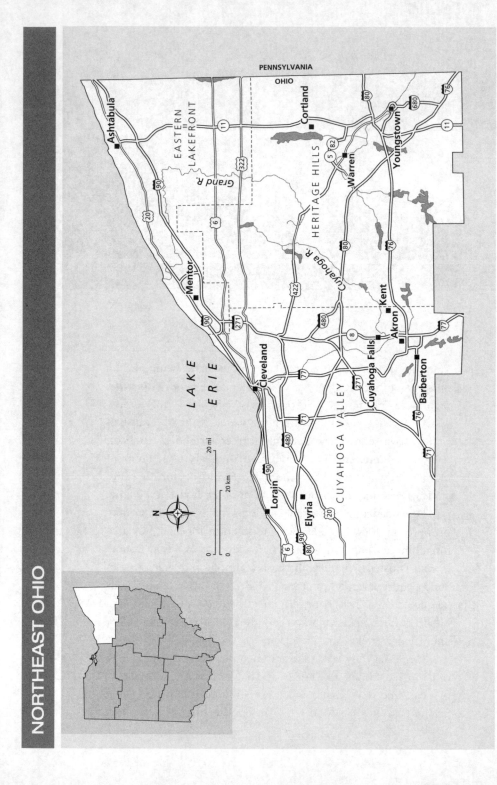

crab legs, fresh pickerel, shrimp tempura, and the broiled shore dinner—a combination of orange roughy, scampi, tomatoes, mushrooms, peppers, and onions served on a skewer. A favorite with many regulars here is the broiled scampi in parsley and garlic butter served in individual chafing dishes.

A fine dinner salad distinguishes a quality restaurant from an ordinary one, and an Oaks Lakeside salad comes brimming with carrots, cucumbers, and tomatoes. For your choice of potato, try the unusual potatoes Anna—pan-fried spuds smothered in onions and peppers. The lodge's luxurious desserts include Grand Marnier chocolate mousse, chocolate cheesecake, and an assortment of parfaits. From the fresh flowers and stylish decor (the lodge has won several awards for interior design) to the culinary expertise, the Oaks Lakeside rates high marks.

The Oaks Lakeside is at 5878 Longacre Lane, Chippewa Lake; (330) 769–2601, (800) 922–5736; www.theoakslodge.com. Open daily from 5:00 P.M. to closing, closed Mondays January through March. American Express, Master-Card, and Visa are accepted.

AUTHORS' FAVORITES

- Oaks Lakeside
- Hickories Museum
- Allen Memorial Art Museum
- Crawford Auto-Aviation Museum
- Healthspace Cleveland
- Rock and Roll Hall of Fame and Museum
- Hale Farm and Village
- Blossom Music Center
- National Inventors Hall of Fame
- Akron Art Museum
- Stan Hywet Hall
- Perkins Stone Mansion
- John Brown House
- Portage House
- Kent State University Museum

- Youngstown Historical Center of Industry and Labor
- Butler Institute of American Art/ Arms Family Museum of Local History
- Mill Creek MetroParks
- Alessi's at the Welshfield Inn
- Middlefield Cheese House
- Burton Sugar Camp
- Century Village
- Richards Maple Products
- Alpine Valley Ski Area
- Holden Arboretum
- Lake Farmpark
- Chalet Debonne Vineyards
- Claire's Grand River Vineyard
- Old Tavern

You have to love a museum whose mission is "preserving a segment of America's dairy heritage and America's love of ice cream and its history for future generations to enjoy." *America's Ice Cream & Dairy Museum* is housed in what used to be an 8,000-square-foot dairy plant. The Abell family, who runs the museum, started in the dairy business in the 1830s delivering milk door to door in Cleveland. In 1927, the family purchased land in Medina County to begin the Elm Farm Dairy. Though the dairy business closed in 1979, the family preserved their dairy heritage by opening the museum and ice-cream parlor. Along with photo displays chronicling the long history of dairy operations and ice cream, there are vehicles and machines that many children of today will not recognize. There is a milk delivery wagon from around 1900— the horse-drawn kind—and a motorized version from the 1930s. Examples of hand-processing equipment, such as butter churns and milk separators, are displayed along with a re-creation of the "modern" dairy operation of the 1930s. Soda fountains from the 1870s and early 1900s give you a glimpse back in time when the best, and often only, ice-cream flavor was vanilla. Of course, once you see all the dairy displays and walk by the ice-cream truck, you may be interesting in living, or at least tasting, the fruits of this ice-cream tradition. The museum has provided for that as well. They have converted the dairy's cooler, or refrigerator, into a working ice-cream parlor, styled after those popular in the 1890s. You can sit at the 20-foot-long marble soda fountain counter and enjoy ice cream that is still hand-made on the premises. Of course, that ice cream can be fashioned into a super soda or a spectacular banana split. For Ohio State fans, try a couple of scoops of Ohio Buckeye (chocolate and peanut butter).

America's Ice Cream & Dairy Museum is at 1050 Lafayette Road, Medina; (330) 722–3839; www.elmfarm.com. Open April through November, Tuesday through Sunday, noon to 5:00 P.M.

Medina County is also the location of a unique annual occurrence—Ohio's equivalent of the swallows returning to Capistrano. Each year on March 15, seventy-five turkey vultures come home to roost in trees by the cliffs and caverns of Whipp's Ledges near Hinckley. With clocklike regularity, the buzzards have returned to this summer home for the past 150 years. Hinckley townspeople mark the occasion with celebrations on the first Sunday after March 15, when a "buzzard breakfast" is served.

The architect was Arthur Oviatt; the owner, Arthur Lovett Garford. The result of their vision: one of the finest residences in northeast Ohio, now the *Hickories Museum.*

Construction on this massive nineteen-room stone-and-shingle home began in 1894 and cost Garford $100,000. On the large corner lot stand many of the original shag-bark hickory trees from which came the name Hickories.

Within its walls are Tiffany-style windows, six fireplaces, twelve built-in seats, and approximately sixty carved faces. Features are the grand staircase, pier mirrors, a Gothic chapel, and a bull moose head given to Mr. Garford by Teddy Roosevelt. An opulent Victorian bathroom as well as a restored master bedroom and guest room can be seen on the second floor.

Garford was a young banker when he hopped on a newfangled high-wheeled vehicle, the bicycle. A rough ride on the bike's hard seat launched a new career for A.L.—he invented a padded bicycle seat, which made him a millionaire. His interests would grow to include such diverse items as golf balls, telephone parts, lighting fixtures, and steel; he also became involved in car and truck manufacturing, mining, and publishing.

The Hickories Museum is at 509 Washington Avenue, Elyria; (440) 322–3341; www.lchs.org. Open for tours Tuesday through Friday, 1:00 to 4:00 P.M.; Saturday, 1:00 to 3:00 P.M. Admission: adults $5.00, children $3.00.

Founded in 1917, the ***Allen Memorial Art Museum*** at Oberlin College is ranked as one of the finest college or university collections in the nation. Cass Gilbert designed the original building; he also designed four other buildings for Oberlin College between 1907 and 1931. The museum's contemporary addition, designed by Robert Venturi, opened in 1977.

The museum's collection consists of some 11,000 objects from ancient Egypt to contemporary America. Collection highlights include Dutch and Flemish paintings of the seventeenth century, European art of the late nineteenth and twentieth centuries, and contemporary American art. Of particular note are the Mary A. Ainsworth collection of Japanese woodblock prints, the Charles Martin Hall collection of Islamic carpets, the Joseph and Enid Bissett collection of modern European paintings, and a comprehensive collection of Old Master prints, including Rembrandt and Dürer. The museum also has a growing collection of African and African-

birthplaceof aluminum

We have Charles M. Hall to thank for a world full of aluminum siding and aluminum everything else. Born in Thompson on December 6, 1863, Hall's family moved to Oberlin. Along with a country full of scientists, he had been trying to find a cheap way to make aluminum; Hall did his experiments in an old woodshed while still in high school.

Hall attended Oberlin College, where he continued to experiment. Eight months after graduating, the twenty-two-year-old discovered the process he and the others had been seeking. After a patent dispute with a French scientist claiming the same invention, Hall secured capital from Andrew Mellon and built what became the American Aluminum Company. Hall died in 1914, leaving a substantial bequest to Oberlin College.

American art. In addition to the galleries, a number of sculptures can be found on the museum's well-manicured grounds. Be sure to tour the Frank Lloyd Wright home on the grounds—built in 1950, this is an example of the compact Usonian houses he created for middle-class families.

The Allen Memorial Art Museum is at 87 North Main Street, Oberlin; (440) 775–8665; www.oberlin.edu/allenart. Open Tuesday through Saturday, 10:00 A.M. to 5:00 P.M.; Sunday, 1:00 to 5:00 P.M. No admission charge. Tours of the Frank Lloyd Wright Usonian House are offered the first and third Sunday of each month, noon to 4:00 P.M.

Take the high road or take the low road, but those wishing for a wee bit of Scotland in Ohio should take to the road in late June to celebrate the Ohio Scottish Game Weekend in Oberlin. Visitors can enjoy the colorful Scottish games and the traditional dress in the parade of clan tartans. In addition there is a competition among the pipe and drum corps. The event is held in late June in Oberlin. Visit www.ohioscottishgames.com for information.

One of the best car collections you'll find is the **Crawford Auto-Aviation Museum** in Cleveland. The collection tells the history of technological as well as stylistic changes and developments in the auto industry. With some 200 cars in the collection, the vehicles range from the famous to the obscure, from a Model T to a modern Jaguar. For example, the visitor can admire a rare 1897 Panhard et Lavassor, which was the first automobile to enclose the passenger area and protect the occupants from the elements. The car enthusiast can also view the 1982 Indy car driven by Ohio's own Bobby Rahal.

Since car manufacturing is now centered on a few dominant companies, many people may not know just how many small automotive manufacturers existed in the early 1900s. The Crawford Auto-Aviation Museum highlights the remarkable number of carmakers that were located in the Cleveland area. Between 1898 and 1931 more than eighty makes of cars were produced here, including the Winton Bullet. Alexander Winton was the leading automotive pioneer in Cleveland, selling his first car in 1898. The Winton Bullet held the land-speed record in 1902 and is on display in the museum.

Along with the car collection, the museum also features bikes, motorcycles, and aircraft. The centerpiece of the aviation collection is a 1912 Curtiss Hydroaeroplane, which was once piloted by Cleveland aviator Al Engel.

This museum is part of a larger complex, the Western Reserve Historical Society's University Circle. This campuslike setting also houses a history museum in a turn-of-the-century mansion. A visitor to this museum can go on a mansion tour and view a costume collection and various special displays. Also nearby is the renowned Cleveland Museum of Art. The Western Reserve Historical Society's library is one of the best genealogical resources in the nation.

The Crawford Auto-Aviation Museum is located at 10825 East Boulevard, Cleveland; (216) 721–5722; www.wrhs.org. Open Monday through Saturday, 10:00 A.M. to 5:00 P.M.; Sunday, noon to 5:00 P.M. Admission: adults $8.50; children (ages 6 to 12) $5.00.

HealthSpace Cleveland is the old Health Museum of Cleveland, reborn from the foundation up in a completely new 81,000-square-foot structure, but still fulfilling the vital mission of educating families and individuals about making healthy choices for life. The museum spans the entire block between East Eighty-ninth and East Ninetieth streets in Cleveland, in the University Circle area.

Hundreds of thousands of people, young and old, remember their school field trip or family visit to the Health Museum of Cleveland, where they met Juno, the Transparent Talking Woman and the Big Tooth. Now at HealthSpace Cleveland, new audiences are experiencing the museum in a more powerful, interactive way—and a new, third-generation Juno is there to greet each guest.

HeadFirst! is a multistory, interactive theater in the form of a stylized walk-in "head" where visitors become immersed in an environment that teaches real-life decision-making scenarios. Stress Yard is a multimedia experience that uses visualization booths and Stress Man, an urban sculpture, to demonstrate how the body reacts to and manages stressful situations. The Go-Go Grill uses a full-sized concession truck with videos, music, and dance to teach young people about healthy, nutritious eating.

HealthSpace of Cleveland is at 8911 Euclid Avenue, Cleveland; (216) 231–5010; www.healthspacecleveland.org. Open Wednesday through Friday, 10:00 A.M. to 4:30 P.M.; Saturday, 10:00 A.M. to 4:30 P.M.; Sunday, noon to 4:30 P.M. Admission: adults $7.00; children $5.00.

If you haven't had your fill of health and science, head down Euclid Avenue to the **Dittrick Museum of Medical History.** This museum presents the medical history of Cleveland and the Western Reserve. Exhibits trace advances in diagnostic technology from the stethoscope to the X-ray machine. Visitors inspect an array of early surgical instruments, bloodletting tools, and the museum's collection of microscopes. Also featured are two complete and furnished doctors' offices, one from 1880 and the other from 1930.

The Dittrick Museum of Medical History is on the third floor of the Allen Memorial Medical Library at 11000 Euclid Avenue, Cleveland; (216) 368–3648; www.cwru.edu/artsci/dittrick/site2/. Open Monday through Friday, 10:00 A.M. to 4:00 P.M. No admission charge.

Most critics have and will continue to debate the location of the birthplace of rock and roll, but there's no debate that Cleveland has now provided a home for rock with the opening of the **Rock and Roll Hall of Fame and Museum.** The spectacular $92 million facility overlooks Lake Erie. Designed by renowned architect I.M. Pei, the 150,000-square-foot building consists of bold geometric forms and dramatic spaces anchored by a 162-foot tower.

Rock fans of all ages will discover memorabilia from all phases of rock and roll, from its birth in the fifties, its explosion in the sixties, and its evolution to the present. Among the highlights of this most extensive collection are John Lennon's Sgt. Pepper uniform and the Rickenbacker guitar he used at the Shea Stadium concert, the black leather stage outfit Elvis wore during his 1968 "comeback" TV special, Tina Turner's "Acid Queen" costume from the movie *Tommy,* Jim Morrison's Cub Scout uniform, and Jimi Hendrix's handwritten lyrics to "Purple Haze." The original recording equipment from Sam Phillips's Memphis Recording Service is on display, along with Janis Joplin's psychedelic Porsche convertible.

Music plays throughout the museum, except in the actual top-floor Hall of Fame. Film and video presentations trace the history of rock and offer snapshots of its various incarnations and tangents. If you are or ever have been a fan of rock and roll, this is a must-see.

The Rock and Roll Hall of Fame and Museum is at One Key Plaza, 751 Erieside Avenue, Cleveland; (216) 781–7625; www.Rockhall.com. Open daily, 10:00 A.M. to 5:30 P.M. (until 9:00 P.M. on Wednesday). Admission: adults $20.00; children (ages 9 to 12) $11.00.

northolmstedto andfrom

Talk about "necessity being the mother of invention"! The mayor of North Olmsted was given one week's notice that the railway connecting his community with Cleveland was calling it quits. Mayor Charles Seltzer had until midnight February 28, 1931, to find a way to get 150 of his constituents to work.

His solution: that North Olmsted start a municipal bus line, the first in Ohio. The City Council concurred, and they all scrambled to purchase two used buses and two sets of license plates and hire two drivers. At 5:00 A.M. March 1, two freshly painted red and white coaches hit the road, changing Ohio transportation history.

Looking for an unusual tour or for a unique setting for lunch or dinner? Then be ready to board the **Goodtime III.** This 1,000-passenger boat offers two-hour sightseeing tours Tuesday through Sunday and has provided a great way to see Cleveland since 1958. As you cruise by, your guide will help you learn more about the area. The boat offers indoor and outdoor seating so you can tour even if the weather is not perfect. Along with sightseeing you can also enjoy a box or buffet lunch. Dance and dinner cruises sail on Friday and Saturday evenings.

Goodtime III is at 825 East Ninth Street Pier, Cleveland; (216) 861–5110; www.goodtimeiii.com. The summer sailing schedule runs from June 15 through Labor Day; limited sailings in May and September. Tours are avail-

ALSO WORTH SEEING

Great Lakes Science Center,
Cleveland

Cleveland Museum of Art

Cleveland MetroPark Zoo

Cleveland Children's Museum

The "Flats" entertainment and dining dining district,
Cleveland

able Tuesday through Sunday at noon and 3:00 P.M. Dinner and dance cruises are offered Friday and Saturday. Tour rates: adults $15.00; children $9.00; luncheon cruise: $24.75; dinner and dance cruise: $45.95. For the luncheon or dinner and dance cruise, be sure to call ahead for reservations. Ask about departure times for the evening cruise.

For more cruising and dining, board the **Nautica Queen.** Buffet lunches, brunches, and dinners are part of the sightseeing experience aboard this pleasure cruise. You glide by the "Flats," parks, and view the Cleveland skyline while munching on a wide variety of salads, entrees, and desserts. There are outdoor observation decks so you can enjoy the sun or stars during your approximately two-hour voyage. The dining areas are enclosed so that a bit of foul weather won't put a damper on the dining experience. When you call for information you might want to ask about the *Nautica's* special events. You might enjoy one of their theme cruises, or have the staff plan something special for a birthday or anniversary.

The *Nautica Queen* is located at 1153 Main Avenue (on the West Bank of the Flats), Cleveland; (216) 696–8888, (800) 837–0604; www.nauticaqueen.com. Sails April through December. Lunch cruises: Monday through Friday, noon; Saturday, 11:00 A.M.; Sunday, 1:00 P.M. Dinner cruises: Monday through Thursday, 7:00 P.M.; Friday and Saturday, 7:30 P.M. Lunch cruise prices: adults $23.95; children $13.95. Dinner cruise prices: adults $39.95 to $44.95; children $18.95 to $22.95. Sunday brunch prices: adults $31.95; children $15.95.

The North Union Colony of Shakers was established here in 1822 and thrived for sixty-seven years. This unique religious group of more than 200 people stressed social justice, freedom, and equality of men and women. They built their own school and cared for orphans. They farmed and sold their apple products, herbs, and high-quality, simple handmade furniture. When the community declined, the Shakers' property was sold to a real estate company and developed to become Shaker Heights.

The ***Shaker Historical Museum*** occupies a Tudor-style mansion facing Horseshoe Lake. The Shaker Historical Society presents exhibits about the

Shakers, the development of Shaker Heights by the Van Sweringen brothers, as well as seasonal displays, programs, and events. The museum shop offers books, herbs, candles, cards, and Shaker-style boxes and carriers.

The Shaker Historical Museum is located at 16740 South Park Boulevard, Shaker Heights; (216) 921–1201; www.ohiohistory.org/places/shaker. Open: Tuesday through Friday and Sunday, 2:00 to 5:00 P.M. Admission: adults $2.00; children (ages six to eighteen) $1.00.

Pigs, ponies, and a gaggle of geese are likely to greet visitors to the **Stearns Homestead.** The Parma Area Historical Society, mostly with a lot of volunteer labor, has saved a little chunk of rural Ohio and preserved the Stearns Homestead in the midst of urban growth. The Stearns family built the farmhouse in 1855. When the Gibbs family bought the farm, they added a second house in 1919. A barn, which is tilting a little to the west, is home to an unlikely vehicle collection: a 1948 fire engine and a horse carriage once used by President William McKinley. The collection of farm animals delights visiting children, and volunteers sell feed so you can offer a treat to one of these four-legged inhabitants. There are also a variety of special events at the farm throughout the summer months, such as ice-cream socials and antiques markets.

The Stearns Homestead is at 6975 Ridge Road, Parma; (440) 845–9770; www.parma-oh.com/stearns/stearns.html. Open late May to late October, Saturday and Sunday, 1:00 to 4:00 P.M. Admission is free but donations are welcomed.

The Western Reserve region of Ohio was "reserved" for settlers moving west from Connecticut after the American Revolution. One of those settlers,

Twins Day Festival

You'll be seeing double, but that's to be expected if you visit Twinsburg for the annual Twins Day Festival. What better place than Twinsburg to host a national gathering of those special siblings whom we call twins?

Matched sets of brothers and sisters come from all over the nation to gather for this celebration of duality. Infants and oldsters and in-betweeners all attend. Some are so close in looks and dress, down to the hat, the socks, or the tie tack, that you have to wonder how even their mothers and fathers tell them apart!

Triplets, quadruplets, and beyond are also welcome. To add to the fun of celebrating these look-alikes, there's a parade, a fireworks display, arts and crafts, food, of course, and even a golf tournament (with identical twins on the course, keeping the scoring straight could be a challenge).

The Twins Day Festival is held the first weekend in August in Twinsburg. For more information call (330) 425–3652 (or get your twin to call) or visit www.twinsday.org.

Medina Ice Festival,
Medina, February;
(800) 463–3462

Geauga County Maple Festival,
Chardon, April;
(440) 286–3007;
www.maplefestival.com

Blossom Time Festival,
Chagrin Falls, May;
(440) 247–1004;
www.cvcc.org/blossomtime.htm

Civil War Days,
Burton, May;
(440) 834–1492;
khillegass@5thohio.com

Great American Rib Cook-off,
Cleveland, May;
(440) 247–4386, (888) 761–SHOW;
www.cleveland.com/rib

Port Fest,
Lorain, June;
(440) 204–2273;
www.cityoflorain.org/calendar

Strawberry Festival and Craft Bazaar,
Jefferson, June;
(440) 576–0133;
www.jeffersonchamber.com

Ohio Scottish Games,
Oberlin, June;
www.ohioscottishgames.com

Lorain International Festival,
Lorain, June;
www.loraininternational.com

Rock and Soul Festival,
Cleveland, June;
(216) 781–7625;
www.rockhall.com

Festival of the Fish,
Vermilion, June;
(440) 967–4477;
www.vermilionohio.com

Home Days Festival,
Garfield Heights, July 4th weekend;
(216) 475–7272;
www.garfieldhts.org/homedays

Shakespeare at Stan Hywet,
Akron, July;
(330) 836–5533, (888) 836–5533;
www.stanhywet.org

Log Cabin and Crafts Show,
Austintown, July;
(586) 726–1125

Civil War Reenactment,
Bath, August;
(330) 666–3711;
www.wrhs.org/halefarm

Twins Festival,
Twinsburg, August;
(330) 425–3652;
www.twinsday.org

North Ridgeville Corn Festival,
North Ridgeville, August;
(440) 327–5144;
www.nrcornfest.org

Vintage Ohio Wine Festival,
Chardon, August;
(800) 227–6972;
www.visitvintageohio.com

Pioneer Days,
Vermilion, September;
(440) 967–4477;
www.vermilionohio.com

Mantua Potato Festival,
Mantua, September;
(330) 274–0770

Grape Jamboree,
Geneva, September;
(440) 466–5262

Ashtabula County Covered Bridge Festival,
Jefferson, October;
(440) 576–3769;
www.coveredbridgefestival.org

Jonathan Hale, relocated his family in 1810, establishing a farm in the rolling acreage of what is today northern Summit County. The Hale property remained in the family until the death of Miss Clara Belle Ritchie, great-granddaughter of Jonathan, in 1956. She willed the farm to the Western Reserve Historical Society, stipulating that it be opened to the public so that as many people as possible could "be informed as to the history and culture of the Western Reserve."

The history and culture of the region are faithfully preserved at the working *Hale Farm and Village.* Guides in period clothing help transport the visitor back to 1848. You will meet Jacob and Hannah Meredith, who will tell you about their prosperous dairy farm and life at their household in the mid-1800s. You will also have the opportunity to chat with the village founder and the town gossip to learn even more about the flavor of the place and the time. The color and scents of the mid-nineteenth century are reflected in the gardens and in the arts on display around the village. You can watch glassblowing, spinning, weaving, candle and basketmaking, and even try your hand at making bricks.

Hale Farm and Village is in the 32,000-acre Cuyahoga Valley National Park at 2686 Oak Hill Road, Bath; (330) 666–3711, (877) 425–3327; www.wrhs .org/halefarm. Open May through October, Wednesday through Saturday, 11:00 A.M. to 5:00 P.M.; Sunday, noon to 5:00 P.M. (shorter hours in the fall). Admission: adults $14.50; children (ages 3 to 12) $7.50.

Cuyahoga Valley National Park follows the Cuyahoga River for 22 miles between Akron and Cleveland. The park offers numerous hiking, nature, and bicycle trails, scenic overlooks, and picnic areas.

The Towpath Trail follows the historic route of the Ohio & Erie Canal, which was built between 1825 and 1832. This canal provided a transportation link between Cleveland, on Lake Erie, and Portsmouth, on the Ohio River, and opened Ohio to the eastern United States. Prior to the canal, Ohio was a sparsely populated wilderness, where travel was difficult and the shipping of crops was nearly impossible.

Today, hikers, joggers, and cyclists follow the same route once used by "canawlers." Locks and related structures are still visible, as you travel through forests, fields, and wetlands brimming with wildlife.

Information about all of the recreational opportunities and programs at this vast park are available at the six visitor centers: Canal Visitor Center, Boston Store, Hunt Farm Visitor Information Center, Happy Days Visitor Center, the Frazer House, and the Peninsula Depot. Or you can call (216) 524–1497, write to Cuyahoga Valley National Park, 15610 Vaughn Road, Brecksville 44141, or visit the Web site at www.nps.gov/cuva or www.dayinthevalley.com. For information on the Cuyahoga Valley Scenic Railroad, call (800) 468–4070, (330) 657–2000, or go to www.cvsr.com.

Winter sports in the park include sledding, ice skating, and cross-country skiing. Two complete ski centers, Brandywine in Sagamore Hills and Boston Mills in nearby Peninsula (both at 330–467–2242 or 800–875–4241), serve downhill skiers with complete ski shops, lifts, instruction, and equipment rentals.

Nestled in 800 acres of rolling hills between Akron and Cleveland is one of America's premier outdoor cultural and entertainment complexes, **Blossom Music Center.** The summer home for the renowned Cleveland Orchestra, Blossom also attracts audiences for performances that range from jazz to rock and roll.

The nation's top artists take the stage in the innovative pavilion, a fan-shaped open-air structure seating 5,281. Its enormous roof rises 94 feet above the stage level (it's the largest shingled area in the country), creating a sound chamber requiring little or no electronic amplification for those seated in the pavilion.

Four acres of lawn on the gentle hillside provide outdoor seating for another 13,500 patrons. A unique computerized sound system has a delay feature that transmits the sound from speakers at precisely the moment the sound from the stage reaches the lawn audience, creating near perfect listening conditions.

settlingakron

The building of the Ohio & Erie Canal spurred the settlement of Akron, named from the Greek word *akros*, meaning "summit" or "high place." Early gristmills were built in the area because of the available water power.

Two entrepreneurs also contributed to the city's development. In 1863, Ferdinand Schumacher constructed the Empire Barley Mill, which supplied cereal to the Union Army and launched the American cereal industry. His enterprise later became known as Quaker Oats.

In 1870, New Yorker Dr. Benjamin Franklin Goodrich moved to Akron and rounded up investors for his company, which produced fire hoses and other rubber products. With the arrival of the auto industry and the demand for rubber tires, the rest of the story is well known, with Akron becoming the rubber capital of the world.

Artists perform almost every evening during the June-through-September season. A full-service restaurant is open on all concert nights. For information and a schedule of coming attractions, write Blossom Music Center, 1145 West Steels Corners Road, Cuyahoga Falls 44223. April through September you can phone the center at (330) 920–8040 or visit www.blossommusic.com.

What do Thomas Edison, Alexander Graham Bell, and Wilbur and Orville Wright have in common? Two things: They were all great American inventors, and they are four of the more than 200 inventors who have been inducted into the **National Inventors Hall of Fame.**

The Hall of Fame, which opened in 1995, is dedicated to the creative process. Inside this interactive science center, you can conduct a symphony with rubber bands and a laser, build your own sound system, strum a laser harp, fire an air cannon, make a movie, transform a toaster into a work of art, animate your own cartoon, construct a computer, or demolish a DVD player. The quality and creativity of the exhibits win over young and old alike.

The National Inventors Hall of Fame is at 221 South Broadway, Akron; (330) 762–4463, (800) 968–4332; www.invent.org. Open Wednesday through Saturday, 10:00 A.M. to 4:30 P.M. Admission: adults $8.75; children and students $6.75.

The *Akron Art Museum* originally was housed in an 1899 Italian Renaissance-style structure that once served as the Akron Post Office. In 2007, the museum opened its new, magnificent Coop Himmelb(l)au-designed building just south of the original. This ultramodern structure provides a compelling contrast with the original museum. The permanent collection boasts more than 3,000 works from the mid-1800s to the present. Much of the collection is dedicated to contemporary painting and photography. Works by photographers Robert Frank, Margaret Bourke-White, and Harry Callahan are featured, along with the contemporary art of Andy Warhol, Frank Stella, and Carrie Mae Weems. The Myers Sculpture Court is an outdoor venue for large-scale sculpture as well as concerts during the spring and summer months. The museum also hosts traveling exhibitions throughout the year.

The Akron Art Museum is at 70 East Market Street, Akron; (330) 376–9185; www.akronartmuseum.org. Open daily, 11:00 A.M. to 5:00 P.M. No admission charge.

Constructed at an estimated cost of $2 million, Frank A. and Gertrude Seiberling's *Stan Hywet Hall* in Akron took four years to build and was completed in 1915. Frank Seiberling founded the Goodyear and Seiberling rubber companies, and this lavish sixty-five-room mansion gives testimony to the personal wealth amassed by industrialists in that era.

Considered to be one of the finest examples of American Tudor Revival architecture, Stan Hywet is patterned after three Tudor estates in England, with elements of each incorporated in the design of the structure. As is typical of Tudor buildings, windows, doors, chimneys, and roof peaks are asymmetrical and appear randomly placed. The name Stan Hywet means "stone quarry" in Anglo-Saxon, a reference to the sandstone quarry once located on the original 3,000-acre estate.

Molded plaster ceilings and hand-carved oak walls, both commonly used in English Tudor residences, can be found throughout the Seiberling home. The Seiberlings went to considerable trouble to make Stan Hywet as faithful as possible to the Tudor style; they concealed telephones behind wall coverings and installed twenty-three working fireplaces, even though the building is equipped with central heating. They also built in a rope elevator for hauling firewood from the basement to the upper floors.

Formal balls and other social functions were held in the large music room, which has three massive crystal chandeliers, sixteen wall sconces, and a second-floor balcony for a small orchestra. The formal dining room seats forty, and an oil-on-canvas mural above the oak walls depicts Chaucer's *Canterbury Tales*. Rare American chestnut, a type of wood that's no longer available because of devastating blight, lines the walls of the billiard room.

The Seiberlings removed the paneling and fireplace from a room in an English manor house scheduled for demolition and installed these materials in the second-floor master bedroom. Also in their bedroom is an original Tudor canopy bed, ca. 1575. Throughout the tour, guides point out many of the outstanding pieces in the Seiberlings' priceless collection of antiques.

stanhywet/ shakespeare

The owners of the impressive Stan Hywet Hall were well known for their love of music and the performing arts. That love continues as the estate hosts Shakespeare at Stan Hywet each July.

Outdoor performances are held in the early evenings on the grounds of the great hall. Generally the performances are held on two consecutive weekends in July. The grand mansion and grounds also are the setting for other special activities, including art shows and teas on the terrace featuring period music and entertainment. For information on Shakespeare and other special events at Stan Hywet, call (330) 836–5533.

Formal gardens, woodlands crisscrossed with paths and trails, and splendid shrubbery surround Stan Hywet Hall. Clear stream water pours over a stone waterfall in a cool pond in the tall trees just behind the Seiberling mansion.

Stan Hywet Hall and Gardens is at 714 North Portage Path, Akron; (330) 836–5533, (888) 836–5533; www.stanhywet.org. Open April through December, daily, 9:00 A.M. to 6:00 P.M. Admission: adults $12.00; children (ages 13 to 17) $6.00; children 12 and under free.

From Stan Hywet Hall, take Portage Path south for a drive past many fine old Akron homes and estates. If you continue south to the intersection of Copley Road and South Portage Path, you will find two museums.

The mansion of Colonel Simon Perkins was constructed adjacent to the historic Portage Path at Akron between the years 1835 and 1837. The home is an example of the Greek Revival style, which had great influence on architecture during the early settlement of the Western Reserve. Built of native sandstone on the brow of a hill, the **Perkins Stone Mansion,** with its two-story portico, overlooks the city of Akron. Through the years, it has become recognized as one of the most imposing homes of northern Ohio.

Colonel Perkins was born to General and Mrs. Simon Perkins at Warren, Ohio, in 1805. His father organized the Western Reserve Bank in 1813, and, in connection with Paul Williams, founded the village of Akron in 1825.

Colonel Perkins, who served in the Ohio legislature and was an active promoter of the Cleveland, Zanesville & Cincinnati Railroad, purchased 115 acres of land on this site in 1832 for $1,300. Perkins and his wife, sister of the future governor of Ohio, David Tod, resided in Warren before moving to Akron in 1835. While the mansion was under construction, they lived in a small frame house, now known as the *John Brown House.*

Surrounded by more than ten acres of beautiful grounds, the mansion today contains some of its original furnishings, as well as items connected with the early history of Summit County. Situated on the grounds are the original carriage house, a combination summer kitchen and laundry built in 1890, the original well—dug through 40 feet of sandstone—and a visitor center, previously the Perkins' woodshed.

allfiredupin barberton

The unusually named Ohio Columbus Barber was a premier matchmaker, but he was not one involved in pairing couples for romance. No, Barber and his company, Diamond Match Company, made fire-starting matches, a quarter-billion a day during the company's heyday.

Barber came from a family of matchmakers: his father made them, too, and peddled them. The younger Barber founded Diamond Match in 1880, and his success resulted in the creation of a new town, Barberton, which he conceived and promoted. He was known during his day as the "Match King."

Across the street is the John Brown House, so named to commemorate the residency of that abolitionist leader from 1844 to 1854. At the time, Brown was associated with Colonel Simon Perkins in the sheep and wool business. The original frame structure, to which several additions have been made, is believed to have been built around 1830. Inside is an exhibit that explains the importance of the canal to the development of Akron, as well as a replica of a canalboat captain's cabin.

Both museums are operated by the Summit County Historical Society, 550 Copley Road, Akron; (330) 535–1120; www.summithistory.org. They are open Wednesday through Friday, with tours at 12:30 and 2:30 P.M. Closed in January and February. Admission (to both museums): adults $5.00; children (ages 6 to 16) and senior citizens $4.00.

Just up the street from the museums, Jeanne Pinnick offers bed-and-breakfast accommodations in her 1918 *Portage House.* This three-story Tudor home provides a pleasant stop in a quiet, parklike setting for weary travelers.

Jeanne and her daughter, Carol, live on the third floor; the second-floor bedrooms are available for guests. Downstairs, the large living room is a quiet place to relax or read the evening paper.

Depending on the number of guests in the house, Jeanne serves a full breakfast either at an island in the center of the kitchen or in the formal dining room. Friendly people like the Pinnicks and modest prices are why bed-and-breakfasts are increasingly popular throughout Ohio.

The Portage House is at 601 Copley Road, Akron; (330) 535–1952; www.members.aol.com/portagehse. Rates: $50 to $60 per night. Personal checks accepted.

Kay and Donna Vaughan have been farming in the Hartville area since the 1960s, and both quit their teaching jobs in the 70s to farm full time. By 2000, their children joined the operation, they purchased a 140-year-old barn and refurbished it, and the Maize Valley Farm Market opened for business. In 2005, the next expansion created what is now known as the *Maize Valley Winery.*

Today the Vaughan family farms 750 acres, including 200 acres of fruits and vegetables. Super-sweet corn and juicy tomatoes grow alongside cantaloupes, watermelons, peppers, green beans, squash, strawberries, raspberries, and blueberries.

The winery produces a crisp, dry, fruity Riesling, and a medium-bodied chambourcin, a spicy dry red with hints of black cherries and raspberries balanced by soft tannins and toasted oak. The Maize Valley cabernet sauvignon is aged in American oak barrels and features rich currant and black-cherry flavors. Among other selections, try the red table wine known as Red Neck Red or one of the many fun fruit wines produced here. The wines are already winning regional awards.

The Vaughans often stage special events at the winery, everything from a performance by an Elvis-tribute artist to hot-air balloons. Fall harvest time means corn mazes and that the Pumpkin Cannon is locked and loaded—be sure not to park down range or plan on a trip to the nearest car wash. Wagon rides around the property are popular with visitors, as is the petting pasture for younger guests.

The Maize Valley Winery is at 6193 Edison Street, Hartville; (330) 877–8344; www.maizevalleywinery.com. Open Monday through Thursday, 9:00 A.M. to 7:00 P.M.; Friday until 10:00 P.M.; Saturday until 11:00 P.M. with live entertainment. Sunday hours for the market are 10:00 A.M. to 4:00 P.M., but there are no wine sales.

Heritage Hills

Founded with an initial gift from Jerry Silverman and Shannon Rodgers, the **Kent State University Museum** opened its doors in 1985. Silverman and Rodgers, New York dress manufacturers, donated 4,000 costumes and accessories, almost 1,000 pieces of decorative art, and a 5,000-volume reference library. Today, the collection consists of more than 20,000 pieces representing the major world cultures.

Highlights of the collection include the black velvet evening cape, trimmed with a band of crystals, worn by Joan Crawford at Truman Capote's Black and White Ball. Another favorite is the eighteenth-century English silk dress, in a style typical of the Spitafields silk-weaving district in London. There's a magnificent uniform of the Chinese Imperial Palace Guard worn at the end of the Manchu dynasty around 1900 and a fancy blue silk ball gown from the French couture house of Balenciaga, ca. 1958.

A second gift to the museum was the Tarter/Miller collection of more than 200,000 pieces of collectible glass. A distinctive part of this collection is the Vaseline glass, so called because of its unusual yellow-green color. The recent acquisition of the Paige Palmer Collection of Ohio art pottery includes exquisite examples of Roseville, Weller, and Rookwood pieces.

The Kent State University Museum is in Rockwell Hall on the corner of East Main and South Lincoln Streets on the Kent State University campus, Kent; (330) 672–3450; www.kent.edu/museum. Open Wednesday, Friday, and Saturday, 10:00 A.M. to 4:45 P.M.; Thursday, 10:00 A.M. to 8:45 P.M.; Sunday, noon to 4:45 P.M. Admission: adults $5.00; seniors $4.00; students $3.00.

The history of the Mahoning Valley is the history of the iron and steel industries. Deposits of black coal suitable for blast furnaces were discovered near Youngstown in 1845, and by the 1850s the Valley was one of the nation's centers of iron production. As technology advanced, the Valley switched to steel production; the Ohio Steel Company, the area's first steel company, was organized in 1892.

Steel mill jobs attracted immigrants from eastern and southern Europe, as well as African Americans from the South. Working conditions for these laborers were appalling: typically twelve-hour days, six or even seven days a week, in an environment of heavy machinery, poisonous gases, and open vats of molten steel. These conditions eventually led to the formation of the United Steelworkers of America in 1936.

Youngstown's steel production and employment soared during the middle of the twentieth century, peaking in 1973. But just four years later, "Black Monday" hit the area on September 19, 1977, with the closing of Youngstown's Sheet and Tube's Campbell Works. Global changes in the steel market, labor-management disputes, and a depletion of high-grade ores all contributed to the death of the Valley's steel industry.

The ups and downs of this pivotal industry are presented at the *Youngstown Historical Center of Industry and Labor.* The museum's permanent exhibit, By the Sweat of Their Brow: Forging the Steel Valley, uses videos, artifacts, photographs, and reconstructed scenes to tell the story of steel in the valley.

The Youngstown Historical Center of Industry and Labor is at 151 West Wood Street, Youngstown; (330) 743–5934, (800) 262–6137; www.ohiohistory .org/places/youngst. Open Wednesday through Saturday, 10:00 A.M. to 4:00 P.M.; Admission: adults $7.00; children (ages 6 to 12) $3.00.

In a city best known for steel and other heavy industry, Youngstown's *Butler Institute of American Art* houses an outstanding permanent collection of more than 10,000 works. From the earliest Limner painters of the colonial period through contemporary masters, the Butler Institute features representative works by Benjamin West, John Singleton Copley, Winslow Homer, Thomas Eakins, Martin Johnson Heade, and Mary Cassatt.

Specialty collections include western art by the likes of Albert Bierstadt, Frederic Remington, and Victor Higgins, and an expansive group of marine paintings featuring the works of Fitzhugh Lane, Edward Moran, William Bradford, and Alfred Bricher. The Lester F. Donnell Gallery of American Sports Art features paintings, sculpture, drawings, and prints of all things sporting, including works by George Bellows, John Steuart Curry, Red Grooms, Robert Riggs, and Roy Lichtenstein.

Founded in 1919 by industrialist Joseph G. Butler, Jr., the Butler Institute is housed in a classic building, the first structure built in the United States specifically to house a collection of American art. Additions to this historic edifice in the 1930s and 1960s preceded the impressive West Wing addition in 1987 and the Beecher Center for Art and Technology in 2000. These postmodern structures, awash in marble and partially lit by soaring skylights, brings to twenty the number of galleries at the Butler Institute.

The Butler Institute of American Art is at 524 Wick Avenue, Youngstown; (330) 743–1107; www.butlerart.com. Open Tuesday and Thursday through Saturday, 11:00 A.M. to 4:00 P.M.; Wednesday, 11:00 A.M. to 8:00 P.M.; Sunday, noon to 4:00 P.M. No admission charge.

Just down the road from the Butler Institute is another Youngstown treasure: the early-twentieth-century mansion of Wilford and Olive Arms, Greystone, now the *Arms Family Museum of Local History.* The three main rooms on the first floor of this elegant mansion preserve the Arms' way of life; their family portraits, furniture, china, glassware, silver, linens, Oriental rugs, and objets d'art are still in place.

On the lower level, a large exhibition room depicts pioneer life in the region, with a collection of farm and household tools, implements and utensils, antique toys, and Native American relics. Second-floor exhibits explore the more recent history of the Mahoning Valley through photographs, costumes, and artifacts.

Period gowns adorn mannequins throughout the museum, and the table setting in the dining room changes periodically to rotate the display of china, crystal, and silver. Special exhibits here include toys and dolls, costumes and accessories, political memorabilia, and works of art.

The Arms Family Museum of Local History is at 648 Wick Avenue, Youngstown; (330) 743–2589; www.mahoninghistory.org. Open Tuesday through Sunday, 1:00 to 5:00 P.M. Admission: adults $4.00; children (up to 18) $2.00.

One of Ohio's greatest regional parks offers visitors 2,530 acres of streams, lakes, gardens, woods, meadows, and wildlife. It's Mahoning County's *Mill Creek MetroParks,* and it features 21 miles of roads and 15 miles of foot trails through truly spectacular scenery. Hiking, picnicking, and boating are popular pastimes on Lake Newport and Lake Glacier.

The central feature of the park is picturesque Mill Creek. Many pioneer industries developed along the creek, and relics still remain to be discovered by visitors. Lanterman's Mill operates today as it did in the early 1800s, grinding corn, wheat, and buckwheat via power driven by a 14-foot oak waterwheel. The mill had ceased operation in 1888, only to reopen a century later. A covered bridge stands just south of the mill and is one of the scenic highlights of the park.

Downstream from the mill is the start of the Gorge Trail. Mill Creek borders one side of this 2-mile trail; a massive wall of sandstone forms the other boundary. The trail takes hikers past a stunning waterfall.

More than 50,000 flowering bulbs announce the arrival of spring each year at the Fellows Riverside Garden. As summer arrives a spectacle of colorful annuals takes over. The wooded setting of the shade garden is a showcase for ornamental plants that thrive in low light. Other park highlights include a golf course, tennis courts, miniature golf, an ice skating rink, ballfields, and basketball courts.

Mill Creek Park is at 810 Glenwood Avenue, Youngstown; (330) 702–3000; www.millcreekmetroparks.com. Open during daylight hours.

The collectibles at the *Hummel Gift Shop* may be diminutive, but the shop that houses them is anything but. With 30,000 square feet of display space, this may be the largest gift shop in the state. Hummel collectors will be instantly attracted by the shop name, but the Hummel Gift Shop also carries a wide range of other gifts and collectibles. There are also year-round displays of ancient artifacts and a Christmas wonderland.

The Hummel Gift Shop is located at 1656 East Garfield Road, New Springfield; (330) 549–3728 or (800) 354–5438; www.hummelgiftshop.com. Open Monday through Saturday from 10:00 A.M. to 5:00 P.M.; from June 1 through December 24, it's also open Sunday from 1:00 to 5:00 P.M.

The Packard automobile may be a thing of America's past, but its history is preserved at the **National Packard Museum.** The museum is located in the community of Warren, and its mission is to document and tell the story of the Packard family, the Packard Electric Company, the Packard Motor Car Company, and the innovations they created. The museum has several wonderfully restored Packards, and plenty of displays and Packard memorabilia, as well as changing exhibits.

The National Packard Museum is at 1899 Mahoning Avenue NW, Warren; (330) 394–1899; www.packardmuseum.org. Open: Tuesday through Saturday, noon to 5:00 P.M.; Sunday, 1:00 to 5:00 P.M. Admission: adults $5.00; children (ages 7 to 12) $3.00.

Where can you see a Water Buffalo and a Weasel together in Ohio? At the **World War II Museum and Learning Center** in Hubbard probably seems an unlikely answer, unless you know the names of military fighting vehicles. History buffs will get a chance to see an eight-inch Howitzer up close, as well as a German Kubelwagen, and many U.S. military vehicles including a Sherman tank and the M-16 half-track. In addition, there are numerous displays of Japanese, German, and British weapons, and an amphibious tank.

The World War II Museum and Learning Center is at 5959 West Liberty Street, Hubbard; (330) 534–8125; www.wwiivehiclemuseum.com. Open Monday through Friday 9:00 A.M. to 5:00 P.M.; closed between noon and 1:00 P.M. Admission: adults $5.00; children (ages 10 and under) $3.00.

Built in the 1840s by Alden J. Nash and originally called the Nash Hotel, the **Welshfield Inn** served as an Underground Railway station for slaves escaping from the South to Canada. Stagecoaches traveling between Cleveland and Pittsburgh also frequently stopped here for food and overnight accommodations.

Although lodging is no longer offered here, the tradition of serving old-fashioned country cooking has been maintained by the owners, but now with an Italian flare. Renamed Alessi's at the Welshfield Inn, the menu features unpretentious comfort food—pastas, steaks, and chops. The large dining room with a fireplace contains an eclectic mix of bentwood chairs and wooden tables; browns, greens, and other earth tones predominate, and fresh flowers dress up each table. One of the smaller dining rooms, called Peddlers Parlor, has Early American decor with antiques, Quaker lace tablecloths, and seasonal flowers. On the front porch, lawn furniture creates a friendly, informal atmosphere under the tall columns. Also under the porch roof is a huge wooden sled named Snowbird capable of carrying twenty to thirty people.

Alessi's at the Welshfield Inn is on Route 422, 14001 Main Market Road, Burton; (440) 834–4164. Open Monday, Wednesday, and Thursday, 11:00 A.M. to 9:00 P.M.; Friday and Saturday, 11:00 A.M. to 10:00 P.M.; and Sunday, 11:00 A.M. to 8:00 P.M. MasterCard, Visa, and American Express are accepted.

Approximately 16,000 Amish live in Geauga County, making it one of the largest Amish communities in the country. Wearing the traditional dark, solid-colored clothing and rejecting modern conveniences such as electricity and automobiles, the "plain people" strive for a simple farming life. Merchants in Middlefield, Ohio, provide hitching posts for their Amish customers.

The Schaden family has a most unique and charming business. They are the owners of the *End of Commons General Store* in picturesque Mesopotamia. Ken Schaden, once a frequent customer, gave up a corporate position with extensive international travel requirements to purchase the store in 1982 and spend more time with his wife Margaret and their eleven children. The Schadens sell more than 800 products in bulk to area Amish families, most arriving at the store in horse-drawn buggies. As its name indicates, the store sits at the end of a parklike commons, surrounded by thirty historic homes, the oldest of which was built in 1816.

When they purchased the store and began to clean out the old storage areas, they found hundreds of items related to the store's and the town's history. Today, visitors find on display old clothes, shoes, a barber chair, a post office, a player piano, and many things of bygone days. Penny candy still lines shelves by the checkout counter (yes, it is still just a penny), where slots and boxes of the old post office remain. In summer, hand-dipped ice cream is dispensed from a window where stamps once were sold. Amish families who host church services in their homes buy pounds and pounds of bologna and cheese here and also bake lots of bread and goodies with the unusual flours they find here in suitable quantities.

The family also operates a truck route that calls on 375 Amish families in the surrounding countryside. It is equipped with a cooler and freezers so they can bring them ice cream and milk along with other essentials. It is a grocery store on wheels.

The End of the Commons General Store is at 8719 Route 534, Mesopotamia; (440) 693–4295; www.endofthecommons.com. Open Monday through Friday, 8:30 A.M. to 8:30 P.M.; Saturday, 8:30 A.M. to 6:00 P.M.

Mid-February through mid-April is a special time in Geauga County—maple syrup season. Those first February thaws start the sap flowing, and farmers throughout the county use special taps and buckets to drain the sap from their sugar maple trees. Once collected it is boiled and evaporated, with thirty to sixty gallons of sap needed to make one gallon of maple syrup. Smoke rising from area sugarhouses means syrup production is underway.

The **Burton Sugar Camp** is the only municipally owned sugar camp in the country. Located in a ten-acre park in the center of Burton, sap from the park's 1,500 sugar maples is boiled into syrup in a rustic log cabin. The cabin is open daily from late February through April, and maple syrup products are sold on weekends from May through the middle of December.

At the south end of Burton's town square is **Century Village**—eighteen restored buildings that provide a glimpse of the Western Reserve in the 1800s. The Blacksmith Shop, built in 1822, has an impressive complement of smithy tools and equipment. For a look at upper-middle-class life in the region, the Boughton House is furnished with pieces typical of the 1840s. The B&O Railroad built the Aultman station after the Civil War, and next to it sits a twenty-ton B&O caboose. Guides from the Geauga County Historical Society conduct one-and-a-half-hour tours of the village.

Century Village is on the town square in Burton; (440) 834–1492; www .geaugahistorical.org. Open mid-April through mid-November, Friday, Saturday, and Sunday, tours at 1:00 and 3:00 P.M. Admission: adults $6.00; children (ages 6 to 12) $4.00.

Working from a small farm in Mantua, Ohio, Jim Stadtlander has been creating intriguing wooden sculptures since the early 1990s. His complex and detailed pieces reflect his love of this medium and his attention to detail—even the smallest elements are carved by hand. The results of his labor of love have been more than fifteen "best of show" awards and numerous other recognitions. Busts and other human subjects are the most frequent of his works, and in each, his goal is to "freeze his subjects into the wood." Jim creates pieces of varying sizes, some like a cigar-store Indian he crafted from butternut wood, standing more than 5 feet tall.

Jim's fellow woodcarver, Diane Harto, started her craft with duck decoys in the 1980s. Her interest in wildlife expanded to carvings of a wide variety of "critters," resulting in her first book, *Carving Wooden Critters*. Her depictions of squirrels, cows, and butterflies display both her craft and her sense of whimsy.

The quality of their work has resulted in long backlogs for commissions to be completed; in Jim's case, the wait can be as long as six years. Carvings are available for viewing and purchase at their gallery, **Stadtlander's Woodcarving Gallery,** or at various shows around the country.

Stadtlander's Woodcarving Gallery is at 2881 Frost Road, Mantua; (330) 274–2671; www.woodcarvedart.com. Open by appointment Monday through Saturday, 8:00 A.M. to 4:00 P.M.

The annual Geauga County Maple Festival, held on the first weekend after Easter, takes place in Chardon, 10 miles north of Burton. Parades, maple syrup contests, a quilt and afghan show, competitions in pancake flipping and eating, wood chopping, rooster crowing, and beard shaving with an ax are just some of the activities at this yearly celebration.

Many of the Amish operate dairy farms, and they bring their milk to the **Middlefield Cheese House** to be manufactured into Swiss cheese. The cheese plant, founded as a cooperative in 1956 by twenty-five area farmers, is one of the largest producers of quality Swiss in the United States, with an output of more than twenty million pounds annually.

Visitors are invited to view a film, *Faith and Teamwork*, which carefully describes each step in the cheese-making process. A tour of the cheese house museum features Old World carvings from Switzerland, antique cheese-making equipment, Amish artifacts, and historical photos. Be sure to stop in the Cheese Chalet Shop, where fresh sausages, homemade breads and pastries, Geauga County maple syrup, plus a wide selection of fine cheeses are available for purchase. A light lunch of soup, sandwiches, muffins, pie, and ice cream is served.

Middlefield Cheese House is on Route 608 at 15815 Nauvoo Road, Middlefield; (440) 632–5228, (800) 327–9477; www.middlefieldcheese.com. Open Monday through Saturday, 8:00 A.M. to 5:30 P.M. No admission charge.

The king of maple products in Geauga County has to be Paul Richards, of **Richards Maple Products**—his family has been in the business since 1910. Paul purchases tens of thousands of gallons of syrup annually from area farmers, syrup that he transforms into pure maple spread (similar to honey butter), maple sugar, maple cream (a fudgelike concoction available with or without black walnuts), maple candy, and, of course, three grades of maple syrup. All of these are produced without the use of preservatives.

Richards Maple Products also sells a wide selection of gift boxes containing endless combinations of their various products. Catalogs of gift box selections are available by mail.

Richards Maple Products is at 545 Water Street (Route 6, west of the central business district), Chardon (440) 286–4160, (800) 352–4052; www.richards mapleproducts.com. Open Monday through Friday, 9:00 A.M. to 6:00 P.M.; Saturday, 9:00 A.M. to 4:30 P.M.; Sunday, 10:00 A.M. to 4:30 P.M. From May 15 through July 15, Richards closes at 5:30 P.M. daily and all day on Wednesdays.

You can return home from your visit to **Fowler's Mill** with a taste of the 1800s. The mill was established in 1834 by Milo and Hiram Fowler and has been operating for almost all of the years since. Currently the millstones grind corn and wheat. You can purchase their stone-ground flours in traditional cloth bags and do some scratch baking. The mill also offers a variety of baking mixes, pastas, and gift items.

Fowler's Mill is at 12500 Fowlers Mill Road, Chardon; (440) 286–2024, (800) 321–2024; www.fowlermill.com. Open Monday through Saturday, 10:00 A.M. to 5:00 P.M.

From late November to the middle of March, skiers hit the powder at the **Alpine Valley Ski Area.** This complete ski resort has six slopes and a back-woods trail, high-powered lighting towers for night skiing, and a 10,000-square-foot rental shop with 1,400 pairs of skis. Their Professional Ski Instructors of America (PSIA) ski school offers both private and group lessons. After a strenuous day on the slopes, a blazing fire in the lodge's fireplace lures skiers there to unwind. The lodge offers a great view of the slopes, as well as a full-service cafeteria, a pizza shop, and a pub called Chaser's.

The Alpine Valley Ski Area is on Route 322, 4 miles east of Chesterland at 10620 Mayfield Road; (440) 285–2211, (440) 729–9775 (ski reports).

Eastern Lakefront

The **Holden Arboretum,** one of the world's largest arboreta, encompasses 3,400 acres of wooded trails, ponds full of ducks and geese, fields, and deep ravines. Dedicated to increasing knowledge of the plant world, Holden has five primary nature trails, which take visitors past the maple collection, renowned for its beauty when the leaves change color in the fall; the conifer collection of pines, firs, spruces, and junipers; and the wildflower garden, where a showcase of Ohio's flora can be enjoyed.

The lilac and rhododendron gardens and crabapple and shrub collections are other examples of the many and varied exhibits in this vast nature preserve. Nature walks and frequent lectures are offered at the arboretum, as are memberships. Membership entitles you to free admission to the grounds, cross-country skiing privileges, and discounts on courses, lectures, and gift shop purchases. Bird-watching and wildflower walks are popular at Holden, and the arboretum has summertime nature discovery sessions as well as special programs for children on subjects such as animal communication.

The Holden Arboretum is at 9500 Sperry Road, Kirtland; (440) 946–4400; www.holdenarb.org. Open daily, 9:00 A.M. to 5:00 P.M. (closed Monday, November through March). Admission: adults $6.00; children (ages 6 to 12) $3.00.

Picture, if you will, a giant tomato plant with vines as thick as your waist, fruit 6 feet across, and leaves up to 12 feet long. The stuff of science fiction?

No, *science,* not *science fiction.* These are features of the creative Great Tomato Works at **Lake Farmpark.** The Farmpark, a Lake Metroparks facility, is an outdoor museum where city folks can learn about and learn to appreciate agriculture—the source of our food supply. The number of farmers among us has declined from more than 90 percent in 1800 to less than 3 percent today. Relatively few Americans have ever met a farmer, let alone understand what he or she does.

Try your hand milking a cow, or just enjoy the 235 acres of fields and forests. Two miles of easy walking roads cross the property, and wagon rides are also offered. You'll discover more than fifty breeds of livestock including cattle, sheep, goats, pigs, and poultry, plus orchards, gardens, and vineyards. You'll leave knowing the difference between strip cropping and contour plowing, and perhaps having seen the planting, cultivating, or harvesting of fields of hay, oats, rye, wheat, corn, and barley.

Lake Farmpark is at 8800 Chardon Road (U.S. Route 6), Kirtland; (440) 256–2122, (800) 366–3276; www.lakemetroparks.com. Open daily, 9:00 A.M. to 5:00 P.M. (Closed on Monday, January through March.) Admission: adults (ages 12 and up) $6.00; children $4.00.

After a day exploring the Lake Farmpark or the Holden Arboretum, you might want to relax with a night's stay at **Rider's Inn.** Rider's Inn has offered hospitality to Ohio visitors since 1812, when Joseph Rider opened it as a stagecoach stop for those heading to the Western Reserve and beyond. The inn provided a different kind of hospitality prior to the Civil War, as it served as a stop on the Underground Railroad, offering safe haven to fleeing slaves. The inn also was briefly a hot springs spa and was reputed to offer yet another kind of hospitality to thirsty drinkers during Prohibition.

The new owners purchased the inn in 1988 and refurbished the ten guest rooms. Some of the guest rooms have private baths, but others share facilities so if you have a preference, be sure and ask when you are making reservations. The Innkeeper's Suite and Suzanne's Suite (named after Joseph Rider's third wife) have some of the Rider's original furnishings. Guests have a gathering room to enjoy and are served a continental breakfast in bed.

Along with the accommodations, the inn also houses Mistress Suzanne's Dining Room, featuring fish and game recipes from the colonial period as well as more traditional dishes. You also can enjoy a game of darts in the English-style pub or just sit and sip your favorite beverage by the old stone fireplace. The innkeepers enjoy outdoor activities, including boating and sailing and are be happy to introduce their guests to the many sporting and cultural activities in the area.

Rider's Inn is located at 792 Mentor Avenue, Painesville; (440) 354–8200; www.ridersinn.com. Rates: $79 to $101 per night. Visa, MasterCard, and American Express are accepted. The restaurant is open for lunch Monday through Saturday, 11:30 A.M. to 4:00 P.M.; dinner, 4:30 to 9:00 P.M.; Sunday brunch, 10:00 A.M. to 3:00 P.M.; Sunday dinner, 5:00 to 9:00 P.M.

The Debevcs have made wine for family and friends for three generations, but it wasn't until 1970 that Tony Sr. and Tony Jr. decided to convert some of their farm acreage into a commercial vineyard. **Debonne Vineyards** produced its first bottle for sale in 1972, and near-constant expansion has taken place ever since. Winemaker Tony Jr. oversees production from one hundred acres of vineyard.

Guests at Debonne sample the twenty-four varieties of Debevc wine—twelve white wines, eight reds, and four blush wines—in a Swiss-style A-frame chalet with a large fireplace, burgundy tablecloths, and weathered barn board siding on the inside walls. Visitors may also sit under the covered patio during warm weather, and snacks such as cheese and sausage and homemade bread are served. Regional bands perform on Wednesday and Friday evenings and Saturday afternoons.

Tours of the winery take place hourly, or as needed, with members of the Debevc family explaining the various steps in winemaking, from grape crushing and filtering to aging and bottling. Debonne holds 100,000 gallons of wine in various stages of fermentation in the cellar and bottled for sale.

Debonne Vineyards is off Route 528 and Griswold Road at 7743 Doty Road, Madison; (440) 466–3485; www.debonne.com. Open Tuesday, noon to 6:00 P.M.; Wednesday and Friday, noon to midnight; Thursday and Saturday, noon to 8:00 P.M. (Open Sunday, Memorial Day through the end of October, 1:00 to 6:00 P.M.).

Acres of vineyards can be seen throughout eastern Lake County, and five minutes from Chalet Debonne is another winery, **Claire's Grand River Vineyard.** After driving past the rows of grapevines, you reach a modern building at the edge of a cool forest. Unlike other wineries, Grand River continually changes the wines it produces, so customers have the opportunity to taste new variations and blends on each visit to this pleasant facility.

Claire's Grand River Vineyard is at 5750 Madison Road (Route 528), Madison; (440) 298–9838. Tours are available by appointment.

His Majesty's Bed and Breakfast has five guest rooms located in two historic homes in Madison. The Paige House, built in 1830, is listed on the National Register of Historic Places, and Queen's Cottage is a charming home, built in 1861, and located on the village square. The three rooms in the Queen's Cottage are more ornate with a Victorian theme, and one room features a whirlpool tub. The two rooms in the Paige House have queen-size beds, a bath with a whirlpool tub and separate shower, and a fireplace. All five rooms have private baths.

A full-course breakfast is included with your stay. In addition, the proprietors will be happy to create a gold package for you, steer you to local wine tastings, or make reservations for that perfect night of dinner and dancing.

The Paige House is located at 25 West Main, and Queen's Cottage is located at 25 Park Street, Madison; (440) 336–1607, (888) 551–3241; www.his majestys.com. Rates: $109 to $139 per night. MasterCard and Visa are accepted.

Two years of extensive renovation of this distinctive French Tudor home, built in 1937, earned the **Fitzgerald's Irish Bed and Breakfast** a "Best Interior Design and Decor" designation, one of fifteen North American bed-and-breakfasts to be so honored in *Arrington's 2004 Book of Lists*. The innkeepers, Tom and Debra Fitzgerald, bought the castlelike home from the original owners and opened it as a bed-and-breakfast in 1998.

The common areas of the home are graced with grand architectural features such as a majestic staircase, a turret, and huge fireplace. The three guest rooms have private baths; one—the Bushmills Room—has a whirlpool tub. Continental breakfasts are served to guests on weekdays and full breakfasts on the weekends. If you would like a traditional Irish breakfast, please request it when you make your reservations. For lunch and dinner, restaurants are within walking distance.

Fitzgerald's Irish Bed and Breakfast is located at 47 Mentor Avenue, Painesville; (440) 639–0845; www.fitzgeraldsbnb.com. Rates: $95 to $130 weeknights and from $110 to $150 on weekends. Major credit cards accepted.

The **Victorian Perambulator Museum of Jefferson** has to be a little girl's or an antique-lover's dream come true. The museum has the largest collection of early wicker baby and doll carriages anywhere—more than 200. The handiwork and shapes are fascinating. One carriage is shaped like a Model T Ford, and another like an Italian gondola. The most recent acquisition is a pram used by Queen Elizabeth and Princess Margaret as children—it was pulled by miniature horses. There are also charming and unusual toys, many from the 1800s. Along with rare dolls, there are rocking horses, sleighs, books, and games. For those who can't resist taking a little bit of the past home, there is a museum store brimming with collectibles and craft items.

The Victorian Perambulator Museum of Jefferson is at 26 East Cedar Street, Jefferson; (440) 576–9588. Open Saturday, May and September through December, from 11:00 A.M. to 4:00 P.M.; Wednesday and Saturday, June through August, 11:00 A.M. to 4:00 P.M.; and by appointment. Admission: adults $4.00; children $3.00.

Places to Stay in Northeast Ohio

AKRON

Akron Hilton Inn at Quaker Square
135 South Broadway
(330) 253–5970

Portage House
601 Copley Road
(330) 535–1952

MADISON

His Majesty's Bed and Breakfast
25 West Main
25 Park Street
(440) 428–7767,
(888) 551–3241

PAINESVILLE

Fitzgerald's Irish Bed and Breakfast
47 Mentor Avenue
(440) 639–0845

Quail Hollow Resort and Country Club
11080 Concord-Hambden Road
(216) 350–3504

Rider's Inn
792 Mentor Avenue
(440) 942–2742

Places to Eat in Northeast Ohio

BURTON

Alessi's at the Welshfield Inn
Route 422
(440) 834–4164

CLEVELAND

Watermark
1250 Old River Road
(216) 241–1600

LAKE AT CHIPPEWA

Oaks Lakeside
5878 Longacre Lane
(330) 769–2601
or (800) 922–2601

HELPFUL WEB SITES

Ohio Division of Travel and Tourism:
www.discoverohio.com

Cleveland Convention and Visitors Bureau:
www.travelcleveland.com

Cleveland Plain Dealer:
www.cleveland.com

Youngstown Convention and Visitors Bureau:
www.youngstowncvb.com

East Central Ohio

Legacy Trail

Stunning natural beauty and re-created pioneer history blend in a state park in the foothills of the Appalachians, **Beaver Creek State Park.** Wide, swift Little Beaver Creek rushes through deep gorges and past pine and fir forests, the locks of the old Sandy and Beaver Canal, and a restored pioneer village.

Private entrepreneurs constructed the canal between 1834 and 1848, connecting the Ohio River with the Ohio and Erie Canal. Though they spent $3 million on the project by its completion, the canal carried paying traffic only until 1852, when competition from the railroad doomed the canal era in this part of the state. Ironically, the directors of the Sandy and Beaver kept the Pennsylvania Railroad out of the county to avoid competition between the railroad and their canal—a move that had dire consequences for the canal towns in Columbiana County after the Sandy and Beaver failed.

Fifteen miles of hiking trails and numerous bridle trails follow Little Beaver Creek and wind through the woods up the steep foothills. Primitive camping areas are scattered throughout the 3,000-acre park. The creek offers anglers a variety of fish, including smallmouth and rock bass.

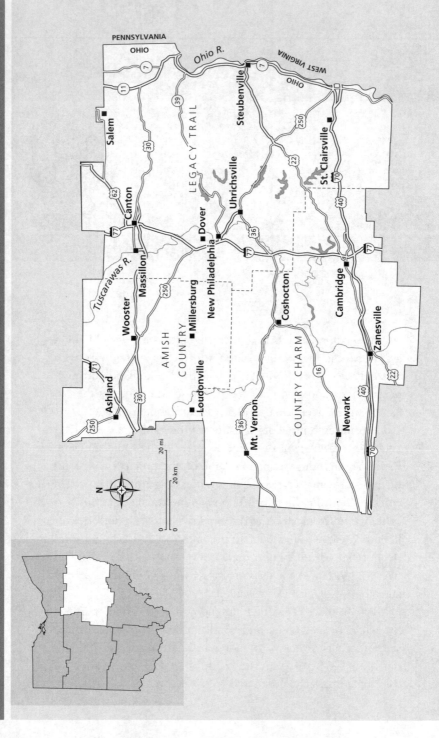

Gaston's Mill, built by Samuel Conkle in 1830, dominates the park's reconstructed pioneer village. Originally powered by a large waterwheel, the mill operated until 1920, though in later years it used steam and gas engines to drive the massive grinding stones. When restored, it was converted back to waterwheel power, and on summer weekends visitors can observe the mill at work and may purchase stone-ground corn, wheat, and buckwheat flour. A pioneer church, schoolhouse, cabin, and blacksmith shop, all filled with antiques from Ohio's early settlement era, surround the historic mill.

Beaver Creek State Park is off Route 7 at 12021 Echo Dell Road, 15 miles east of Lisbon; (330) 385–3091; www.dnr.state.oh.us/parks/parks/beaverck.htm. Open year-round.

Perched on a hilltop overlooking 8,000 acres of rolling hills and water is a great getaway destination, ***Atwood Lake Resort.*** This complete resort complex features a rustic yet modern lodge with 100 guest rooms and 17 four-bedroom cottages in quiet lakefront woods.

Atwood Lake is 1,540 acres of boating, swimming, and fishing, with sailboat and powerboat rentals available. Golfers will enjoy the 6,007-yard, par-70 course, which features challenging doglegs, rolling fairways, and gorgeous greens, as well as the lighted nine-hole par three. Other amenities include five lighted tennis courts, bike rentals, hiking trails, and indoor and outdoor swimming pools.

AUTHORS' FAVORITES

Beaver Creek State Park

Atwood Lake Resort

Cibo's Restaurant

The McKinley Museum

Pro Football Hall of Fame

Canton Classic Car Museum

Hoover Historical Center

Canal Fulton

Amish Door Restaurant and Village

Warther's

J.E. Reeves Victorian Home and Museum

Zoar Village

Fort Laurens

Schoenbrunn Village

Quaker Meeting House

Lehman's/Kidron Town and Country Store

Pine Tree Barn

Quailcrest Farm

Delagrange Antiques

Mohican State Park

Blackfork Inn

Beaver Creek Ghost

Visitors to Beaver Creek State Park will want to bring a camera to get some pictures of the restored mill and locks, but be prepared to miss at least one of those shots if one of the park's ghosts is in residence. At Beaver Creek one of the men who was a lock keeper is said to continue to work shifts along the water's edge. If you visit "Jake's Lock," you may become part of his legend. In life, he sometimes worked the day shift; sometimes at night. At night he would light a lantern and keep watch for boats needing his services to transverse the lock. But one night, it is said, a bolt of lightning shot from the sky and hit poor Jake, killing him and propelling his body into the lock.

Visitors say that to this day they occasionally see the light from Jake's lantern bobbing along the side of the canal or even under the water where Jake fell that night. If you try to take a picture near the lock, the legend says that your camera may malfunction if Jake is working his shift. Be careful that your flash doesn't remind Jake of the fateful flash of lightning!

One of the 1830s locks is nicknamed "Gretchen's Lock." Tales say that Gretchen was the daughter of Gill Hans, an engineer who came from Holland to build the lock. His daughter never adjusted to the move to America and eventually grew sick and died in 1838.

Her family made plans to return to Holland to bury their daughter. Until they could, the coffin was temporarily placed in the stone sides of the lock. The arrangements were made and the family set sail with the coffin containing the remains of their homesick daughter.

But as fate would have it, their ship was sunk in a storm in the Atlantic. Legend says the girl named Gretchen has not found her rest, and instead she walks the lock that was her last, unhappy home.

Atwood Lake Resort is at 2650 Lodge Road, Dellroy; (330) 735–2211, (800) 362–6406; www .atwoodlakeresort.com. Lodge rates: $79 to $179 per night, double occupancy; cottage rates from $135 per night to $1,175 per week, depending on season. Visa, MasterCard, and American Express accepted.

The family known as the Fighting McCooks did not earn that moniker in barroom brawls. Rather, the Ohio McCooks earned that distinction because of their incredible family commitment to the United States military before and during the Civil War. In fact, Daniel McCook and his eight sons and the five sons of Daniel's brother John all served in the Union army. The Daniel McCook family included three major generals, two brigadier generals, one colonel, two majors, and one private. John McCook's sons served as a major general, two lieutenants, a commander, and a brigadier general.

About 1837 Daniel McCook erected the large brick home on the southwest corner of the public square in Carrollton. The *McCook House* was in the family until 1853, and it was acquired by the state of Ohio more than a century later. It is furnished with period pieces and relics from the McCook family.

The McCook House is on the square in Carrollton; (330) 627–3345, (800) 600–7172; www.ohiohistory.org/places/mcookhse. Open Memorial Day to Labor Day, Friday and Saturday, 10:00 A.M. to 5:00 P.M.; Sunday, 1:00 to 5:00 P.M.; Labor Day to mid-October, Saturday, 10:00 A.M. to 5:00 P.M.; Sunday, 1:00 to 5:00 P.M. Admission: adults $3.00; children (ages 6 to 12) $1.00.

It's not usual to see cows and bulls in farm fields in Ohio, so you might do a double take when heading down Muskrat Road toward the *Dickinson Cattle Ranch.* During summer months, visitors can take bus tours through this working cattle ranch to see not only prize-winning cattle, but breeds that are not common in the Midwest. Perhaps the most striking of those is the Texas Longhorn. These magnificent creatures have horns that are about 5 or 6 feet from tip to tip. Longhorns can be many colors: speckled, brown, black, blue, even an orange color. Rivaling the Texas Longhorns for, well, long horns, is the ranch's herd of Watusi cattle. The horns of Watusi bulls measure 6 feet or more from tip to tip, while the base of the horns can be more than 2 feet around. These cattle are tall, too. Looking out the bus window will put you right about at horn-level with these huge animals. Another interesting breed at the ranch is the Blue Lingo. Unlike the multicolored and speckled Longhorn, Blue Lingos look like dark cows wearing a white cummerbund. They are more docile animals, but the big, white stripe around their middles certainly makes them striking.

This is not a tourist attraction, but a working cattle ranch. The owners breed animals for sale internationally. The ranch features the

barnesville's "gay '90s mansion"

Founded in 1808 by James Barnes, a Quaker from Maryland, Barnesville prospered as a producer of tobacco and strawberries during the nineteenth century. As the town flourished, so did its banks. It was the Bradfields, the owners of the First National Bank, who built the town's most dramatic residence, what's known as the "Gay '90s Mansion."

This elegant, twenty-six room, eleven-thousand-square-foot structure, complete with dramatic turret, took five years to construct, and cost $60,000 when completed in 1893. In its prime, the mansion hosted Barnesville's most important dinners and parties, guests climbing the massive oak staircase to the third-floor ballroom. Today, the mansion is a museum and the restored home of the local historical society.

Longhorn Head to Tail Store where you can purchase souvenirs and beef products. An example is the Barrel O' Beef, featuring longhorn jerky, longhorn beef
sticks and longhorn pepper stick summer sausage.

The Dickinson Cattle Ranch is at 35000 Muskrat Road, Barnesville; (740)
758–5050; www.texaslonghorn.net. Open June through August, Monday
through Saturday, 10:00 A.M. to 5:00 P.M.; Sunday, 1:00 to 6:00 P.M. Bus tour
ticket: $10.

Cibo's Restaurant serves authentic Italian cooking in a very unusual
setting—an old movie theater. The Mohawk Theater, built in the early 1940s,
presented feature films for the people of Waynesburg for decades. But since
1971 it has been spaghetti the pasta, not spaghetti the western, that attracts
crowds at 134 West Lisbon Street.

At first, dining was limited to the Mohawk's old lobby, but now the entire
theater has been remodeled and converted to a multilevel eating area, complete
with ceiling fans and oak dividers. Italian favorites such as antipasto, pasta fagi-
oli (beans), spezzato (wedding) soup, and homemade chicken noodles constitute the list of appetizers. The reasonably priced entrees include spaghetti,
rigatoni, cavatelli, lasagna, ravioli, and cannelloni, and for those who have trouble choosing from that list, a combination plate offers a sample of all the above.
Cibo's offers American dishes as well—baked steak and chicken, plus family-
style combinations of spaghetti, ravioli, chicken, lasagna, and baked steak.
Pizza and sandwiches are also served.

Cibo's is at 134 West Lisbon Street, Waynesburg; (330) 866–3838. Open
Thursday and Sunday, 11:00 A.M. to 8:00 P.M.; Friday and Saturday, 11:00 A.M. to
9:00 P.M. Personal checks are accepted.

The quaint village of Magnolia was established in 1834. The picturesque,
bright-red, four-story Elson Mill has been in continuous operation since that
date, always in the hands of the Elson family. Next door to the mill is a truly
memorable bed-and-breakfast, the *Elson Inn.* A stately Victorian Italianate constructed in 1879, it too has always been in the Richard Elson family. You enter
through ten-foot leaded glass doors into this period masterpiece. The decor is
faithful to the home's Victorian vintage, truly a step back in time. Common
areas include a parlor with piano, sitting room with fireplace and board games,
library with comfy leather chairs, outdoor garden room, and a large wraparound porch with swings and comfortable rockers. After breakfast, enjoy a
stroll along the mill pond or a more rigorous 1.5-mile hike along the towpath
of the Sandy Beaver Canal to Elson Dam.

The Elson Inn is at 255 North Main Street, Magnolia; (330) 866–9242; www
.elsoninn.com. Rates: $110 to $130 per night double occupancy including
breakfast.

William McKinley was elected the twenty-fifth president of the United States in 1896. Five years later he was assassinated at the Pan-American Exposition in Buffalo, New York. He died in office on September 14, 1901. The story of this Ohio native's life and public career is preserved at *The McKinley Museum,* a multifaceted complex that also includes the McKinley National Memorial, a hands-on science center for kids of all ages, a history museum, and a 65-seat planetarium.

Perhaps the most dramatic section of this vast museum is the Street of Shops. Visitors stroll down a nineteenth-century boulevard that is complete with a pioneer home; a general store; an early print shop; dentist's, physician's, and lawyer's offices; a photography studio; a hotel; a fire station; and a toy company and shop. There is also an 84-foot model train layout, including a Pennsylvania Railroad train station.

Included in this impressive complex is Discover World, an interactive scientific program geared for children and the young at heart. At the entrance to Discover World, you're greeted by the spine-tingling roar of a life-sized allosaurus, with jaws that open and legs that move thanks to the magic of robotics. Ingenious in-verted periscopes let you check out the plant and animal life in a series of ponds. Once aboard Space Station Earth, you find yourself in a scientific laboratory, where you can activate demonstrations on lasers and light waves, water in motion, and air under pressure.

kilnsaplenty

As early as 1806, small kilns were fired in East Liverpool to take advantage of the area's unique clay and produce the popular "yellow ware" pottery. James Bennett, a potter from England, walked into town in 1839 determined to build a pottery empire. Profits from his effort the first year were $250, a huge sum in those days and just the beginning of a dramatic expansion for East Liverpool's pottery industry. By the end of the century, more than one-third of all the kilns operating in the United States were in East Liverpool—239 of them.

The McKinley Museum is at 800 McKinley Monument Drive NW, Canton; (330) 455–7043; www.mckinleymuseum.org. Summer hours: Monday through Saturday, 9:00 A.M. to 6:00 P.M.; Sunday, noon to 6:00 P.M. The rest of the year: Monday through Saturday, 9:00 A.M. to 5:00 P.M.; Sunday, noon to 5:00 P.M. Admission: adults $7.00; children (ages 3 to 18) $5.00.

You might think that the likely home for the *First Ladies National Historic Site* would be somewhere in Washington, D.C. You might think that, but you would be incorrect. It is actually in downtown Canton. The mission of the First Ladies National Historic Site is to create a central location where people can explore the lives of our nation's first ladies and their contributions to our nation's history. The site is both a primary research facility and an educational center that includes three major components: the National First Ladies' Library online bibliographic database, the library in the historically documented Saxton McKinley home, and an educational center adjacent to the Saxton McKinley home in the former City National Bank Building.

The Saxton McKinley house is a two- and three-story brick building of irregular massing. It was constructed in two segments in 1841 and ca. 1865. It is significant as the only remaining residence with direct historical ties to President William McKinley in his hometown of Canton. It was the family home of McKinley's wife, Ida, and he and his wife lived in the house between 1878 and 1891.

The Saxton McKinley House in Canton celebrated its national debut as the home of the National First Ladies' Library with a dedication ceremony and Victorian Gala in June, 1998, with former First Lady Rosalynn Carter. The public rooms of the house have been restored to their original splendor, complete with ornate historical wallpapers and period furniture. Great care has been taken to ensure that all design elements, including patterns of wallpaper, carpets, and area rugs, are authentic.

stateflower timestwo

President William McKinley wore a red carnation in his lapel every day for twenty-nine years. After McKinley's assassination in 1901, Ohio legislators searched for a fitting tribute to the fallen president. In his honor, they made the red carnation Ohio's state flower in 1904. Their resolution read: "for its beauty, its fragrance and its fitness, let it be adopted as the state flower of Ohio; and let the action of its adoption be to the memory of William McKinley."

Not contented with a single state flower, Ohio lawmakers declared the trillium grandiflorum the state wildflower in 1987. They noted that the large-flowered or white trillium is found in all eighty-eight Ohio counties and is easy to identify.

The renovated ballroom is, and always has been, located on the third floor of the house. Many parties were held in this ballroom, since the Saxtons were among the most prominent families in Canton. In President McKinley's study, all of the wallpapers were custom-made by historic merchants to replicate wallpaper depicted in an early photograph of the study taken during his official residence. The photo revealed a wallpaper that resembles an intricate quilt of Oriental scenes.

The library and parlor are decorated in the more opulent Italianate style that became popular after the Civil War. In this area there are twenty-three different wallpaper patterns in subtle shades of tan, grayish green, rose, and warm beige. The flow of the color and pattern creates an ambiance that is feminine, but understated and elegant. Lace curtains, authentically reproduced from an 1876 pattern, are thrown over rods and pinned in place—just as the Victorians did it. The chrysanthemum-patterned Wilton Carpet was loomed in the same mill that provided carpet for the White House at First Lady Dolly Madison's request.

The building housing the educational and research center was constructed in 1895 and has seven floors with approximately 20,000 square feet of usable space. It had a large skylight over the main banking room on the first floor that has been fully restored, as well as an extensive glass block floor under the skylight. There is extensive use of marble on the first floor foyer/lobby and main banking room, as well as in the lobbies on the upper floors of the building. There is a 91-seat Victorian theater on the lower level, where films and documentaries on first ladies are shown, and author presentations and live lectures take place. The center also houses a collection of books that replicates the first White House library created by First Lady Abigail Fillmore.

The First Ladies National Historic Site is at 331 Market Avenue South, Canton; (330) 452–0876; www.firstladies.org. Tours are given Tuesday through Saturday at 9:30 and 10:30 A.M. and at 12:30, 1:30, and 2:30 P.M. (Sunday tours are offered in the summer). Admission: adults $7.00; children (under age 18), $5.00.

Canton was once home to the Canton Bulldogs, an early-day powerhouse in professional football. Today Canton, where the National Football League began in 1920, is the home of the national shrine of professional football, the *Pro Football Hall of Fame.* This five-building complex delights every pigskin addict, with action films, displays, and gridiron history. Expanded in 1995, the highlight of the hall is the GameDay Stadium Theater, where visitors are treated to a unique rotating theater. The extravaganza begins with rare training-camp footage few "outsiders" ever see. The theater then rotates 180 degrees into the stadium, where NFL football is presented in Cinemascope on a screen almost two stories high.

A 7-foot bronze rendition of Jim Thorpe greets visitors to this comprehensive museum. Exhibits trace the history of the sport from the first game in 1892 to the latest teams. In the Pro Football Photo Art Gallery, you'll find the best of professional sports photography. The African-American Pioneers display tells the story of African Americans in the NFL. A favorite here are the twin Enshrinee Galleries, where the best of the best are honored. Each year a new class is enshrined, to join the ranks of pro football legends. After your tour, stop by the museum store for those can't-be-passed-up football souvenirs.

The Pro Football Hall of Fame is at 2121 George Halas Drive NW, Canton; (330) 456–8207; www.profootballhof.com. Open daily, 9:00 A.M. to 5:00 P.M. (closing at 8:00 P.M. during the summer). Admission: adults $15.00; children (ages 6 to 14) $8.00.

For those who appreciate the rumble seats, wooden-spoke wheels, and V-16 engines of antique automobiles, a stop at the ***Canton Classic Car Museum*** is a must. The museum, housed in one of Ohio's earliest Ford-Lincoln dealerships (1914–29), comprises dozens of meticulously restored vehicles, from a blue 1906 Reo to a 1938 Cadillac convertible with a 452-cubic-inch, 185-horsepower engine.

Six Packard automobiles, from model years between 1920 and 1937, trace the evolution of that distinctive make. For elegant driving, the museum contains a Rolls-Royce—a red and white 1929 Phantom I convertible. The museum also has a rare Marmon Sixteen, which, according to an advertisement used at a 1931 automobile show, "looks and performs like no other car—16 cylinders, 200 horsepower and under $5,000."

The two-seat 1929 Kissel White Eagle Speedster (available with rumble seat) conjures up images of goggles, blowing scarves, and deserted country roads. The very rare 1914 Benham is the only survivor of the nineteen cars produced by the short-lived automaker, which folded after only one year in business. Celebrity cars include Amelia Earhart's 1916 Pierce Arrow, Queen Elizabeth's 1939 Canadian tour car, and a movie car from *Those Daring Young Men in Their Jaunty Jalopies*. The museum also has an armor-plated, bulletproof 1937 Studebaker from the Canton Police Department.

In addition to the fine old cars, vintage gas and steam engines and other automotive paraphernalia are on display. In the restoration shop, future classics await rejuvenation.

The Canton Classic Car Museum is at 555 Market Avenue South, Canton; (330) 455–3603; www.cantonclassiccar.org. Open daily, 10:00 A.M. to 5:00 P.M. Admission: adults $7.50; students $5.00.

Daniel and Mary Hoover arrived in 1852 on their eighty-two-acre farm, where Daniel's father had established a leather tannery. At the turn of the century, Daniel's son, W.H. Hoover, realized that the coming age of automobiles would drastically reduce the demand for leather goods such as harnesses and

Canton Classic Car Museum

saddles. So W.H. Hoover searched for a new product for the Hoover Company, and bought the rights to inventor Murray Spangler's upright vacuum cleaner. In 1908 Hoover offered the public the first commercially viable upright vacuum cleaner, the Hoover Suction Sweeper Model O.

In less than a decade, the Hoover Company blossomed into an international concern. With its world headquarters in North Canton, the company has established the **Hoover Historical Center** on the family's original Stark County farmstead. Hoover history unfolds in the Italianate-style farmhouse accented with elegant Victorian decor.

A six-minute video presentation details the history of the company, and guided tours begin in the tannery, which was the original family home, where many leather-working tools and artifacts from the late 1800s are displayed. The two-story white farmhouse contains what has to be the world's most complete collection of antique vacuums, ranging from the 1869 Whirlwind Cleaner, which was the first manual vacuum cleaner offered for sale that picked up dust with suction, to modern Hoover units.

The Kotten Suction Cleaner, built in 1910, required the operator to stand and rock on the bellows to create suction—it sold for $25. The 1905 Skinner electric vacuum was advertised as a portable, but weighed more than a hundred pounds! Murray Spangler's original 1907 upright stands next to the Hoover Model O, which launched this multinational corporation. Other Hoover exhibits include old photos of W.H. Hoover and various Hoover factories around the world, early advertisements for Hoover products, World War II memorabilia, and some furnishings used by the family in the farmhouse. Herb and flower gardens surround the museum, which hosts changing exhibits throughout the year.

The Hoover Historical Center is located at 1875 East Maple Street NW, North Canton; (330) 499–0287; www.hoover.com/dbPages/history_9.asp. It's open Wednesday through Saturday, with tours conducted hourly from 1:00 to 4:00 P.M. No admission charge.

As the mules clip-clop down the towpath, for a moment you can imagine yourself back in the days of Ohio's canal era—people waving, men tossing horseshoes, barefoot boys fishing. The captain points out the sights, such as a drydock where canal boats were built and repaired. In less than thirty minutes, you reach the Lock 4 turning basin. The captain describes how the lock works as the skillful crew poles the boat around for the scenic trip home. You float along in the *St. Helena III*, a 60-foot replica of the freight barges that slipped through the canal network crisscrossing the state more than a hundred years ago.

Canal Fulton is a living canal town of 3,500 residents, where tourism and historical appreciation have replaced the commerce that once thrived on this section of the Ohio and Erie Canal. In addition to the authentic canalboat rides,

Canal Fulton features an inviting nineteenth-century business district, listed on the National Register of Historic Places, with everything from antiques and gifts to candy and ice cream.

Other attractions include a Canal Days Museum and tours of a saltbox-style residence built in 1847. Biking along a section of the Cardinal Trail and canoeing on the Tuscarawas River are popular.

Canal Fulton is between Barberton and Massillon on State Route 93; (330) 854–3808. Canalboat rides are given daily in the summer, plus on weekends in May, September, and October.

For charming accommodations in the area, try the ***Canal House Bed and Breakfast.*** This ca. 1865 Georgian-style post-and-beam home offers three guest rooms with private baths. A hot tub provides more modern creature comforts.

The Canal House Bed and Breakfast is at 306 South Canal Street, Canal Fulton; (330) 854–6229, (888) 875–2021; www.bbonline.com/oh/canalhouse. Rates: $65 to $100 per night.

If cooking is the way to your heart, you will find just what you're looking for at the ***Amish Door Restaurant & Village.*** The restaurant features family-style meals as well as a standard menu. This is Amish country, so fresh baked breads and real mashed potatoes have got to be part of your meal, along with a country-fresh salad from the salad bar. Inside the restaurant is a bakery, so you can take some of those fresh baked goodies with you.

If you're spending some time in the area, the Amish Door Village offers two choices of accommodations. The Hasseman Bed and Breakfast has four guest rooms in an early 1900 Victorian home. The most unusual is the "Attic" room, which is the inn's honeymoon suite. Breakfast is served at the B & B.

The Inn at Amish Door offers fifty-two Victorian-style rooms in a modern inn. Your stay includes a continental breakfast, and the inn offers such amenities as a heated indoor pool and a fitness room.

The Amish Door Restaurant & Village is located at 1210 Winesburg Street, Wilmot; (330) 359–5464, (330) 359–7904; www.amishdoor.com. Rates: $69 to $119 per night.

Europe's foremost woodcarvers proclaimed Ernest Warther "the world's master carver," and the intricately crafted carvings displayed at ***Warther's*** museum give credence to that proclamation. Born near Dover, Ohio, in 1885, Ernest started carving at age five, when he found an old pocketknife while tending the family's cow. His formal education ended in the second grade, and at the age of fourteen he went to work in the American Sheet and Tin Plate Company's mill. During his twenty years at the plant, he used his spare time to perfect his craft.

That steel-rolling mill is preserved today in a 3-by-5-foot working model carved by Warther—a model built with thousands of small, handmade walnut parts. Warther mechanized not only the model's steel-rolling equipment, but also many of the workers, including the foreman raising a sandwich to his mouth, a second worker nodding off on the job, and a third "drinking" his lunch by raising a tiny bottle to his lips. An intricate belt-drive system designed by Warther and a sewing-machine motor power the model's many moving parts.

Warther's most widely acclaimed carvings, however, are the series he created tracing the history of steam power, particularly his many steam locomotives and trains. Starting with working models of the simplest steam devices dating from 250 B.C., Warther produced models of the various developmental stages of the steam era. By far the most impressive of these are the dozens of steam railroad locomotives on display at the museum, many with hundreds of moving parts.

Warther used walnut for the dark pieces of his models and, in the early part of his career, pieces of bone for the white pieces. In later years, he could afford ivory and carved entire trains, some with as many as 10,000 parts, from pure white ivory. Warther used arguto, an oil-bearing wood, for the moving parts of his carvings, some of which have run for eighty years without repair.

Of the steam locomotives displayed at Warther's, perhaps the most intriguing is the 8-foot replica of Abraham Lincoln's funeral train. An avid admirer of Lincoln, Warther spent a year at age eighty carving the ebony and ivory locomotive, coal car, funeral car, and passenger cars. Thousands of miniature parts make up the magnificent carving. As an example of the extraordinary detail work done by Warther, outside the restroom in one of the passenger cars there is even a tiny ivory key hanging on a hook on the wall.

Warther's exacting craft demanded fine precision knives and blades, and, not satisfied with those commercially available, he created his own custom cutlery. In fact, he supplemented his income by selling this cutlery, a business still operated by his family today. Ernest Warther died at the age of eighty-seven in 1973, leaving his sixty-fourth carving incomplete. Footage of Warther working at his craft is shown in the Warther theater.

The small original museum behind the present one houses Mrs. Warther's button collection—more than 70,000 buttons, no two alike. Beautiful Swiss-style gardens surround the museums and the Warther home.

Warther's is at 331 Karl Avenue, Dover; (330) 343–7513; www.warthers .com. Open daily, 9:00 A.M. to 5:00 P.M., except for major holidays (10:00 A.M. to 4:00 P.M. December through February, closed Sunday January through February). Admission: adults $9.50; children $5.50.

TOP ANNUAL EVENTS

Maple Syrup Guided Walking Tour,
Newark, March;
(740) 323–2355, (800) 443–2937;
www.dawesarb.org

Dennison Railroad Festival,
Dennison, May;
http://web.tusco.net/drrf

Utica Old Fashioned Ice Cream Festival,
Utica, May;
(740) 892–4272;
www.uticaoldfashionedicecream
festival.com

Dulcimer Days,
Coshocton, May;
(740) 622–9310, (800) 877–1830;
www.roscoevillage.com

Buckeye Central Scenic Railroad,
Hebron, May to December;
(800) 970–5242;
http://home.insight.rr.com/pcaravan

Trumpet in the Land,
New Philadelphia, June to August;
(330) 339–1132;
www.trumpetintheland.com

Cows and Curds,
Zoar, June;
(330) 874–4336, (800) 874–4336;
www.ohiohistory.org/places/zoar

The Living Word Outdoor Drama,
Cambridge, June to September;
(740) 439–2761;
www.livingworddrama.org

First Town Days Festival,
New Philadelphia, 4th of July weekend;
(330) 343–6814;
http://web.tusco.net/ftd

Ohio Hills Folk Festival,
Quaker City, July;
(740) 679–2704

Jamboree in the Hills,
Morristown, July;
(800) 624–5456;
www.jamboreeinthehills.com

A new century was just beginning when Jeremiah E. Reeves moved his family into a newly remodeled home in 1901. Originally built as a stately eight-room farmhouse around 1870, the house was expanded into a magnificent seventeen-room mansion by Reeves, Dover's wealthiest citizen. Its gleaming white exterior is enhanced by dormers, bays, turrets, classical columns, and a porte cochere. To the rear of this Victorian mansion is a large turreted carriage house.

Today, the Dover Historical Society invites you to tour the *J.E. Reeves Victorian Home and Museum* for a magnificent look at turn-of-the-century elegance. Lush drawing-room draperies, gleaming windows of stained and leaded glass, luxurious parquet floors, and artistic mementos of the Reeves family all greet the eye. Nearly all of the furnishings on display belong to the Reeveses and are placed where they were when the family lived here. Other special features include a distinctive hand-carved oak grand stairway and a delightful third-floor ballroom.

Pro Football Hall of Fame Festival,
Canton, late July to August;
(330) 456–7253, (800) 533–4302;
www.profootballhoffestival.com

Coshocton Canal Festival,
Coshocton, August;
(740) 622–9310, (800) 877–1830;
www.roscoevillage.com

Tuscarawas County Italian-American Festival,
Dover, August;
(330) 339–6405

Fredericktown Tomato Show,
Fredericktown, September;
www.tomatoshow.com

Ohio Swiss Festival,
Sugarcreek, September;
(330) 852–4113, (888) 609–7592;
www.sugarcreekohio.org

Barnesville Pumpkin Festival,
Barnesville, September;
(740) 425–2593, (740) 425–3331;
www.barnesvillepumpkinfestival.com

Holmes County Antique Festival,
Millersburg, October;
(330) 674–6781;
www.holmescountyantiquefestival.com

Algonquin Mill Fall Festival,
Carrollton, October;
(330) 627–5910;
www.carrollcountyohio.com/history

Buckeye Book Fair,
Wooster, November;
(330) 262–3244;
www.buckeyebookfair.com

Holiday Open House at the Orville Depot,
Orville, November;
(330) 683–2426;
www.orvillerailroad.com

Dalton Holidays Festival,
Dalton, December;
(330) 828–9543

Out in the carriage house, built in 1902, the first floor houses a marvelous 1892 two-horse carriage that belonged to the Reeves family, a one-horse sleigh, and a 1922 automobile. Upstairs, visitors find remnants of the old Dover post office, along with displays of early household tools and sports memorabilia, plus historic maps, photographs, and documents. Following the crooked stairs to the Tower Rooms rewards the visitor with collections of old-fashioned cameras and radios.

The J.E. Reeves Victorian Home and Museum is at 325 East Iron Avenue, Dover; (330) 343–7040, (800) 815–2794; www.doverhistory.org. Open June through October, Thursday through Sunday, noon to 4:00 P.M. and December, 1:00 to 7:00 P.M. daily. Open other times of the year by appointment. Admission: adults $6.00; children $2.00.

More than 100 years after this Victorian home welcomed a farm family after a hard day's work, the ***1881 Olde World Bed and Breakfast*** now welcomes travelers for a peaceful retreat. The home, constructed of sun-baked brick and hand-hewn hardwood beams, was built, as you might have guessed, in 1881. Original features, such as pocket doors and the solid walnut staircase, have been restored. The guest rooms have been updated, and the suites have a private bath and are air-conditioned. Each of the rooms is decorated in a theme: the Victorian, the Parisian, the Mediterranean, and the Alpine. Some have old-fashioned claw-foot tubs, fireplaces, and king-size beds.

Guests are treated to a family-style breakfast every morning and can relax in the hot tub. "Queen's Tea" is served in the Tea Room Wednesday through Saturday and includes a three-course luncheon. Reservations are recommended; romantic escape packages also are available.

The 1881 Olde World Bed and Breakfast is at 2982 Route 516 NW, Dover; (330) 343-1333, (800) 447-1273; www.oldeworldbb.com. Rates: $95 to $125 per night.

Seeking freedom from the new religious tenets in their native Kingdom of Wurttemburg in Germany, 300 men, women, and children known as Separatists, led by Joseph Baumeler, came to 5,500 acres they had purchased along the Tuscarawas River and established *Zoar Village* in 1817. Two years later, frustrated by their progress, the Zoarites abandoned personal property ownership in order to establish a communal system. Under the new system, all property in the village was owned by the Society of Separatists at Zoar, with men and women each given a vote in the election of a board of trustees. The board governed the day-to-day operations of the community, and under this system, with Baumeler remaining as leader of the group, Zoar flourished.

The community established its own farms for food products, a tin shop, a blacksmith shop, two blast furnaces, a bakery, a garden with greenhouse, and a wagon shop. Many of these enterprises produced more goods than needed by the village, with the surplus sold for profit at a store established by the villagers. The Zoarites even landed the contract to build a section of the Ohio and Erie Canal, which passed through their land.

In 1852, the assets of the society were more than a million dollars, and the future appeared bright for this hard-working community. But a year later, Joseph Baumeler was dead, leaving a serious leadership void at Zoar. Baumeler had served as the inspiration of the village, as well as its financial administrator. After his death, Zoar began a gradual decline, which persisted for forty years. Finally, in 1898, having lost its competitive edge both in agriculture and in industry, the community disbanded.

Many of the original Zoar buildings have been restored or reconstructed, allowing visitors to better understand the unique experiment that took place here. Inside the Number One House, an audiovisual presentation provides the history of the village. The rooms in this rambling two-story brick building, which once housed the aged and infirm, contain many original furnishings. In the music room, for example, is Peter Bimeler's magnificent hand-built pipe organ. Bimeler was the village miller, and he powered the organ with the mill's water turbine.

The second-floor windows provide a splendid view of the adjacent gardens and greenhouse. A guide at the greenhouse explains the religious significance of the formal gardens, with the large Norway spruce symbolizing Christ and the twelve slip junipers representing the apostles. The greenhouse, constructed in 1835, utilized a unique heating system—charcoal fires burned under the floor; vents funneled the warm air into the greenhouse—allowing the Zoarites to cultivate a wide variety of fruits and vegetables, including tropical fruits. In the Zoar bakery, huge wooden bins stored flour and meal, and the brick oven baked eighty loaves of bread per day.

Other buildings in the village include a tin shop, which has the tools, patterns, and products used and produced by the tinsmith, and the Bimeler House, with its outstanding collection of wool coverlets woven at the community's woolen mill. Knowledgeable guides provide information and answer questions in each building of the village.

Zoar Village is on Route 212, Zoar; (330) 874–4336, (800) 874–4336; www.ohiohistory .org/places/zoar. Open from Memorial Day to Labor Day, Wednesday through Saturday, 9:30 A.M. to 5:00 P.M.; Sunday, noon to 5:00 P.M. Open weekends in April, May, September, and October. Admission: adults $7.00; children (ages 6 to 12) $3.00.

cows'ncurds

Quick, what is the month of June? If you said "Dairy Month" you'd be right. But whether you guessed correctly or not, you are still welcome to celebrate the dairy industry's history during Cows and Curds at Zoar Village Memorial.

The renovated dairy at Zoar Village is the backdrop for demonstrations of old-time dairy processing and practices, such as butter churning. Cows and Curds is celebrated in June at the Zoar Village Memorial on Route 212, Zoar. Call (800) 874–4336 for details.

The *Zoar Tavern & Inn,* built in 1831, was once the home of Dr. Clemens Breil, who lived here for many years—in fact, well after the dissolution of the Zoar Society. Today, the Zoar Tavern & Inn features solid oak booths and hardwood floors and serves soups, appetizers, salads, and a wide variety of sandwiches. Entrees such as char-grilled chicken breasts, pork chops, and prime rib au jus round out the menu, as do a selection of fresh-cut steaks and broiled seafood. For dessert, try the homemade gingerbread or a hot apple dumpling topped with ice cream, a French silk chocolate pie, or a hot peanut butter fudge sundae.

Overnight accommodations consist of nine guest rooms at two separate properties. The Inn, with original hand-hewn beams and exposed brick and stone walls, is decorated with period antiques. The Guest House features standard and Jacuzzi suites, each with a king-size bed and a gas fireplace.

The Zoar Tavern & Inn is at 162 Main Street, Zoar; (330) 874–2170; www .zoar-tavern-inn.com. The tavern is open daily, 11:00 A.M. to 10:00 P.M. Lodging rates: $85 to $150 per night. Visa, MasterCard, and American Express are accepted.

Named for Henry Laurens, then president of the Continental Congress, Fort Laurens, Ohio's only Revolutionary War fort, was constructed in 1778 as part of an ill-fated campaign to attack the British at Detroit. The 1,200 troops under the command of General Lachlan McIntosh, who built the fort, dubbed it "Fort Nonsense," since no attack on Detroit was ever executed. Supplying this wilderness outpost proved impossible, forcing the starving troops to survive on boiled moccasins while under siege from British-led Indians for a month. The fort was abandoned one year after it was built.

Today visitors to **Fort Laurens State Memorial** find the outline of the old fort, and a small museum that commemorates the conflict with both video and artifacts from the fort's excavation. The remains of soldiers who died defending Fort Laurens are buried in a crypt in the museum wall and at the Tomb of the Unknown Patriot of the American Revolution.

Fort Laurens State Memorial is at 11067 Fort Laurens Road NW, Bolivar; (330) 874–2059, (800) 283–8914; www.ohiohistory.org/places/ftlauren. Open Memorial Day through Labor Day, Wednesday through Saturday, 9:30 A.M. to 5:00 P.M.; Sunday, noon to 5:00 P.M. Open weekends only in September and October. Admission: adults $4.00; children (ages 6 to 12) $3.00.

Nestled on a wooded and secluded six-acre site, **Enchanted Pines Bed and Breakfast** was constructed with the visitor in mind. Built in 1981 in Yankee Barn design, the home features post-and-beam openness throughout. A living room with thirty-five foot ceilings and impressive fireplace is the heart of this 5,000-square-foot home. There is plenty of room to get away on your own on the home's grounds, or to join hosts Linda and Earl Menges for traditional high tea. Other amenities include a swimming pool, hot tub, and screened porch.

The three Key West rooms have second-floor views of the woods. The English Ivy Suite features separate sleeping and living areas, private porch with swing, and easy access to the pool.

Enchanted Pines Bed and Breakfast is at 1862 Old Trail Road NE, Bolivar; (330) 874–3197, (877) 536–7508; www.enchantedpines.com. Rates: $85 to $155 per night double occupancy including breakfast.

Missionary David Zeisberger migrated to the United States in 1737 to work with the American Moravian Church in Bethlehem, Pennsylvania. In

Schoenbrunn Village

1772, accompanied by a band of Delaware Indians, Zeisberger traveled to the wilderness in Ohio to convert other Indians to Christianity, founding *Schoenbrunn Village.*

The efforts at Schoenbrunn were interrupted by the coming of the Revolutionary War. The village was on the trail between the American outpost at Fort Pitt and the British at Fort Detroit, and neither side trusted the Moravians or their Christian Indians. Harassment eventually forced Zeisberger to abandon Schoenbrunn Village in 1777 and to relocate to a new settlement at nearby Gnadenhutten. Even there, they were not safe. The British arrested Zeisberger and other village leaders and transported them to Detroit for trial on charges of treason. While the leaders were away, American troops, seeking revenge for the death of a settler's wife and children, massacred the Christian Indians at Gnadenhutten by striking them with heavy coopers' mallets.

Schoenbrunn Village today contains eighteen reconstructed rustic log buildings, the original village cemetery, and two and a half acres of planted fields. Log cots with stretched animal skins and a firepit in the center of the floor (with a hole in the roof for smoke to escape) are the only conveniences in some of these cabins. Others feature modest pioneer furnishings such as rough rope-spring beds, wooden baby cradles, spinning and flax wheels, and butter churns. Schoenbrunn's settlers constructed Ohio's first schoolhouse, a one-room building completed in 1773. In addition to the log structures, a museum displays Schoenbrunn artifacts excavated from the site, including nails, knives, horseshoes, and chips of cups, jars, and a kettle used at the village more than 200 years ago.

Mingo Junction

George Washington slept here—actually he camped here in the fall of 1770. He came via canoe to scout the land in the Ohio Valley, and he found rugged country and plenty of Indians. He was here to secure land for the officers and soldiers of the Virginia Regiment before the British tried to claim it.

Upon his arrival in poor weather, Washington and his party heard of a killing down river, the direction they were heading. It was unclear if it was an Indian dispute or a simple homicide. After one night's rest, they left the spot that is known today as Mingo Junction and paddled downstream.

They arrived at Powhatan Point, from which Washington dispatched several in his party to uncover the truth about the alleged murder. They returned and told Washington that the rumors were untrue; the death had been an accidental drowning. On October 25, 1770, they departed, continuing their journey down the Ohio River.

Schoenbrunn Village is on Route 259 on the southeast edge of New Philadelphia; (330) 339–3636, (800) 752–2711; www.ohiohistory.org/places/schoenbr. Open Memorial Day to Labor Day, Wednesday through Saturday, 9:30 A.M. to 5:00 P.M.; Sunday, noon to 5:00 P.M. Admission: adults $7.00; children (ages 6 to 12) $3.00.

For a dramatic presentation of the story of David Zeisberger and the settlement of Schoenbrunn and Gnadenhutten, attend a performance of Paul Green's **Trumpet in the Land.** Staged in a lovely hilltop outdoor amphitheater, this spirited drama uses a mix of song and dance, humor, adventure, and ultimately tragedy to tell of Zeisberger's missionary work in frontier Ohio.

Trumpet in the Land is presented in repertoire with *The White Savage* at the Schoenbrunn Amphitheatre on University Drive, just off U.S. Route 250, New Philadelphia; (330) 339–1132; www.trumpetintheland.com. Performances from June through August, Monday through Saturday at 8:30 P.M. Admission: adults $15.00; children $7.00. Reserved tickets available. MasterCard and Visa are accepted.

The *Dennison Railroad Depot Museum* has been drawing people from all across the United States since it opened in 1989. This fully restored railroad station gives the visitor a glimpse into the role that railroads played in America's past. At the turn of the twentieth century this depot was a busy crossroads, hosting twenty-two arrivals daily. In the 1940s the station became an oasis of homegrown comfort for many World War II service men and women passing through on the National Defense Railroad Route. The depot grew famous as more and more military men and women were welcomed by scores of volunteers at the Salvation Army Servicemen's Canteen. This canteen was the third largest in the country and served free food and a little hometown warmth to thousands passing through on their way to and from the fronts.

Visitors can relive the early eras of railroad travel by visiting the museum and the various restored areas, including the women's lounge and the ticket booth. The large model N-scale train display will fascinate children, even the adult kind. You can also experience the flavor of the 1940s in the Pennsy Dining Company, which is filled with photos, hosts a documentary video, and serves pasta, seafood, and steaks.

The Dennison Railroad Depot Museum is at 400 Center Street, Dennison; (740) 922–6776, (877) 278–8020; www.dennisondepot.org. Open Tuesday through Saturday, 11:00 A.M. to 5:00 P.M.; Sunday, 11:00 A.M. to 3:00 P.M. Admission: adults $3.00; children (ages 7 to 17) $1.75.

The depot is also the place to begin a real railroad journey into the past. From May to December, the *Ohio Central Railroad* offers special railroad excursions. These trips may be on trains powered by diesel or steam locomotives, and last from one hour to a full day. Dinner and mystery trips, as well as autumn color tours, are just some of the special offerings. Prices range from $5.00 to around $100.00 depending on the type and duration of the trip. Reservations are recommended.

The Ohio Central Railroad trips originate and terminate at the Dennison Railroad Depot Museum. For schedules and trip rates, call (740) 922–6776 or (877) 278–8020; www .dennisondepot.org or www.amish steamtrain.com.

The *Quaker Meeting House,* set in a field in a hilly section of Jefferson County, housed the annual

famouspeople fromlittlecadiz

The little town of Cadiz boasts an impressive roster of native sons. Clark Gable was from this town, as was Edward Stanton, President Lincoln's Secretary of War during the Civil War, and John Bingham, who also has a Lincoln connection. Bingham, an attorney, worked in William Henry Harrison's presidential campaign and was elected to Congress in 1854. During his tenure in Washington, he served as special-judge advocate in the trial of Lincoln's assassins. He also was minister to Japan from 1873 to 1885.

August meeting of 2,000 Ohio and Pennsylvania Quakers for nearly a century. Constructed in 1814, this impressive three-story brick structure measures 92 feet by 60 feet and has walls 2 feet thick.

The Society of Friends relocated an entire meeting from North Carolina to Jefferson County in 1813 and built the meetinghouse of brick fired right on the

thehousethatjack built

You might know that Bellaire is the site of the original "house that Jack built." But did you know that "Jack" was a mule? Englishman Jacob Heatherington immigrated to this area and worked his way up from a laborer hauling coal to an industrialist. His faithful mule, Jack, helped him move coal in those early years, and Jacob never forgot this. So, when he erected a mansion in 1870, he referred to it as the "house that Jack built" and even took the old mule on a tour of the home's interior, describing the features as they clip-clopped through the magnificent residence. Jack died shortly afterward, and Jacob, grief-stricken, buried him nearby under an apple tree.

site. The interior of the building is one large room, with the original floors, poplar benches, and a large balcony. A massive wooden center divider splits the room—four men in the attic raised and lowered this divider as needed. Men sat on one side of the room during the meetings, women on the other side, and young men and women sat in their respective balconies. The elders and overseers used the facing benches— benches resting on a small platform and facing the congregation. "Strict services" took place here until 1909, with no formal ceremony or music; the group simply meditated in silence until a member felt moved to speak out. The interior of the meetinghouse is exactly as it was 170 years ago, though it has been more than 70 years since the Quakers last gathered in Jefferson County.

The Quaker Meeting House is just off Route 150 in Mount Pleasant. Open by appointmet April through October; call Sherry Sawchuk, (740) 769–2893, (800) 752–2631; www.ohiohistory.org/places/quaker. Admission: adults $4.00; children $2.00.

Amish Country

Ohio's largest Amish and Swiss Mennonite communities are in four east central Ohio counties: Holmes, Wayne, Tuscarawas, and Stark. The Amish espouse a simple agrarian lifestyle and reject the use of automobiles and electricity as potentially disruptive to that lifestyle. Living in the twentieth century without electricity creates a demand for unusual products, such as kerosene-powered refrigerators, and one Wayne County business, **Lehman's,** has established itself as the nonelectric appliance and equipment supplier for the area's substantial Amish population.

Although Lehman's stocks the nails, wire, and garden tools found in every hardware store, the bulk of the floor space is dedicated to merchandise such as gas-powered washing machines, and gas and kerosene lamps. Wood- and coal-burning cooking and heating stoves fill one large showroom, with many of the cooking stoves ornately trimmed in chrome and costing from $700 to $3,000.

Other items in Lehman's inventory include hardwood fruit presses, an apple parer, a cherry stoner, and a bottle capper. How many other stores carry a variety of hand-crank butter churns and a hand-powered cream separator that produces eighty-five liters of milk per hour?

The store's crowded hitching posts, used by the Amish to secure their horse-drawn buggies, indicate the popularity of Lehman's with the local Amish population, but in recent years Lehman's has attracted another type of customer—people drawn to wood- and coal-burning appliances because of the increasing cost of utilities. Lehman's sells a 160-page catalog called *Lehman's Non-Electric Good Neighbor Heritage Catalog* for $3.00. It's full of major appliances, small gristmills, copper wash boilers, sausage stuffers, noodle makers, and carbide lamps. And city people have been known to purchase unique non-electric devices, particularly the fancy chrome cooking stoves, simply for use as decorative pieces.

Lehman's is 2 miles west of Route 94 in downtown Kidron; (330) 857–5757; www.lehmans.com. Open Monday through Saturday, 8:00 A.M. to 5:30 P.M.; Thursday until 8:00 P.M.

Just down the street is the ***Kidron Town and Country Store,*** where you can purchase an array of Amish clothing—men's broadfall barndoor pants, black felt church hats, and wide-rimmed flat or mushroom-top straw hats.

Upstairs you'll find quilting supplies, and the store also offers fresh-cut meats, fresh fruits and vegetables, and other bulk food items. It has long been the custom of the Amish to come in from the fields at noon and enjoy *es midaugh*. They continue that tradition at the store, serving a hearty midday meal prepared by local Amish women in their restaurant.

The Kidron Town and Country Store is at 4959 Kidron Road, Kidron; (330) 857–2131; www.kidrontc.com. Open Monday through Saturday, 8:00 A.M. to 7:00 P.M.

After establishing their Christmas tree farm, Robert Dush and his son Roger's next challenge was to convert a barn built in the 1860s into a Christmas shop and country store, the ***Pine Tree Barn.*** This massive old barn has been designated a Wayne County Historic Landmark, and its original rough-hewn beams and floors create a rustic atmosphere.

What started as a gift shop in 1980 has evolved into a complete home furnishing and accessories center, featuring indoor and outdoor lighting, carpeting, floor coverings, and window treatments, plus gifts and accessories, all displayed on three floors in this marvelous historic structure. In fact, Roger Dush and his wife, Rita, offer a complete interior decorating and design service.

The gift shops at Pine Tree include a Colonial Williamsburg shop; a floral shop featuring silk and dried flowers, wreaths and garlands, and a year-round Christmas shop. Christmas is a special time of year at Pine Tree; you'll find thirty or more fully decorated trees throughout the structure, along with hundreds of unique ornaments and baubles.

A similar transformation took place at The Granary, the Pine Tree's dining facility. In the early '80s, this former dairy barn's old grain bins were converted into a small kitchen, serving simple refreshments. Today, The Granary presents gourmet lunches of crepes, quiches, soups, salads, fresh breads and muffins, and sandwiches. Top off your meal with a slice of one of the sour cream fruit pies, a Pine Tree Barn tradition for more than twenty years.

Large windows along the back wall of the barn provide those eating lunch with a view down the hill to the private forty-acre lake and rows of young Christmas trees. Diners also see antique farm implements on the walls of the barn and the block and tackle that once hauled bales of hay up from the ground level to the second-floor loft.

The Pine Tree Barn is on Route 226, 4374 Shreve Road, 4 miles south of Wooster; (330) 264–1014; www.pinetreebarn.com. Open Monday through Saturday, 9:00 A.M. to 5:00 P.M.; Sunday, 10:00 A.M. to 5:00 P.M.

The Charles Randolph Compton family built a Victorian farmhouse in 1881, and the family owned the property for more than ninety years. Two of Compton's descendants, Leila and Mary Belle, lived in the home until 1990. Leila was a recognized authority on herbs, and she and her sister often served syrups and jams made from their garden herbs when they entertained. A few of the apple and cherry trees remain to this day.

Jim and Marty Taggart were living in the Taggart family home (built in 1883) next door to the Compton house in 1990 when Leila and Mary were no longer able to live on their own. They purchased the property and began a massive, two-year renovation inside and out. They opened the *Leila Belle Inn* as a bed-and-breakfast in 1993.

Today, visitors enjoy four bedrooms, each with private bath, in this revitalized Victorian home. Its three acres include redbud and dogwood trees, restored gardens, walking paths, porches, and patios. Enjoy a leisurely breakfast of juice, fresh fruit compote, homemade granola with yogurt, and assorted goodies such as blueberry lemon bread, lemon crumb muffins, or apple strudel coffeecake, plus eggs and breakfast meats.

The Leila Belle Inn is at 846 East Bowman Street, Wooster; (330) 262–8866, (888) 430–7378; www.wooster-bnb.com. Rates: $70 to $95 per night. Visa and MasterCard accepted.

Before Deanna and Andy Troutman converted their property into a vine-yard, the previous owner used it to raise chickens and sell produce. The win-ery building formerly served as one of the chicken coops. The Troutmans moved in back in 1997 and began planting their vineyard the next year. By the fall of 2000, the first crop was harvested, and *Troutman Vineyards* unveiled their first three wines the following summer.

Deanna and Andy, who also serves as vineyard manager at Wolf Creek Vine-yards, currently have seven different wines ready to pour. During the holidays, try their Chambourcin Ice Wine, aged in French oak barrels with a hint of raisin and walnut. Another favorite is their White Menagerie seyval blanc, an award-winning fruity yet dry German-style white. Visitors are encouraged to take a self-guided tour of the vineyard's operations.

Troutman Vineyards is at 4243 Columbus Road, Wooster; (330) 263–4345; www.troutmanvineyards.com. Open April through December, Wednesday through Saturday, 1:00 to 6:00 P.M.; Saturday only January through March.

Set in rolling Wayne County farmland is charming *Quailcrest Farm.* More than six hundred different herbs and perennial plants, both potted and field grown, are cultivated here, ready for transplanting to your backyard garden. Flowering shrubs and trees are also available. April through June is the peak season for plants at Quailcrest, but a good selection is available throughout the summer and into fall.

Avid gardeners will love browsing through the various shops. The Garden Barn contains pottery and several garden ornaments. A newly built 12,000-square-foot greenhouse solarium displays a wide variety of perennials and herbs for sale. Another restored building, the 170-year-old Tracy Barn, sells contemporary gift items, including books, jewelry, gourmet foods, linens, and pet and children's items.

Outside, even people without green thumbs can enjoy wandering through five acres of display gardens overlooking the Killbuck Valley. You can view herb gardens, perennial plantings, and water gardens, or just sit and relax in the gazebo.

Quailcrest Farm is just off Route 83 at 2810 Armstrong Road, 5 miles north of Wooster; (330) 345–6722; www.quailcrest.com. Open late March through December, Tuesday through Saturday, 9:00 A.M. to 5:00 P.M. (extended and Sunday hours from the end of April through June and also after Thanksgiving).

Out-of-state antique dealers have frequented Jeromesville, Ohio, for years, but most native Ohioans are unaware of the town's reputation as an antiques stop. George Delagrange owns one of Jeromesville's more intriguing shops,

Delagrange Antiques, which is in an 1870s storefront that originally housed the town's drugstore.

Delagrange's business specializes in the poplar, cherry, and walnut pieces so in demand with East Coast buyers. Delagrange (whose name means "from the farm" in French) purchases four-poster rope-spring beds, cupboards, tables, and chests from area farms, selling scores of major pieces each year. In addition, George and his wife, Susan, always are delighted to chat with visitors about tidbits of local history that pertain to the pieces in the shop.

stateflag/pennant

Flying overhead at public buildings and parks in Ohio, visitors may be surprised to see what appears to be a pennant where they would expect a state flag to fly. That is Ohio's state flag. No other state flag has a pennant shape.

Cleveland designer John Eisenmann created this unusual design in the 1880s. At the wide end of the pennant is a blue triangle with a large circle and seventeen stars. The thirteen stars clustered closest to the circle represent the thirteen colonies. The four stars at the apex of the triangle represent the next four states admitted to the Union, since Ohio was the seventeenth state to join the Union. The circle represents the Northwest Territory, but with a smaller red circle at its center; it also forms an O for "Ohio."

Delagrange Antiques is at 12 North High Street (Route 89), Jeromesville; (330) 294–0778; www .ohioantiques.com. Open Saturday and Sunday, noon to 5:00 P.M.

The natural beauty of the Mohican area, with its steep and rolling hills, swift rivers, and deep forests, once prompted author Louis Bromfield to remark, "I live on the edge of paradise." Visitors to the area quickly realize that statement was no exaggeration. White pines flourish along the ridges of the ***Mohican State Park,*** while hemlock abounds in the hollows and gorges.

Cabins in Ohio's state parks typically are located in scenic surroundings, but the twenty-five two-bedroom Mohican State Park cabins, isolated from the rest of the park in woodlands along the bank of Clear Fork Creek, may just be in the most picturesque setting of any cabins in Ohio. They come furnished with all linens, blankets, and kitchen equipment, and may be rented in the summer for full weeks only. (There are no restrictions on the length of stay the rest of the year.) Canoeing and rafting are favorite summertime activities on Clear Fork Creek, and hiking, fishing, and camping are also popular in the park.

Mohican State Park cabins are on Route 3, just north of Route 97, Loudonville; (419) 994–5125, (866) 644–6727; www.dnr.state.oh.us/parks/ parks/mohican.htm. Open year-round. Rates range from $90 to $110 per night; early reservations are a must.

Another lodging option in the lush Mohican State Park is the impressive stone-and-timber Mohican Lodge, perched on a bluff overlooking Pleasant Hill Lake. Each room in the lodge has a private balcony or patio, many with views of either the lake or the woods surrounding the lodge. Facilities include indoor and outdoor pools, two tennis courts, shuffleboard, and a game room. In addition to the meals served in the dining room, poolside barbecues are offered occasionally during summer months.

The Mohican State Park Lodge is on Route 97, 6 miles west of Loudonville; (419) 938–5411, (800) 282–7275; www.mohicanresort.com. Open year-round. Rates: $110 to $180 per night, double occupancy.

The confluence of Black Fork River and Clear Fork Creek forms the scenic Mohican River, probably Ohio's most popular stream for canoeing, kayaking, and rafting. Canoe liveries rent hundreds of canoes and kayaks in the Loudonville area, from as early as April to as late as November. With prices of $15 and up per canoe and trips lasting from two hours to several days, the liveries provide access to these scenic waterways. One of the liveries, on Route 3 south of Loudonville and north of Route 97, is the *Mohican Canoe Livery and Fun Center,* which also has cabins, go-karts, horseback rides, water slides, and miniature golf; (419) 994–4097, (800) 662–2663; www.canoemohican.com. Many other liveries operate in the area, and a complete list is available from the Loudonville Chamber of Commerce, Loudonville 44842, or by calling (800) BUCKEYE, Ohio's tourism information center.

Another enjoyable way to explore the 4,000-acre Mohican State Forest is on horseback, and *Bit 'N Bridle Stables* offers guided trail rides through sections of this vast wooded preserve. Along the paths, riders enjoy deer, rabbits, and multicolored wildflowers in this peaceful state forest. Trail rides cost $23.00 for the first hour.

Bit 'N Bridle Stables is at 996 County Road 3275, off Route 3 south of Route 97, Perrysville; (419) 938–8681. Open daily, April through November.

It's a dream you may have had, too: Purchase one of those charming Victorian houses on a quiet street in a small Ohio town and restore it to create the perfect bed-and-breakfast. City people would flock to your new establishment, attracted by the charm of your stately residence, not to mention your gracious hospitality. You would earn extra income while enjoying the company of "new friends."

I'm sure that's what the couple who originally restored the *Blackfork Inn* believed when they acquired this 1865-vintage property on Water Street in Loudonville. Built by Philip J. Black, this delightful brick three-story home seemed destined to be a fine small inn. And the couple restoring it decided to "do it right" by importing antiques from Europe, installing a complete commercial kitchen,

Blackfork Inn

securing accurate reproductions of period wallpapers, and updating the six guest rooms with private baths, while retaining the high ceilings and natural woodwork that make such properties both distinctive and desirable. It's rumored they spent upwards of a half-million dollars on this project, and that may have been their undoing. Less than a year from their grand opening, the Blackfork Inn was closed down and boarded up—its brief resurrection snuffed out.

On Labor Day weekend in 1982, Al and Sue Gorisek arrived at the sheriff's auction at the Blackfork hoping to pick up some good deals on antiques, which they have collected for years. But they walked away as the proud new owners of the entire inn.

The inn they acquired was orginally the home of Philip Black who built it from the profits he made during the Civil War selling groceries and such to Federal troops. It's said he was instrumental in bringing the railroad to Loudonville, so it seems appropriate that railroad tracks are next door—it's the main line between New York and Chicago, so trains do rumble by!

Both Goriseks are from the publishing world: Al is a retired editor for the *Cleveland Plain Dealer;* Sue writes for *Ohio Magazine* and other publications. And the Blackfork has become Sue's other career—she splits her time between their home in Cleveland and the inn. Sue is perhaps the perfect host for such a place, for as a freelance writer, she travels the state extensively and has plenty of tips for guests on where to go and what to see in the area.

Accommodations at the Blackfork Inn—six rooms plus two large suites— include exquisite breakfasts featuring fresh fruit, a breakfast entree, and a raspberry crepe. Although no other meals are routinely served, an area chef is available to prepare elegant meals for guests with approximately one week's notice.

The Blackfork Inn is at 303 North Water Street, Loudonville; (419) 994–3252; www.blackforkinn.com. Rates: $75 to $140 per night, including breakfast. MasterCard and Visa are accepted. Open year-round.

The fertile, rolling farmland of Holmes County is the center of Ohio's largest Amish community, with 20,000 of the 145,000 Amish in the United States living in the area. Amish men and women can be seen in the markets, restaurants, and shops, or driving their black horse-drawn buggies through the pastoral countryside.

Amish restaurants in Holmes and surrounding counties serve simple country cooking at reasonable prices, and shops sell Amish goods, such as quilts. This section of east central Ohio also contains a sizable Swiss Mennonite population, and there are many cheese houses producing Swiss cheese from the milk brought in by Amish dairy farmers.

The Amish were the largest group of the 1694 Swiss Brethren split, following the leadership of Jacob Ammann, from whom the sect gets its name. Facing religious persecution in their native Germany and Switzerland, they began a migration to the United States in the 1730s, settling in Pennsylvania. The move to Ohio took place in 1808, and Holmes County, Ohio, now is the world's largest community of Amish. The Amish continue the agricultural traditions of the past 200 years.

Artist Heinz Gaugel painted the history of the Amish-Mennonite-Hutterite people in a spectacular 10-foot-by-265-foot cyclorama called **Behalt,** which means "to remember." Completed in 1992 after four years' labor, Behalt spans the centuries from the time of Christ to the Amish migration to the New World to the present day. *Behalt* is permanently displayed at the Mennonite Information Center, where guides use the cyclorama to educate visitors about Amish history, culture, and lifestyle.

Behalt and the Mennonite Information Center are at 5798 County Road 77, Berlin; (330) 893–3192; www.pages.sssnet.com/behalt. Open Monday through Saturday, 9:00 A.M. to 5:00 P.M.; extended hours until 8:00 P.M., Friday and Saturday, June through October. Admission: adults $5.50; children (ages 6 to 12) $2.50.

Gloria and Eli *Yoder's Amish Home* is a hundred-acre working farm that can be explored by visitors to Amish country. Children will enjoy the horses, rabbits, chickens, sheep, cows, pigs, and goats that fill the barn. Adults will probably be more interested in the two farmhouses, both built more than one hundred years ago. The first home on your tour contains furnishings typical of an Amish farmhouse in the late 1800s. Built in 1866, this home last served as a residence more than thirty years ago. Its wood floors, simple heavy furniture, wood-burning stove, and people-powered appliances (such as a pump sewing machine) give a glimpse of the lifestyle of Amish farm families.

The larger home, constructed in 1885 and occupied for one hundred years, is similarly furnished but contains some unusual items such as gas floor lamps. Religious services have been held here many times, as in most Amish homes and barns. These services take three full hours to complete.

Many who visit here enjoy buggy tours of the property, which even has a hilltop family cemetery. Inside the craft shop, you'll discover quilts, dolls, pottery, woodwork, and many other country favorites. And be sure to pick up a copy of the *Downhome Shoppers Guide*. This hundred-page magazine-style publication is the guide to Ohio's Amish settlements. It's packed with information on Amish restaurants, tours, crafts, quilts, cheese, and the like, with hundreds of entries and very detailed maps.

Yoder's Amish Home is on Route 515 between Trail and Walnut Creek; (330) 893–2541; www.yodersamishhome.com. Open mid-April through October, Monday through Saturday, 10:00 A.M. to 5:00 P.M. Tours: adults $4.50; children $2.50. Buggy rides: adults $3.00; children $2.00.

If you admire fine handmade quilts, stop by the ***Helping Hands Quilt Shop.*** A nonprofit enterprise with all proceeds donated to charities and missions, the shop stocks hundreds of marvelous quilts in every conceivable pattern and color combination. Many of these are sewn in the large, sunlit quilting room in the back of the shop, where Helping Hands serves a social function in addition to its contributions to charity.

Helping Hands will quilt your quilt top, custom design a quilt for you, or even finish a quilt you have already started. The shop also sells quilted pillow covers, quilting books, embroidery kits and floss, quilting needles, thread, fabrics, stencils, and patterns—in short, everything a quilter could need. Also visit the Quilt Museum, with its many antique quilts.

The Helping Hands Quilt Shop is on Route 39 at 4826 Main Street, Berlin; (330) 893–2233. Open Monday through Saturday, 9:00 A.M. to 5:00 P.M.

A variety of romantic options await guests of ***Donna's Premier Lodging*** in the heart of Amish country. Along with rooms in the main building, Donna's offers a variety of upscale log cabins, chalets, villas, and bridal suites. Honeymoon and anniversary chalets are two-level, brick, free-standing guest cottages located on a wooded hillside. Designed as luxurious retreats, they feature a main level with a king-size bed, a brick fireplace, and a heart-shaped Jacuzzi for two. The lower level is a recreation room with another fireplace and a billiard table. Throughout the chalets you will find elegant touches such as leaded glass windows, chandeliers, and homemade cookies for your late-night snack. Chalets are equipped with two televisions, stereo, CD player, microwave, coffeemaker, and a refrigerator. The log cabin is similarly equipped but has a queen-size bed tucked in a loft.

Whether summer or winter, the cabin, cottages, and chalets offer guests natural views and a good opportunity to wander just outside the door to visit with the birds or enjoy the woodland displays.

Donna's Premier Lodging is located ½ block off Main Street on East Street, just behind the Helping Hands Quilt Shop, Berlin; (330) 893–3068, (800) 320–3338; www.donnasofberlin.com. Rates: $129 to $369 per night.

Opened for guests in 1996, *Garden Gate Get-A-Way* has a surprisingly long history. Many elements in the home are from a dismantled one-room schoolhouse. The original bell tower is now perched on the roof's south peak, and the original foundation stones now form many of the retaining walls and line the flowerbeds. Inside, lumber, oak flooring, tongue-and-groove ceiling, and wainscoting have found new uses in this modern facility.

Roger and Laverta Steiner (and their children) are your innkeepers, offering four very different guest rooms, each with a garden theme. The Potting Shed Room features a picket fence headboard, a cane chair, and a hickory rocker. A white iron bed is the centerpiece of the Rose Garden Room, flanked by an antique tapestry chair and chest. The Briar Patch Room and the Grape Arbor Room both feature engraved headboards and individual furnishings. All four have private baths, queen-size beds, and coffeemakers.

The beautiful gardens include a grape arbor, birdhouses, and porch swings. Roger's design talent is on display with the fieldstone landscaping and winding brick paths through the lush gardens.

Garden Gate Get-A-Way is located just outside Berlin at 6041 Township Road 310; (330) 893–3999, (330) 674–7608; www.garden-gate.com. Rates: $99 to $179 per night.

If you look for an antique dealer at the *Antique Emporium,* you'll be in for more than you bargained for. The shop, located 2 blocks west of the Town Square in Millersburg, is really two buildings next door to one another, and is home to more than sixty different antiques dealers.

The wide range of antiques dealers in this historic hardware store building gives the shop a particularly broad range of merchandise. Since dealers are

ALSO WORTH SEEING

Salt Fork State Park,
Cambridge

Fort Steuben,
Steubenville

Steubenville Murals,
Steubenville

always on the lookout for the next unique item, the stock in the shop is ever changing. The discriminating buyer can seek out china, textiles, Victorian and country furniture, toys, primitives, books, glassware, and a range of collectibles.

Do-it-yourselfers can find great raw material in the "Furniture in the Rough" section. The gift shop is stocked with pencil Christmas trees, old wooden spools, candle lights, and garden and folk-art accents. Delivery service is available for shoppers who purchase more than the car trunk or van can handle.

The Antique Emporium is located at 113 West Jackson Street, Millersburg; (330) 674–0510; www.millersburgae.com. Open Monday through Saturday, 10:00 A.M. to 5:00 P.M.; Sunday 10:00 A.M. to 4:00 P.M.

When I first heard about a "modern" inn that opened outside Millersburg, right in the heart of Amish country, I must admit I was skeptical. I envisioned a motel-like structure on a bulldozed and paved chunk of earth, and I wasn't thrilled by the prospect.

The Inn at Honey Run does not fit that description in the least. As you motor up a winding county road, through dense vegetation, your curiosity can't help but be aroused. And when you reach the tasteful contemporary structure that is the Inn at Honey Run, it's difficult not to let out a sigh of approval. Carefully blended into the surrounding trees—trees so close that I'm not sure how they managed to get the inn up without disturbing them—is a truly unique getaway. Lots of exposed wood, inside and out, creates a harmony between the inn and the peaceful forest. The inn's twenty-five guest rooms combine a potpourri of styles—everything from Shaker and Early American to very contemporary. Cherry, pine, oak, and walnut furnishings complete these rooms; some feature bi-level floor plans with skylights. All have living areas and tabletop space for work (if absolutely necessary), writing, card playing, or whatever.

Up a hill from the main inn are twelve additional guest rooms in a most unusual setting—dug into the hillside. Called the Honeycomb, this earth-sheltered building looks down onto a peaceful landscape. Each room has a stone patio, gas log fire-

statebird/fish/insect

The designation of the cardinal as Ohio's state bird was uncontroversial; the Ohio General Assembly unanimously made it official in 1933. Lawmakers deemed the choice appropriate because the cardinal is a permanent resident of the state, its song is pleasing to hear, and its coloring is impressive. But other species have not had it so easy. A debate in the 1980s between fans of the walleye and boosters of the small-mouth bass resulted in a legislative standoff; neither side could muster the votes to be declared Ohio's state fish. One species did make the cut: the ladybug. Legislators declared it the state insect in 1975.

place, and a bath with a whirlpool tub. And breakfast is brought right to your door. The newest accommodations are three cabins nestled in the woods. The Trillium is a one-bedroom unit with large Jacuzzi tub; the Cardinal and Woods House feature two bedrooms.

If you can't stay the night, then come by and enjoy an excellent meal in the dining room, which has a wall of glass for viewing the trees and wildflowers. The inn prides itself on its from-scratch recipes, including some spectacular pastries and desserts, and regional specialties like pan-fried trout. The dining room is open to all for lunch and dinner, by reservation, Monday through Saturday. Overnight guests have the place to themselves on Sunday.

The Inn at Honey Run is 3 miles northeast of Millersburg off Route 241 on County Road 203; (330) 674–0011, (800) 708–9394; www.innathoneyrun.com. Lodging rates: $104 to $320 per night for two people, including continental breakfast. Visa, MasterCard, and American Express are accepted.

Charm is the state's only predominantly Amish town, and evidence of that fact includes the popularity of the local icehouse (since the Amish don't use electric refrigerators), the town's harness shop (for the horse-drawn buggies and field horses' leather needs), and the hitching posts behind **Grandma's Homestead Restaurant.**

This is not the largest Amish restaurant in the county, nor the fanciest, but it does serve authentic Amish cooking at reasonable prices. The menu features a variety of sandwiches, and the dinner entrees include country favorites such as fried chicken, pork tenderloin, fresh lake perch, beef tenderloin, ham, and fish. Family-style dinners of chicken, roast beef, and ham, or any combination of the three, include potatoes, gravy, noodles, salad, and dressing. Fresh desserts are one of the trademarks of Amish restaurants, and the Grandma's Homestead is no exception, offering very tasty peanut butter cream and pecan pies, plus date pudding, sundaes, and Amish cracker pudding. Homemade breads are also available to carry out.

For a total immersion into the life of Charm, spend the night in the accommodations offered in the cottage across the street. The cottage has a private bath with Jacuzzi tub, a sitting room, a great fireplace, and rents for $125 per night. Lodging includes a breakfast buffet and dinner at the restaurant.

Grandma's Homestead Restaurant is on Route 557 in Charm; (330) 893–2717; www.grandmashomestead.com. Open Monday through Saturday, 6:30 A.M. to 7:30 P.M.

Just up the road is the "home of Ohio Baby Swiss Cheese," the **Guggisberg Cheese Company,** owned and operated by Alfred and Margaret Guggisberg. Born in Switzerland, Alfred began work in a cheese factory more than forty years ago at the age of sixteen.

Today, their plant produces 1,000 five-pound wheels of baby Swiss each day between 10:00 A.M. and noon, cheese that is then shipped worldwide. Local Amish dairy farmers supply the milk, which arrives daily in horse-pulled wagons. Visitors to the plant can see the cheese forming in large stainless-steel vats by looking through the windows that connect the plant with the retail store. Guggisberg stocks a wide variety of cheeses in addition to Ohio baby Swiss, and cuckoo clocks, books, gift items, and ice cream are also sold.

Guggisberg Cheese Company is at 5060 Route 557, north of Charm; (330) 893–2500, (800) 262–2505; www.babyswiss.com. Open from April through December, Monday through Saturday, 8:00 A.M. to 6:00 P.M.; Sunday, 11:00 A.M. to 4:00 P.M. Open the rest of the year Monday through Saturday, 8:00 A.M. to 5:00 P.M.

If you want to unwind after a day of touring Amish country, the ***Guggisberg Swiss Inn*** is waiting to welcome you with a comfortable room and a country-style breakfast. The inn is a modern structure set in Amish farming country. You can hike or picnic nearby or just take a walk around the inn pond to watch the swans. In the winter months sleigh rides take guests into the rolling countryside.

Rooms are air-conditioned and all have private baths and in-room coffee. Breakfast is included in the room rate and takes advantage of the wonderful, fresh goodies available in farm country.

The Guggisberg Swiss Inn is at 5025 Route 557, Charm; (330) 893–3600, (877) 467–9477; www.guggisbergswissinn.com. Rates: $100 to $200 per night.

One of Ashland's best-known landmark homes is now a delightful bed-and-breakfast, the ***Winfield Bed & Breakfast.*** Built in 1876 in the Victorian Italianate style, it's perched on two acres of well-manicured lawns and gardens surrounded by green pastures.

Visitors have a choice of three very different rooms, each with a private bath. Light pours into the Garden Suite, which features English country decor, a fireplace, and a private sitting room with French doors that open to a garden terrace. The East Room is more formal, with its magnificent eighteenth-century French armoire and wingback chairs. Tucked up high in the front of the house, the Crow's Nest features rich cocoa walls, fresh white moldings, a washed pine armoire, and a polished mahogany queen-size bed.

You will be greeted with a fresh fruit and cheese plate, and each morning starts with a gourmet breakfast. The nightly turndown service includes fine French chocolate mints.

The Winfield Bed & Breakfast is at 1568 Route 60, Ashland; (419) 281–5587, (800) 269–7166; www.bbonline.com/oh/winfield/. Rates: $85 to $150 per night. Visa, MasterCard, and American Express accepted.

Country Charm

The nearly 10,000 acres that constitute **The Wilds** have made a dramatic transformation—from an open strip mine to North America's largest preserve for endangered species. American Electric Power reclaimed the land and then gave it as a gift to the public to spur the creation of this unique facility. Animals from around the world are free to roam the rolling hills; visitors observe them from buses, which take them past every species imaginable.

The preserve is divided in large sections where African, Asian, and North American wildlife live and thrive. During your visit, you might encounter camel, exotic deer, wild horses, or rhinos. Zebras and giraffes mingle with gazelles and antelopes in the preserve's African environment. During your visit, you'll learn the issues affecting the survival of each species.

The Wilds is at 14000 International Road, Cumberland; (740) 638–5030; www.thewilds.org. Open May through October, Saturday and Sunday, 10:00 A.M. to 4:00 P.M. Also open Wednesday, Thursday, and Friday, June through August, 10:00 A.M. to 4:00 P.M. Admission: adults $14.00; children (ages 4 to 12) $9.00.

Eastern Ohio, western Pennsylvania, and northern West Virginia were once the center of the U.S. glassware industry, and Cambridge, Ohio, was an important city for the glass business. The large Cambridge Glass Company dominated glass production in Guernsey County, opening in the spring of 1902 and shutting down half a century later. Although the boom in glassmaking has since passed, the **Degenhart Paperweight and Glass Museum** preserves the heritage of the industry.

By a bequest in her will, Elizabeth Degenhart established the museum. Born in 1889, she had been associated with the glass business most of her life. She went to work at Cambridge Glass at age sixteen and married John Degenhart in 1908. John's father, Andrew, had been a mold maker in several glass factories, and John worked for the Cambridge Glass Company for forty-six years, until his retirement. John and Elizabeth established the Crystal Art Glass Company, which Elizabeth took over after John's death in 1964.

The museum contains Elizabeth Degenhart's personal collection of paperweights, plus pieces from Cambridge Glass and Crystal Art Glass. Various cut- and blown-glass pieces are displayed, as is an antique glass mold built 150 years ago. An audiovisual presentation explains the history and importance of the glass industry to the area and describes the glassmaking still taking place in Guernsey County.

The Degenhart Paperweight and Glass Museum is on Route 22, just west of Interstate 77 at 65323 Highland Hills Road, Cambridge; (740) 432–2626; www.degenhartmuseum.com. The museum is open Monday through Saturday,

9:00 A.M. to 5:00 P.M.; Sunday, 1:00 to 5:00 P.M., April through December; Monday through Friday, 10:00 A.M. to 5:00 P.M., January through March. Admission: adults $1.50; children (under 18) free.

Just down the street from the museum, *Mosser Glass* offers free tours of their factory to the public. Mosser manufactures glass pitchers, goblets, candleholders, lamps, and animal figures such as frogs, owls, cats, and rabbits.

During the tour, guides explain glassmaking, from heating glass powder to 2,000 degrees in the furnace to forming molten glass in a cast-iron mold. After being pressed in a mold, the shaped glass goes under a flame "glazer," which smooths the surface by reheating the exterior. From there, the molded hot glass cools in a special oven called a Lehr, which uniformly reduces the temperature to prevent shattering. Mosser Glass cranks out 150 pieces of glass per hour.

Mosser Glass is ½ mile west of I–77 on Route 22 at 9279 Cadiz Road, Cambridge; (740) 439–1827; www.mosserglass.com. Tours are given from 8:00 to 10:00 A.M. and 11:00 A.M. to 2:30 P.M. Monday through Friday. No tours the first two weeks of July or Christmas week. No admission charge.

You will find *Georgetown Vineyards* surrounded by five acres of planted grapes, sitting on top of a ridge overlooking the city of Cambridge. The family-owned business produces a variety of wines. The list includes familiar whites, reds, and blushes. However, in addition to that more familiar chardonnay or merlot, those looking for something a little different will find sweet fruit wines such as apple, cherry, or blackberry as well. The wines, along with selected Ohio-made and grown products, are available in the retail shop. You can also tour the winemaking facilities and see both the modern equipment and oak barrels where the wine is aged in the time-honored tradition.

Georgetown Vineyards is located at 62920 Georgetown Road, Cambridge; (740) 435–3222, (866) 435–3222; www.georgetownvineyards.com. Open Tuesday through Saturday from 11:00 A.M. to 5:00 P.M.

The *Pine Lakes Lodge* gives you both the chance to work up an appetite and the chance to satisfy it with gourmet meals. Guests at the lodge can hike the trails and bird-watch while walking the grounds of this 550-acre working cattle ranch. If the view across the stocked ponds or fields isn't quite expansive enough, you can climb up the wildlife observation tower. For the less adventurous, a visit to the petting zoo will give you a close-up encounter with white-tailed deer, goats, emus, llamas, donkeys, and miniature horses.

After all this communing with nature, you can settle in to one of the five suites. A plush robe is provided so you can wrap up after your relaxing bath in a two-person whirlpool tub. Each suite is well appointed and decorated using a ranch-rustic motif, and each suite also has a balcony or deck.

But don't get so comfortable in your room that you miss the gourmet dinner that is included with your stay. Breakfast is also included with your accommodations. For an additional charge you can also have a luncheon picnic basket prepared for your tours around the area or for a quiet lunch on the meadows near the lodge. Indoor areas in the lodge also are very welcoming with three fireplaces and warm, inviting areas to sit and relax.

Pine Lakes Lodge is located at 61680 Buskirk Lane, Salesville; (740) 679–3617; www.pinelakeslodge.com. Rates: $150 to $395 per night. Reservations are required.

Roscoe Village served as an important canal port during the Ohio and Erie Canal's boom years in the 1840s and 1850s, with wheat and wool exports traded for coffee and calico. The 308-mile canal extended from Cleveland to Portsmouth, contained 146 locks, and cost more than $7 million to build. Construction of the canal took seven years, ending in 1832 when the canal completed the link between Lake Erie and the Ohio River.

Located near the confluence of the Muskingum, Walhonding, and Tuscarawas Rivers, the twenty-three brick and frame buildings in the village have been restored to their appearance during the canal's heyday, making Roscoe Village (originally called Caldersburgh) Ohio's only complete canal town restoration. Seven new buildings also have been added to this historic village.

Seven exhibit buildings, a cozy country inn, shops, restaurants, and horse-drawn canalboat rides on the replica *Monticello III* all contribute to the appeal of this unique village. You can purchase tickets to the exhibit buildings and craft demonstrations at the Edward E. and Frances B. Montgomery Visitor Center. This three-story structure offers a wide-screen film presentation of the history of the canal and the village, and displays a large, detailed map of the locks and elevation changes along the canal's more than 300-mile span.

Costumed interpreters and craftspeople welcome visitors to the nineteenth-century buildings, including the blacksmith's shop, the print shop, the one-room schoolhouse, and the 1840s period home of Dr. Maro Johnson. You'll see rugs and wall hangings being woven on two antique looms, and the village potter throwing pots, bowls, and vases on an old-fashioned kick wheel.

In one of the exhibit buildings, the Toll House, Roscoe's first toll collector, Jacob Welsh, registered incoming canalboats and collected passage fees. Also on display is the compass used in the construction of the canal in the 1820s and 1830s, a canalboat model that travels through a set of double locks, and a working model of a gristmill.

Roscoe Village is on Routes 16 and 83 near Route 36, Coshocton; (740) 622–9310, (800) 877–1830; www.roscoevillage.com. Open year-round with tours daily April through December and festivals and special events held May through February. Admission to exhibit buildings: adults $8.95; children (ages 5 to 12) $3.95.

Those fond of guitars, dulcimers, and the like will want to stop in at **Wildwood Music.** Here you will find one of the largest selections of acoustic guitars in the United States. More than 600 instruments fill five showrooms. Owner and musician Marty Rodabaugh carries a large stock of handcrafted fretted and hammered dulcimers. Fine mandolins, banjos, autoharps, specialty tapes and CDs, and music books round out the inventory.

Wildwood Music is at 672 Whitewoman Street, by the Roscoe Village Visitor Center, Coshocton; (740) 622–4224; www.wildwoodmusic.com. Open Wednesday through Friday, noon to 6:00 P.M.; Saturday, noon to 5:00 P.M.

The **Johnson-Humrickhouse Museum,** located in Roscoe Village, contains five major galleries, each with its own theme. North American Indian artifacts including baskets, pottery, beadwork, blankets, and weapons are represented and range from prehistoric to more recent times. Of particular note are the Inuit totem poles, scrimshaw, and carved argilite, ivory, and bone artifacts.

The Historic Ohio Gallery celebrates yesterday in Ohio with a re-created pioneer home and furnishings, plus antique tools, farm implements, rare firearms, dolls, clocks, pottery, and glassware. An extensive treasury of Asian artifacts features Chinese and Japanese porcelains, lacquerware, embroidery, metals, wood sculptures, and splendid carvings in jade, bone, ivory, soapstone, and horn. A Japanese samurai warrior, fully armored, stands guard beside a case filled with Japanese swords.

One gallery is devoted to fine European and American decorative arts and includes cut and pressed glassware, delicate china, precious metals, wood carvings, and an unusual collection of knife rests.

The Johnson-Humrickhouse Museum is located at 300 North Whitewoman Street, Roscoe Village, Coshocton; (740) 622–8710; www.jhmuseum.org. Open daily, May through October, noon to 5:00 P.M.; November through April, 1:00 to 4:30 P.M. Admission: adults $3.00; children (ages 5 to 16) $2.00.

Farmer and engineer George Crise took three years, from 1915 to 1918, to build the fine old structure that is today the **White Oak Inn.** He used white oak from his land for the soul of his home and red oak to produce intricate flooring. Some of the antiques that complete the ten guest rooms at the White Oak Inn are Crise family originals, and each room in the main building is named for the type of wood that predominates in it. All rooms have private baths; the queen-size first-floor suite features a wood-burning fireplace and whirlpool tub. The former chicken house has become a spacious guest house with three rooms, all with fireplaces. The latest additions to the inn are two luxury cottages of log cabin construction, each with fireplace, two-person whirlpool tub, and private deck.

Guests congregate in the light and spacious living room, mingling, reading, or just rocking in front of the fire. Innkeepers Ian and Yvonne Martin offer full breakfasts for their guests, and dinners can be arranged by advance reservation. The inn's remote location invites walks or bicycle rides down country roads, far away from city noise and hassle. On clear nights, the sky dazzles with brilliant star displays.

The White Oak Inn is 4 miles east of the junction of Routes 36 and 62 at 29683 Walhonding Road (Route 715), near Millwood; (740) 599–6107, (877) 908–5923; www.whiteoakinn.com. Rates: $105 to $215 per night, double occupancy, with full breakfast. Cash, checks, American Express, MasterCard, and Visa are accepted. Reservations and a deposit are required; there is a two-night minimum stay most weekends.

Tim and Maureen Tyler undertook a country inn/bed-and-breakfast odyssey; they spent two and a half years and traveled more than 20,000 miles searching for the perfect home to restore as a bed-and-breakfast. Determined to abandon the rat race of New York City, they stumbled on Mount Vernon en route to Kentucky and discovered what is today the ***Russell-Cooper House.***

This ornate structure grew in stages over a period of sixty years, originally constructed in 1829 as a modest Federal-style residence. By 1895, the dwelling had been transformed into a one-of-a-kind mansion masterpiece, a Tudor-Italianate Victorian Gothic villa! The Russell-Cooper House is the former home of two prominent Ohio families. Dr. John Russell, physician and surgeon, was the first American to employ a female physician, Dr. Jane Payne, in 1852. His son-in-law, Colonel William Cooper, had a distinguished career as an attorney, U.S. congressman, and Ohio's adjutant general.

When the Tylers acquired the property in 1987, it was no longer the proud residence of the past, but three "modern" apartments. Their restoration of the home's Victorian grandeur was massive, necessitating the removal of thirteen major walls, three baths, five closets, five furnaces, and three water heaters. After nine months of seven-days-a-week restoration, this award-winning mansion inn now boasts six guest rooms with private baths, a cherry-bookcased library, a dining hall with

yankeepens "dixie"

I wonder how Confederate soldiers and sympathizers would have reacted if they had known that a Yankee from Mount Vernon, Ohio, had written their beloved anthem, "Dixie"? Probably would have spit out their grits.

Daniel Decatur Emmett was a minstrel performer who had moved to New York City when he penned "Dixie" in 1859. It later was played in the South and was quickly adopted as the battle cry for secession. Dan Emmett returned to Mount Vernon and died there in 1904.

an embossed tin ceiling, a grand ballroom with a restored 1856 hand-painted ceiling, a four-season sunroom, and a professional art gallery and studio.

The inn is furnished almost entirely with nineteenth-century antiques, many recovered from Russell-Cooper descendants. The two third-floor guest rooms, accessed via a new grand staircase of cherry and sassafras, offer a primitive, pre-Victorian style, with hand-hewn beams.

The Russell-Cooper House is at 115 East Gambier Street, Mount Vernon; (740) 397–8638; www.russell-cooper.com. Rates: $75 to $85 per night, double occupancy, including breakfast. Reservations and a deposit required; cash, Visa, and MasterCard accepted.

Approximately 200 million years ago, a layer of hard flint pushed toward the earth's surface in an area now known as Flint Ridge. Erosion exposed some of the flint, attracting Native Americans to the area 8,000 to 10,000 years ago. Although the weathered flint on the surface was too brittle to be of much value, the Native Americans discovered a vein of high-quality flint 1 to 10 feet below and established crude quarries to extract the material. Using tremendous physical effort and large hammer stones, they pounded bone and wooden wedges into the flint, breaking it into removable chunks.

They used the flint to form arrowheads and spear points, scrapers, and other tools, and to start fires. Because of the demand for flint in prehistoric times, Flint Ridge was considered neutral ground, with members of any tribe allowed to quarry there. White settlers later rediscovered Flint Ridge, using the mineral for buhrstones in gristmills and as roadbed on a nearby section of the National Road.

Today, the ***Flint Ridge State Memorial*** museum is built around one of the prehistoric Native American quarries, and native mannequins stand ready

State Gemstone and Fossil

The Columbus Rock and Mineral Society led the charge to honor flint as Ohio's official state gemstone. They pointed to its importance to Native Americans in Ohio for making knives, arrowheads, and spear points, its use for flintlock guns and millstones by early white settlers, and its value as a semiprecious stone when cut and polished. In 1965, the Ohio General Assembly concurred, designating flint as Ohio's state stone.

Twenty years later, lawmakers were at it again, this time to recognize a state fossil. Despite numerous jokes suggesting that some of the older members of the General Assembly were in the running for this honor, the actual winner was the trilobite, an extinct marine crustacean found in the limestone and shale beds of southwestern Ohio, among other places.

to break up the rock with a stone maul. The museum features an impressive collection of scrapers, drills, hoes, knives, and projectile points. One flint sample contains an excellent impression of a coral animal, created during one of the times when this part of Ohio was under the sea.

A large topographical map illustrates the extent of the ridge in eastern Licking and western Muskingum Counties. Other displays include an explanation of the calendar of geological time and descriptions of the various layers of rock in the region, from the surface to 468 feet underground.

A thick forest of beech, maple, and oak surrounds the museum, and hiking trails pass by old quarries and exposed outcroppings of red, yellow, brown, and creamy flint. One trail takes hikers by two small streams, and abundant wildlife, including deer, squirrels, chipmunks, and birds, can be observed in the park.

Flint Ridge State Memorial is at 7091 Brownsville Road SE (County Road 668), 3 miles north of Brownsville; (740) 787–2476, (800) 283–8707; www.ohio history.org/places/flint. The museum is open from Memorial Day through Labor Day, Wednesday through Saturday, 9:30 A.M. to 5:00 P.M.; Sunday, noon to 5:00 P.M. Admission: adults $4.00; children (ages 6 to 12) $3.00.

Built in 1900, the Brownsville School educated local youngsters until its closing in 1948. It served grades one through twelve until 1934, and one through eight for the last fourteen years of its school days. Then, this remarkable property sat, vacant . . . for more than 50 years! Larry and Brenda Shrider acquired the school in 2001 and completed a massive renovation, creating the *National Trail Schoolhouse Inn Bed and Breakfast.* Even the school bell, perched in its bell tower, is back in operating order.

Today, the 5000-plus-square-foot home is furnished with a mix of primitive and country pieces. Guests frequently enjoy fresh bread from the inn's country kitchen and can unwind in nearly 2,000 square feet of public space, which includes the old schoolhouse stage. The upstairs common area includes a big-screen TV and pool table; downstairs is a grand piano and fireplace. Guest rooms also offer elegant and comfortable amenities, such as four poster and sleigh beds, huge overstuffed chairs, Jacuzzi tubs, and fireplaces.

The National Trail Schoolhouse Bed and Breakfast is at 10251 Third Street, Brownsville; (740) 787–1808; www.brownsvilleschool.com. Rates: from $69 to $129 per night double occupancy with breakfast.

August Heisey was born in Hanover, Germany, in 1842 and came to America with his family a year later. His career in the glass industry began in Pittsburgh in 1861, but was interrupted by his service with the Union Army during the Civil War.

After the war and several sales positions in the glass business, in 1893 Heisey began formulating plans for his own glass company. He chose Newark as the site for this new enterprise because of its abundance of natural gas and low-cost labor. The factory opened in 1896 and grew to employ several hundred workers.

In 1900, the famous "H within a diamond" trademark was designed by Heisey's son, George Duncan Heisey. Two other sons ran the company, which produced the colored glass and glass animals so popular with collectors today. The company closed for Christmas vacation in 1957 and never reopened; it was no longer competitive in world markets.

Today, the best of Heisey Glass is on display at the **National Heisey Glass Museum.** The museum is housed in what was once the home of Samuel Dennis King, a prominent Newark attorney. It was built in 1831 and was moved to Veterans Park in 1973. The museum is run by the Heisey Collectors of America. In 1993 the collectors constructed a new wing at the museum, adding two large galleries and a media center where a twenty-six-minute video is shown. Inside, you browse through room after room of Heisey glass; hundreds of patterns are displayed, including pieces in all production colors. Examples of experimental pieces, photographs, molds, and tools complete the collection.

The National Heisey Glass Museum is at 169 West Church Street, Newark; (740) 345–2932; www.heiseymuseum.org. Open Tuesday through Saturday, 10:00 A.M. to 4:00 P.M.; Sunday, 1:00 to 4:00 P.M. Admission: adults $4.00; children free if accompanied by an adult.

Housed in a block-long complex of historic buildings, **The Works: The Ohio Center of History, Art, and Technology** is a unique center dedicated to lifelong learning. Through its four primary subject areas—Digital Works, Glass Works, Art Works, and Museum Works, students of all ages experience technology and the arts in provocative settings. The state-of-the-art digital lab enables students to create multimedia presentations using Photoshop, Freehand, Illustrator, Flash, InDesign, and other software. Design students from area colleges work on real projects for real clients in the community. Art Works classes include everything from watercolors to papier-mâché sculpture, from beadwork to painting with dyes on silk.

In the Glass Works, the furnace melts the batch at 2,300 degrees Fahrenheit and keeps it at a 2,100-degree working temperature. The studio has one glory hole, which heats the glass as it is being formed, and a bench equipped with basic glass tools—blowpipes, jacks, shears, etc. Students learn time-honored glass-blowing techniques, and some of the work is available for purchase in the gift shop. The Museum Works occupies the Scheidler Machine Works building, which was constructed in 1861. Built by Reinhard Scheidler, the factory was used to manufacture steam engines and line shaft sawmills. On display are a renovated interurban car, an operating factory, historical landmarks of Licking County and Ohio, Shops of Yesterday, plus many other exhibits.

The Works is at 55 South First Street, Newark; (740) 349–9277; www.atthe works.org. Open Tuesday through Saturday, 9:00 A.M. to 5:00 P.M.

The 1,650-acre *Dawes Arboretum,* established by Bertie Burr and Beman Gates Dawes in 1929, blends rolling meadows, deep woods, and cultivated gardens. Perhaps the most beautiful area is the Japanese garden designed by noted landscape architect Makoto Nakamura. In Nakamura's design, a small lake with islands connected by arched bridges and plantings of pine, flowering cherries, Japanese yew, and Japanese maple creates a tranquil environment. Another popular area is the cypress swamp, where Southern native bald cypress trees grow and produce "knees."

The holly collection contains more than one hundred distinct types of holly, and the sugar maples at Dawes provide the sap for the annual production of maple syrup. One section of the arboretum consists of the deciduous climax forest that once blanketed central Ohio. In a climax forest, tree seedlings are able to grow in the shade of parent trees, thus reproducing the forest indefinitely in a cycle of growth and regeneration.

One feature of the arboretum can be fully appreciated only from the air—a 2,100-foot-long series of hedges that spells out "Dawes Arboretum." Other collections at Dawes include oaks, crabapples, flowering shrubs, and conifers. In addition to the forests, meadows, and gardens, there are three ponds and a lake. The visitor center offers nature exhibits, a bird-watching area, an indoor beehive, which the bees enter from the outside through a clear plastic tube, and a fine bonsai display.

Beman and Bertie Dawes moved into the Daweswood House in 1916. Built in 1867, this two-story brick home contains antique furnishings and other of the Daweses' possessions, including portraits of

ohio'sstatetree/ juice

There was a time when being called a "buckeye" was an insult, the equivalent of being labeled a "hick." Its origin as a put-down comes from the fact that rural Ohio pioneers used wood from buckeye trees to build their cabins and carve their furniture.

Attitudes about the term gradually changed, and the tree's fruit—a brown nut—was described as resembling the eye of the noble buck deer. In 1953, the buckeye was officially designated Ohio's state tree, and Ohio has been the Buckeye State ever since.

The recognition of Ohio's state beverage has been less successful. In 1963, Governor James Rhodes took office and launched a campaign to promote the consumption of Ohio products. Since tomatoes are a significant crop, he encouraged the drinking of tomato juice. What started as a joke—the naming of tomato juice as Ohio's state beverage—became law in 1965. Cheers.

famous family members William Dawes, who rode with Paul Revere, and Charles Gates Dawes, who served as vice president in the Coolidge administration. Guides conduct tours of the home on Saturday and Sunday at 3:15 P.M.

The Dawes Arboretum is on Route 13, 5 miles south of Newark at 7770 Jacksontown Road, SE; (740) 323–2355, (800) 443–2937; www.dawesarb.org. The visitor center is open Monday through Saturday, 8:00 A.M. to 5:00 P.M.; Sunday and holidays, 1:00 to 5:00 P.M. Grounds are open during daylight hours. No admission charge except at Daweswood House.

Perhaps Ohio's prettiest small town, Granville dates its founding to 1805, by settlers from Granville, Massachusetts, and Granby, Connecticut. The nineteenth-century shops and homes in the picture-postcard community are painstakingly maintained. Up on a hill is Denison University, and a more perfect setting for spending college years is difficult to imagine.

In addition to the crafts and antiques shops, Granville boasts historic inns providing overnight accommodations. Orrin Granger built the ***Buxton Inn*** (known as The Tavern in Granger's day) in 1812, and the inn has operated continuously since then. The inn housed Granville's first post office and served as a stagecoach stop on the Columbus-Newark line. An addition in 1851 formed the U-shaped structure with center courtyard that exists today. The Buxton is named for one of its more colorful proprietors, Major Buxton, who owned the inn from the close of the Civil War until his death in 1905. The present owners, Mr. and Mrs. Orville Orr, purchased it in 1972 and spent two years researching and completely restoring this outstanding structure, which is now listed on the National Register of Historic Places.

The Buxton serves fine cuisine in tasteful period dining rooms, each unique in mood and ambience. Antiques are proudly displayed throughout the inn, and the brick-floored center courtyard provides a delightful outdoor din-

Buxton Inn

Buxton Inn's Bonnie Ghost

If an inn has a ghost or two in residence, it is best if they are happy lodgers! Such is the case at the Buxton Inn. According to legend, and those who have had the pleasure of a meeting, the resident spirits of the Buxton Inn are just continuing to play the role of host and hostess.

If the feminine fragrance of gardenia perfume wafts heavily across the air on the stairway, the Lady in Blue is nearby. This spirit is supposed to be that of Ethel Bounell, better known as "Bonnie." The former actress turned innkeeper was the owner and operator of the inn from 1934 until 1960. She died in room nine. She is reported to have had a theatrical streak and was known for both her gardenia perfume and her love of blue dresses.

In life and death she apparently loves the inn. According to staff and guests, she often is heard walking up and down the stairs or opening and closing doors. Guests have reported being wakened by a woman, who generally expresses concern over their comfort.

While Bonnie may be tending guests, the tales of the inn say that she doesn't have to handle that duty alone. The first innkeeper, Major Buxton, also has appeared to both staff and guests. The nattily attired gentleman, sporting a mustache, is apt to show up in the bar or come up behind staff, perhaps just to check that all is running smoothly.

While the occasional ghostly footsteps, door banging, or mysteriously rearranged objects sometimes have given visitors a start, the ghosts also give the Buxton a unique character. Since the inn traditionally receives high ratings for service, who can blame the former innkeepers for hanging around just to make sure that your stay is something special.

ing area. Blooming plants in hanging baskets and small potted trees combine with the splash of a nearby fountain and candlelit tables to make the courtyard a most pleasing place.

For dinner, choose from seafood such as the fresh catch of the day, coquille of seafood cardinal (shrimp, scallops, crabmeat, and mushrooms in mornay), and, one of our favorites, the wild mushroom stroganoff. Other dinner menu options include roast duckling with orange-cranberry sauce; chicken Victoria with mushrooms, cheese, and ham; and lemon pepper primavera. Be sure to order the special baked potato, which comes stuffed with cheddar cheese, bacon, chopped onions, sour cream, chives, and butter. The tempting desserts include gingerbread with hot lemon sauce and the triple chocolate mousse cake.

Luncheon selections such as salads, soups, and sandwiches like the chicken cordon bleu join entrees that include quiche, crepes, eggs Benedict, and seafood Chesapeake.

Stagecoach drivers once cooked their meals on an open fire in the stone-walled basement of the inn and slept on straw beds around that fire. With its rough beams and imposing stone fireplace, the basement tavern retains the flavor of those early years. The tavern serves a casual menu of sandwiches and appetizers.

The Buxton Inn also offers overnight accommodations in guest rooms furnished with antiques. Lodging ranges in price from $100 to $110 per night for two people. A continental breakfast is included with lodging.

The Buxton Inn is at 313 East Broadway, Granville; (740) 587–0001; www.buxtoninn.com. The inn serves a continental breakfast daily, full breakfasts Saturday and Sunday mornings. Lunch is served Monday through Saturday, 11:00 A.M. to 2:00 P.M.; Sunday brunch, 11:00 A.M. to 3:00 P.M. Dinner hours are Monday through Thursday, 5:30 to 9:00 P.M.; Friday and Saturday, 5:30 to 10:00 P.M.; Sunday, 4:00 to 8:00 P.M. The Buxton Tavern is open Tuesday through Saturday, 5:00 P.M. to midnight. MasterCard and Visa are accepted.

Across the street from the Buxton sits the Tudor-style *Granville Inn,* built in 1924 by the president of the Sunday Creek Coal Company, John Sutphin Jones. Offering the elegance of an English manor house, the lobby is furnished with splendid antiques and lush Oriental rugs. The dining room features high ceilings, ornate brass chandeliers, and sandstone fireplaces. In warm weather, meals are also served outside the tall French doors on the flagstone terrace, which is surrounded by a manicured lawn, gardens, and towering trees.

The evening menu at the Granville Inn features a variety of steaks, chops, seafood, chicken, and house specialties such as prime rib and flounder Belle Franklin. Another favorite is the roast serenade of duckling burgundy, served over a wild rice blend. All dinners are served with the much-acclaimed fresh raisin bread and honey butter. For a unique appetizer, try a sampler platter that features shrimp, mushrooms Rockefeller, oysters wrapped in bacon, and marinated herring.

Luncheon selections include soups, salads, and sandwiches. With any meal at the Granville Inn, the house specialty desserts are English walnut pie, served warm, and creamy cheesecake.

Individually decorated, the Granville Inn's twenty-seven guest rooms and three suites have an understated charm and dignity. Prices range from $120 to $200 per night, including a continental breakfast.

The Granville Inn is at 314 East Broadway, Granville; (740) 587–3333, (888) 472–6855; www.granvilleinn.com. Lunch is served Monday through Saturday, 11:30 A.M. to 2:00 P.M. Dinner is served Monday through Saturday, 5:00 to 9:00 P.M. (until 10:00 P.M. on Friday and Saturday) MasterCard, Visa, and American Express are accepted.

For more personal accommodations, spend the night in Kirsten and Jurgen Pape's historic *Follett-Wright House Bed & Breakfast.* Situated at the base of Mount Parnassus within easy walking distance of all of Granville's charms, this gracious structure was built in 1860 and is now listed on the National Register of Historic Places. Its lovely garden provides a tranquil retreat.

Twelve-foot ceilings typical of the era grace the living and dining rooms, permitting large floor-to-ceiling windows. A breakfast of Danish rolls, coffeecake, and other specialties are served in the dining room, which is furnished with a blend of American and European antiques. The kitchen, originally a porch, now is a modern yet charming functional facility.

The Papes offer a good night's rest in two spacious guest rooms, both with private baths and queen-size beds. The upstairs Lincoln Room features Ohio antiques and a view from the bay window of tree-lined East Broadway. Downstairs, the Madison Room has a private access from the front porch.

The Follett-Wright House Bed & Breakfast is at 403 East Broadway, Granville; (740) 587–0941; www.bbonline.com/oh/follett-wright. Rates: $70 per night. No credit cards accepted.

Down the street is a red-painted brick home, which is today the *Granville Life Style Museum.* Built in 1869, it remains furnished as it was while the home of Hubert and Oese Robinson, who lived here from 1918 until their deaths in 1960 and 1981 respectively. Nine rooms of this stately residence are filled with personal and household items from four generations of Hubert Robinson's Granville heritage, many documented with photographs and letters. Visitors also enjoy an old-fashioned garden.

The Granville Life Style Museum is at 121 South Main Street, Granville; (740) 587–0373. Open April through September, the second Saturday each month, 1:00 to 4:00 P.M.

The growing season in Ohio welcomes a variety of fruits and flowers to *Lynd Fruit Farm,* and Lynd Fruit Farm welcomes visitors to pick the best from the fields. Home of Ohio's largest apple orchard, Lynd has 80,000 trees, and during September and October, you can pick your own apples. Fall also brings pumpkins and squash to pick or cornstalks to use for autumn decorating. In July, daylilies are ready for you to scrutinize and then "dig your own."

A "show" apple orchard tells the history of the fruit. Apples from colonial times hang on trees next to the latest test varieties. You may also want to hop on a hayride, and let one of the farm's ten antique John Deere tractors give you a ride around the farm. In addition to these seasonal activities, the farm hosts other events, such as cooking and plant propagation demonstrations. Call ahead for dates and times.

Lynd Fruit Farm is located at 9090 Morse Road, Pataskala; (740) 927–1333; www.lyndfruitfarm.com. Open Friday through Sunday, 9:00 A.M. to 6:00 P.M. No admission charge.

A devastating fire at *Ye Olde Mill* near Utica in April 1986 completely destroyed the hundred-year-old structure. Only the 18-foot, 2,000-pound water-wheel and the quarry stone survived the blaze.

But the Velvet Ice Cream Company, which operates the mill and has its headquarters next door, set about building a new Ye Olde Mill of rough-sawed oak and poplar. This new building now sells country crafts and other gift items, and, not surprisingly, Velvet Ice Cream, a Dager family tradition since 1914.

The 1870-vintage building destroyed by fire was not the first mill on this site—a sawmill was erected here in 1817, and a larger one went up in 1827. You can find out about this and more at the museum of milling history and ice cream that is part of Ye Olde Mill. In fact, the ice-cream museum, Ohio's first and only, traces the history of ice cream from Roman times to the present.

Once you've picked up a cone full of your favorite ice-cream flavor, step outside to the twenty-acre parklike picnic area. Relax at the picnic tables while watching the ducks frolic in a picturesque pond. The mill also houses a down-home restaurant, complete with deli sandwiches, soups and salads, and finger food. A petting zoo, nature trail, and tours of the ice-cream factory round out your visit.

Ye Olde Mill is located 10 miles north of Newark on Route 13, Utica, (800) 589–5000; www.velveticecream.com/olde_mill.asp. Open daily, May through October, 11:00 A.M. to 8:00 P.M. (to 9:00 P.M. during the summer).

Ye Olde Mill

Imports dominate the basket industry in the United States today, but one Ohio family continues four generations of handcrafted basket making. Before the turn of the century, John Longaberger began weaving baskets for his neighbors and local potteries, which used them for storing and shipping their fragile products. John's son, J.W. Longaberger, expanded the business after World War I and taught his twelve children the art of basket making in the evening, after he worked a full day at a nearby paper mill. But over the years, inexpensive cardboard, plastic, and metal containers drastically reduced the industrial demand for Longaberger's baskets, and production slowed to a trickle.

In the 1970s, however, J.W.'s son, Dave, revived the business after becoming convinced a new market existed for good quality, handmade baskets. Today, nearly 1,750 weavers produce an average of 35,000 baskets each day at the Longaberger Company. The baskets are constructed of hard maple from Ohio, Michigan, Pennsylvania, Wisconsin, New York, and Maine. As a testament to the emphasis on quality at Longaberger, each weaver initials and dates each basket. Nearly 70,000 independent Longaberger home consultants sell the baskets, along with pottery, wrought-iron products, and fabric accessories in home shows throughout the United States.

Upon a visit to the headquarters, shaped like a giant basket including the handles, visitors can see baskets being made and see product displays at the Longaberger Manufacturing Campus before heading next door to the **Longaberger Homestead.** You can dine at the Terrace Cafe, the Longaberger Heartland Deli, or the Longaberger Homestead Restaurant. For a sip of tea and something sweet, you may want to drop in to the Sentimental Rose Tea Garden. The Longaberger at Home Building features unique gifts and home decorations.

The Longaberger Homestead is on State Route 16 at 5563 Raiders Road in Frazeyburg; (740) 322–5588; www.longaberger.com. Open Monday through Saturday, 9:00 A.M. to 5:00 P.M. (to 7:00 P.M. on Friday and Saturday, April through December); Sunday, noon to 5:00 P.M.

As the name indicates, the **National Road–Zane Grey Museum** actually houses two museums—one presenting the story of the building of the National Road connecting the western territories with the original eastern states, and the other commemorating author Zane Grey, the Zanesville, Ohio, native known through his travels and writing as the High Priest of the Outdoors.

Built in stages from 1811 to 1838, the National Road stretched from Cumberland, Maryland, to Vandalia, Illinois. George Washington originally conceived the idea of constructing a road into the new nation's western lands, and the ninth Congress of the United States approved funds for this first federally supported road in 1806.

Workers earned a dollar per day to clear a 66-foot-wide path and to build a 30-foot-wide roadbed of broken stone using hand tools, mules, oxen, and horses. The National Road was vital to the development of the frontier—as each section of the road opened, settlers loaded their Conestoga wagons and headed west.

The museum displays horse-drawn carts, buggies, and wagons (including a Conestoga wagon), plus antique bicycles and automobiles—all methods of transportation utilized on the National Road (which eventually became U.S. Route 40 and reached all the way to California). A 136-foot diorama depicts the chronology of the road, from its construction and use by early settlers moving west to farmers herding their livestock on the road and the road's revival after the invention of the bicycle and automobile. Other exhibits include photographs of sections of the road under construction and fully equipped interiors of blacksmith and wheelwright shops.

Author Zane Grey, born in 1875, acquired his passion for hunting and fishing around Dillon Falls, near his home in Zanesville. Grey attended dental school at the University of Pennsylvania, where he also played on the college baseball team. But he abandoned his dental career to write, achieving national prominence with his sixty western novels, many of which were later filmed as motion pictures. He used the money from his books and movies to finance his worldwide fishing trips and big-game hunting expeditions.

The museum displays many of Zane Grey's books, magazine articles, and posters from his motion pictures, plus the lures and hunting rifles used on his travels. There is also a complete replica of the study he added to his Altadena, California, home, where he penned many of his works.

The National Road–Zane Grey Museum is at the Norwich exit of Interstate 70, 10 miles east of Zanesville at 8850 East Pike; (740) 872–3143, (800) 752–2602; www.ohiohistory.org/places/natlroad. Open from Memorial Day to Labor Day, Wednesday through Saturday, 9:30 A.M. to 5:00 P.M.; Sunday, noon to 5:00 P.M. Admission: adults $7.00; children $3.00.

A fairly unremarkable brick building in downtown Zanesville houses a very unique enterprise. The *Alan Cotrill Sculpture Studio and Gallery* is where the Zanesville artist both creates and displays his art. Cotrill and a cadre of artists and artisans bring his work from idea to bronze.

The second-floor gallery shows off numerous bronze sculptures created by Cotrill, as well as photographs of larger Cotrill pices and installations. But visitors can also get a unique look behind the scenes by visiting areas of the studio to see how the process of creating a bronze sculpture begins, from drawing to preparing molds for casting. While the actual pouring of the bronze is done at a foundry, most other steps are undertaken at the studio.

The Alan Cotrill Studio and Gallery is located at 110 South Sixth Street, Zanesville; (740) 453–9822; www.alancottrill.com. Open Tuesday through Sunday, 10:00 A.M. to 5:00 P.M.

Combining their love of antiques with their meticulously restored 1830 Federal-style home, the innkeepers at the *Friendship House* have created a jewel. The four guest rooms, each with private bath, are furnished with select period pieces. Visitors cozy up on the massive 70-foot wraparound-screened porch for a morning coffee or an afternoon read. An evening snack and a candlelight breakfast top off your stay.

The Friendship House is at 62 West Main Street, New Concord; (740) 826–7397, (877) 968–5501; www.bedandbreakfastohio.com. Rates: $75 to $95 per night. Visa and MasterCard accepted.

The Friendship House is across the street from the entrance to Muskingum College, alma mater of senator, astronaut, and former resident John Glenn. Glenn's boyhood home was donated to Muskingum College in 1999. The college leased the building to the John and Annie Glenn Foundation, which moved the house to its current site and restored it to its late 1930s condition. The building is now home to the *John and Annie Glenn Historic Site.*

Senator Glenn's father built the home in 1923. The modest-looking frame house was opened as the John and Annie Glenn Historic Site in 2002. Visitors to the site will see a twenty-minute video presentation on the lives of John and Annie Glenn and can tour the first-floor rooms. Glenn's bedroom looks much like it did in his boyhood, complete with model airplanes and a crystal radio set. Exhibits showcasing the Glenns' hometown of Concord are also part of the site's displays of Ohio living history.

The John and Annie Glenn Historic Site is located at 72 West Main Street, New Concord; (740) 826–3305, (740) 826–0220; www.johnglennhome.org. Open mid-April through Labor Day, Wednesday through Saturday, 10:00 A.M. to 4:00 P.M.; Sunday, 1:00 to 4:00 P.M.; Labor Day through mid-October, Wednesday through Saturday, 10:00 A.M. to 3:00 P.M., Sunday, 1:00 to 4:00 P.M. Admission: adults $6.00; students $3.00; children younger than age 6 free.

Places to Stay in East Central Ohio

ASHLAND
The Winfield Bed & Breakfast
1568 State Route 60
(419) 281–5587,
(800) 269–7166

BERLIN
Donna's Premier Lodging
½ block off Main Street on
East Street
(330) 893–3068,
(800) 320–3338

Garden Gate Get-A-Way
just outside of Berlin
(330) 893–3999,
(330) 674–7608

Pomerance House
Junction of Routes 62
and 39, Main Street
(216) 893–2842

BOLIVAR
Enchanted Pines Bed and Breakfast
1862 Old Trail NE
(330) 874–3197,
(877) 536–7508

CANAL FULTON
The Canal House Bed and Breakfast
306 South Canal Street
(330) 854–6229

CHARM
The Guggisberg Swiss Inn
5025 State Route 557
(330) 893–3600

DELLROY
Atwood Lake Resort
2650 Lodge Road
(800) 735–3596

DOVER
1881 Olde World Bed and Breakfast
2982 Route 516 NW
(330) 343–1333,
(800) 447–1273

GRANVILLE
Follett-Wright House Bed & Breakfast
403 East Broadway
(740) 587–0941

LOUDONVILLE
Blackfork Inn
303 North Water Street
(419) 994–3252

Mohican State Park Lodge and Cabins
Route 3, just North of
Loudonville
(419) 994–4290,
(800) 282–7275

MAGNOLIA
Elson Inn
255 North Main Street
(330) 866–9242

MILLERSBURG
Inn at Honey Run
3 miles northeast of
Millersburg, off Route 214 on
Country Road 203
(330) 674–0011,
(800) 468–6639 in Ohio

HELPFUL WEB SITES

Ohio Division of Travel and Tourism:
www.ohiotourism.com

Canton/Stark County Visitors Bureau:
www.visitcantonohio.com

Holmes County Visitors Bureau:
www.visitamishcountry.com

Tuscarawas County Visitors Bureau:
web.tusco.net/tourism

Wayne County Visitors Bureau:
www.wooster-wayne.com/wccvb

MILLWOOD

White Oak Inn
29683 Walhonding Road
(Route 715)
4 miles east of junction of
Routes 36 and 62
(740) 599–6107

MOUNT VERNON

Russell-Cooper House
115 East Gambier Street
(740) 397–8638

NEW CONCORD

Friendship House
62 West Main Street,
(740) 826–7397

SALESVILLE

Pine Lakes Lodge
61680 Burskirk Lane
(740) 679–3617

WOOSTER

The Leila Belle Inn
846 East Bowman Street
(330) 262–8866,
(888) 430–7378

Places to Eat in East Central Ohio

CHARM

Grandma's Homestead Restaurant
Route 557
(330) 893–2717

GRANVILLE

Buxton Inn
313 East Broadway
(740) 587–0001
Lodging is also available.

Granville Inn
314 East Broadway
(740) 587–3333
Lodging is also available.

WAYNESBURG

Cibo's Restaurant
134 West Lisbon Street
(330) 866–3838

WILMOT

The Amish Door Restaurant & Village
1210 Winesburg Street
(330) 359–5464,
(888) 246–7436
Lodging is also available.

ZOAR

Zoar Tavern & Inn
162 Main Street
(330) 874–2170,
(888) 874–2170

River Region

At the conclusion of the Revolutionary War, Congress passed the Ordinance of 1787, which opened up new land west and north of the Ohio River for settlement. A group of soldiers and officers from the Revolutionary conflict, along with other New Englanders, formed the Ohio Company of Associates to settle in this frontier territory. On April 7, 1788, a party of forty-eight men on a crude barge followed the Ohio River to the Muskingum River, arriving at today's location of Marietta, Ohio. By July of that year, Governor Arthur St. Clair had established the first civil government west of the Allegheny Mountains in Marietta, with the settlement destined to be Ohio's first city and gateway to the Northwest Territory (Ohio, Michigan, Indiana, Illinois, Wisconsin, and part of Minnesota). The city was named for Queen Marie Antoinette, in gratitude for the support France had provided the colonies during the war with the British.

Rufus Putnam, a general under George Washington during the Revolution, led that forty-eight-man party in April 1788 and supervised the construction of a walled fortification with four blockhouses to discourage Indian attacks. Putnam's home was part of that fortification and still exists today, completely

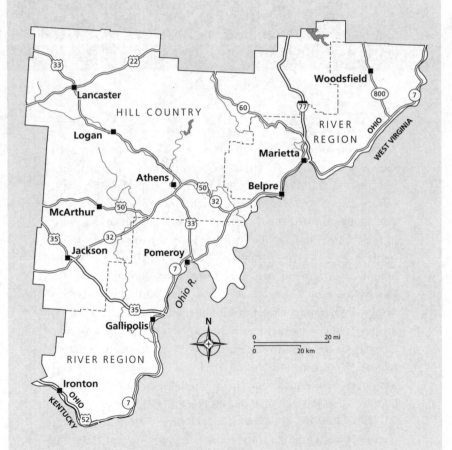

Woodsfield

Lancaster

HILL COUNTRY

Logan

Athens

McArthur

Jackson

Pomeroy

Gallipolis

RIVER REGION

Ironton

Marietta

Belpre

RIVER REGION

OHIO

WEST VIRGINIA

Ohio R.

OHIO

KENTUCKY

N

0   20 mi
0   20 km

enclosed in the *Campus Martius Museum.* Putnam coined the name Campus Martius, which means "field of wars," but the Treaty of Greene Ville in 1795 virtually ended hostilities in the region.

Putnam's 200-year-old home rests on its original foundation and contains furnishings from the Putnam family. Guides describe the hardships of early pioneer life and explain the use of the various kitchen and household implements on display.

The museum also exhibits hundreds of items from Marietta's early days, such as the compasses and surveyors' chains used to plat the city. Other collections include Dr. John Cotton's surgical equipment (he practiced medicine in Marietta from 1815 to 1847), antique musical instruments, and a very unusual studio portrait camera from the early 1900s.

One entire gallery contains nineteenth-century ladies' apparel—the lavish gowns and dresses worn during that era. An outdoor patio features an outstanding assortment of Franklin stoves, a water pumper (ca. 1853) used to fight fires, and the enormous pilot wheel from the stern-wheel towboat *J.C. Risher,* which worked the Ohio River from 1873 until it sank in 1919. A military display includes the sword used by General Putnam during the Revolutionary War (he later gave this sword to George Washington), old rifles and muskets used by early settlers in the area, uniforms and dress swords from the War of 1812, and a Confederate flag captured at the Civil War battle of Chancellorsville, plus uniforms, saddlebags, and a fife and drum used by Civil War soldiers.

The Campus Martius Museum is at the corner of Washington (Route 7) and Second Streets at 601 Second Street, Marietta; (740) 373–3750, (800) 860–0145; www.ohiohistory.org/places/campus. The museum is open from March through October, Wednesday through Saturday, 9:30 A.M. to 5:00 P.M.; Sunday, noon to 5:00 P.M. Admission: adults $7.00; children (ages 6 to 12) $3.00.

AUTHORS' FAVORITES

Campus Martius Museum	Lee Middleton Original Doll Company
Ohio River Museum	Our House
Valley Gem	Bob Evans Farm
Levee House Cafe	Buckeye Furnace
Rossi Pasta	Lake Katharine State Nature Preserve
Lafayette Hotel	

With their tall smokestacks puffing black ash and their paddleboards splashing the waters of the Ohio and Muskingum Rivers, the great stern-wheelers plied these waterways carrying freight and passengers during the nineteenth century. Marietta was once a thriving port; its history is interwoven with that of the rivers and the steamboat era.

The *Ohio River Museum* stands on the bank of the Muskingum River, just down the street from Campus Martius. The museum actually consists of four separate buildings connected with covered outdoor walkways. One building's maps, models, and illustrations trace the origins of the Ohio River—the role of glaciers in its development and the natural history of the region. A half-hour multimedia presentation describes the river's more recent past, from its early exploration to modern-day commercial and recreational usage.

The most popular building features dozens of detailed models of stern-wheeled paddleboats, with the statistics and a narrative of each vessel provided, plus other riverboat memorabilia such as newspaper clippings, passenger tickets, bills of lading, and stern-wheeler travel brochures. The museum also houses a fine collection of steam whistles and a complete set of woodworking tools used for shipbuilding.

ohio'sstatesong

Ohio's state song, "Beautiful Ohio," was written in 1918 by Ballard McDonald and Mary Earl. But the song is not about the state of Ohio; rather, its focus is the Ohio River. That did not stop the General Assembly from designating it as Ohio's official state song on October 24, 1969.

Even more curious was the selection of "Hang on Sloopy" as Ohio's state rock song in 1985. Made popular by the McCoys, a Dayton rock band, "Sloopy" is a favorite of the Ohio State University Marching Band.

The major outdoor attraction at the Ohio River Museum—the 175-foot, 342-ton *W.P. Snyder, Jr.*—was the last steam-powered stern-wheeled towboat to operate in America. It is now permanently docked on the Muskingum River right behind the museum; visitors walk the gangplank to explore this proud vessel from engine room to pilot house. Built in 1918, the *W. P. Snyder, Jr.* plied America's rivers until 1955.

Other outdoor exhibits include a skiff built in 1885, believed to be the oldest such boat in the inland lakes region, which was used during one of the many floods that rampaged in Marietta prior to the installation of flood-control dams. The museum also has a replica of an early flatboat, the flat-bottomed, square-cornered boat used to float heavy cargo downstream. Propelled only by the river's current, flatboats were dismantled (their wood sold for construction projects) upon arriving at their destination.

The Ohio River Museum is at the corner of Front and Saint Clair Streets, Marietta; (740) 373–3750, (800) 860–0145; www.ohiohistory.org/places/ohriver. Open Memorial Day through October, Saturday, 9:30 A.M. to 5:00 P.M.; Sunday, noon to 5:00 P.M. Admission: adults $7.00; children (ages 6 to 12) $3.00.

Given the importance of stern-wheelers to Marietta's past, it seems only proper to survey the city and surrounding area from aboard one—the **Valley Gem,** which docks adjacent to the Ohio River Museum. The ship's captain pilots this 300-passenger excursion vessel down the Muskingum and Ohio Rivers on fifty-minute cruises.

During the trips, he points out the historic places of interest along the shoreline, including the location of Fort Harmar (built in 1785) and the showboat *Becky Thatcher,* a popular restaurant that presents melodrama theater during the summer months. Large stone blocks spelling "Marietta" mark the landing once used by arriving steamboats, and this landing is now the site of the annual stern-wheeler festival. Graceful stern-wheelers come from all parts of the inland waterway system to compete in races, and generally show off during this annual weekend of activities.

Johnny Appleseed Apparition

As you travel throughout Ohio, you may want to conjure up a mental image of the famous Johnny Appleseed. Many of the state's apple orchards, as well as countless lone apple trees, stand as a monument to the man who brought seeds to the farmers of Ohio. A more formal monument at the Washington and Noble County line was dedicated to his memory on September 25, 1942, the 168th anniversary of his birth.

Some say that this is not the only reminder of the famous wanderer that a visitor can experience in this area of Ohio. Just after the monument was dedicated, people began reporting that the man himself was coming back to visit. Some folks were pretty amazed to look up into one of Johnny's apple trees and see a smiling man with a long gray beard swinging his legs and calling out a greeting.

Because Johnny adhered to a religious sect that believed in communication with the departed, local tale tellers say it seems natural that he would try to make an appearance in some of his former haunts.

If you travel through Appleseed country, you may catch a glimpse of a shadow of a man in baggy pants held up with one suspender. You may wonder at the appearance of a man who reaches up to adjust the cooking pot he wears for a hat. But whether or not you see Johnny's spirit as an apparition, you certainly will see his spirit in the strong limbs and the glistening fruits of Johnny's apple trees.

capital of the territory

During the days of the Northwest Territory, the capital of the territory was wherever the territorial governor and judges convened. In July of 1788, Arthur St. Clair, the first territorial governor, arrived in Marietta and instituted the first government under the Ordinance of 1787. By 1790, Governor St. Clair had moved his headquarters to Cincinnati, making it the capital of the territory.

By 1798, the territory had 5,000 white male inhabitants, and Congress gave it permission to elect a legislature. In 1799, twenty-two representatives and Governor St. Clair met in Yeatmen's Tavern in Cincinnati. By the September session, when William Henry Harrison was elected the first territorial delegate to Congress, a new two-story frame building on Main Street was the home of the new legislature.

The *Valley Gem* departs from the landing under the Washington Street Bridge at Front Street, Marietta; (740) 373–7862; www.valleygemsterwheeler .com. During the summer, she sails Tuesday through Sunday at 1:00, 2:00, 3:00, and 4:00 P.M. In April, May, and September, river trips depart on weekends and holidays at 1:00, 2:00, 3:00, and 4:00 P.M. Rates: adults $6.50; children $4.00. Three-hour fall foliage tours leave the landing on Saturday and Sunday in October at noon. Rates: adults $17.00; children $10.00. (Reservations are recommended for foliage tours.) Dinner cruises are offered every Saturday evening, June through October, from 5:30 to 7:30 P.M. Rates: adults $29; children $13.

A delightful dining option is the *Levee House Cafe,* the only remaining original Marietta riverfront structure. Built in 1826 or earlier for Dudley Woodbridge Jr., the first merchant in the Northwest Territory, this historic building later served as a hotel, restaurant, and saloon.

Today the menu changes seasonally and features entrees as varied as four-cheese pasta, garlic shrimp, chicken Parmesan, and tenderloin tips in Dijon sauce. The adventurous might want to sample the enraged pasta—a spicy-hot blend of jalapeño peppers, mushrooms, bacon, and basil, or seafood entrees in a variety of tasty sauces, such as fresh salmon with bourbon sauce.

Your dinner starts with appetizers such as fritto calamari, mousse pâté, or picante shrimp and concludes with your choice of freshly baked pies and cakes. For those guests who only want a sample, you can buy desserts "by the inch."

The Levee House Cafe is at 127 Ohio Street, Marietta; (740) 374–2233; www.mariettaohio.org/leveehousecafe. Open Monday through Thursday, 11:30 A.M. to 9:30 P.M.; Friday and Saturday, 11:30 A.M. to 10:00 P.M. Cash, checks, Visa, and MasterCard accepted. Reservations recommended for dinner.

One of the finest examples of Gothic Revival architecture in Ohio can be found in a mansion in Marietta known as *The Castle.* The Castle was built in

1855 and was home to Ohio senator Theodore Davis. The house, listed on the National Historic Register, had fallen into disrepair, but was rescued by the Bosley family, who began renovations in the seventies. Some restoration projects continued past the year 2000. The home's distinctive features make it easy to see why it's called the "castle." It has a wonderful octagonal tower and stone-capped spires. The attic has a trefoil window and the master bedroom and other rooms have stained glass windows, which have been salvaged and returned to their former glory. Mosaics and intricate woodwork have also been restored or replaced. The fireplace has a scagliola fireplace surround, which is plaster carefully colored and polished to resemble marble. The papier-mâché moldings are another unusual feature. They follow a fashion begun in the mid-eighteenth century when papier-mâché was used to craft delicate and detailed molding and painted to resemble wood or precious metals. On the grounds, a lovely gazebo, once the covering for the well, has been returned to the mansion grounds to grace the gardens. The cast iron fence and herb garden have been restored as well. Decorations and furnishings reflect the period in which Senator Davis would have occupied the home.

Start your tour in the restored carriage house, where a videotape presentation and introductory exhibits will set the scene. Check the Web site for seasonal and special programs at the Castle. Holidays such as Christmas and Easter mean special decorations, and exhibits and musical programs are often held during the winter months. Tours are offered every half hour and take about fifty minutes.

The Castle is at 418 Fourth Street, Marietta; (740) 373–4180; www.marietta castle.org. Open June through August, Monday through Friday, 10:00 A.M. to 4:00 P.M. and Saturday and Sunday, 1:00 to 4:00 P.M.; April, May, and September through December, Thursday through Monday. Admission: adults $5.00; children (ages 6 to 17) $2.50, children 5 and under free.

Marietta is also home to a world-famous gourmet pasta maker, *Rossi Pasta*. Though most of its pasta is sold by catalog and through upscale restaurants and retailers like Williams-Sonoma, in Marietta you can stop by the Rossi Pasta factory and outlet shop.

The success of Rossi Pasta can be attributed to a high-quality product and an intriguing selection of pasta cuts and flavors. These include everything from spinach basil garlic fettuccini to Italian spice linguini, from vino Rosso linguini made with cabernet sauvignon to calamari fettucini. Not only does Rossi have three sauces to top off the pasta, they also will recommend the perfect wine to complete your meal.

Rossi Pasta is at 106 Front Street, Marietta; (740) 376–2065, (800) 227–6774; www.rossipasta.com. Open Monday through Saturday, 9:00 A.M. to 6:00 P.M. (Pasta-making times are variable, typically before noon.)

During your visit be sure to take a walking or driving tour of Marietta's stately residential neighborhoods. The city contains hundreds of nineteenth-century homes, many on charming brick streets.

For overnight accommodations, the **Lafayette Hotel** is at the landing where steamboats once unloaded their passengers and cargoes on cruises between Pittsburgh and Cincinnati. Nautical memorabilia decorate the lobby, restaurants, and lounge in this building, including brass pilot instruments, a pilot wheel, and paintings and photographs of the stern-wheelers that once traveled the nation's rivers.

The hotel's seventy-seven guest rooms have been renovated and feature classy Victorian-style furnishings. Four even offer private balconies facing the river. Special Marietta lodging and entertainment packages are also available at the historic Lafayette.

The Lafayette Hotel is at the corner of Front and Greene Streets at 101 Front Street, Marietta; (740) 373–5522; www.lafayettehotel.com. Rates: $75 to $280 per night. MasterCard, Visa, and American Express are accepted.

How many people can say that they had a massage in a grain bin? You can as a guest at the **Stockport Mill Country Inn.** The inn is housed in an impressive mill built in 1906, the last surviving mill building on the Muskingum River. After its long career as, primarily, a flourmill, the building now houses an inn with fourteen guest rooms and a restaurant, the Restaurant on the Dam. In the basement of the mill, safely located behind glass, guests can view the one-hundred-year-old twin turbines that generate hydroelectric power. Too corroded to restore and use, the mill's original turbines have been replaced by these twins from the same era, which now produce about 800,000 kilowatt hours of electricity each year—enough to supply the electrical needs of the mill, with some extra to sell to the local utility company.

A restaurant, gift shop, and a handicapped-accessible guest room are housed on the first floor. The original train bin that is now home to the massage therapy room is on the second floor. Unique guest rooms are on the second floor too as well as the third and fourth, and even the cupola. The riverboat rooms are named for Ohio riverboats and have private baths with claw foot tubs, all with private terraces with views of the river. One suite, the Captain Hook Suite, which sleeps eight, has a large sitting area, and a stairway up to the Mill's cupola. No, it was not named for the famous fictional pirate. It was named for Isaac Newton Hook, a riverboat captain in the 1800s. A couple of notes for the traveler. Stockport is a dry town, so do not plan to order wine or a drink with dinner. Also, this is an inn in an historic building, so don't expect the uniformity in heating and ventilation systems as you would expect in a more modern building.

The Stockport Mill Country Inn is at 1995 Broadway, Stockport; (740) 559–2822; www.stockportmill.com. Rates: $132 to $349 per night.

Like many innovators, Lee Middleton started work on her dream at her kitchen table. In the late seventies, she began creating porcelain dolls, sculpting her first dolls to resemble her daughter, Brynn, and her son, Michael. Her craftsmanship was obvious to friends, neighbors, and eventually doll collectors, all of whom wanted to order dolls from Lee.

By 1980, Lee had taught others her techniques and moved her operation out of the kitchen and into the basement of a local bank. Five moves later, *Lee Middleton Original Doll Company* began operation in its present 50,000-square-foot factory and doll store.

Today, visitors tour Lee's factory and observe the techniques that make Middleton dolls so distinctive. The most popular part of the tour is when visitors see the hand-painting of each doll's face, the most challenging step in the production process.

Each Lee Middleton doll leaves the factory with a miniature Bible in its hands. Middleton dolls retail for $120 to $228, but are available at the factory outlet store from $50 and up.

The Lee Middleton Original Doll Company is at 1301 Washington Boulevard, Belpre; (740) 423–1481, (800) 233–7479; www.leemiddleton.com. Open Monday through Saturday, 9:00 A.M. to 5:00 P.M. (noon to 5:00 P.M. Sundays, March through December). Tours Monday through Friday, 9:00 A.M. to 3:15 P.M., March through December. Reservations recommended. No admission charge.

The settlement of Gallipolis resulted directly from what had to be one of the first land speculation schemes in the history of the United States. A congressman and his business associates received a congressional grant for 3.5 million acres in southern Ohio. These investors planned to secure the funds to pay for this land by reselling large tracts to Europeans. They formed the Scioto Company and dispatched a sales representative to France, who easily sold tracts to 500 upper-class French citizens ready to leave the turmoil in their country. These 500 men, women, and children set sail for America in 1790, but by the time they arrived in the New World, the Scioto Company had failed, leaving the immigrants without their property.

After negotiations with Congress, the French were given frontier land on the Ohio River. Since these immigrants were largely noblemen, professionals, and artisans, pioneer life quickly took its toll. Half of the party deserted the frontier during the first two years for "more civilized" areas.

But those remaining in what is today Gallipolis endured, and the town's strategic location on the river spurred its growth. In 1819, Henry Cushing constructed a tavern and inn, and that two-story building still exists, now a museum known as *Our House.*

The doors, floors, and even the lock on the front door at Our House are all original. A grandfather clock built in 1780 still keeps time, and the museum contains Chippendale and Hepplewhite furnishings that belonged to early Gallipolis settlers. In the dining room, for example, is a magnificent cherry dining room table set with delicate French plates and serving trays. The second-floor ballroom still has the original carved wooden chandeliers.

The name Our House comes from the sales pitch its owner, Henry Cushing, would give when he met boats arriving at the docks. To keep the newcomers from going to the other inn in town, he would tell them, "Come to our house." The inn's most famous guest was the French general and statesman Marquis de Lafayette. Lafayette, after his first trip to the colonies in 1777 to fight with the Americans against the British, returned to France and convinced his countrymen to enter the war against England. America never forgot Lafayette's aid during the Revolution, and in 1825 he made a triumphant return to the United States, which included a two-and-a-half-hour visit to Gallipolis and Our House on May 22. The coat he wore and one of the violins used to entertain him are displayed at the museum.

Another important Frenchman planned to come to Gallipolis with the original 500 settlers but at the last minute he let his fiancée go without him. Had he made the trip to America, history would have been dramatically altered. His name was Napoleon Bonaparte; his fiancée's portrait hangs above a fireplace at Our House.

Our House is at 434 First Avenue, Gallipolis; (740) 446–0586, (800) 752–2618; www.ohiohistory.org/places/ourhouse. The museum is open Memorial Day through October, Saturday, 10:00 A.M. to 4:00 P.M.; Sunday, 1:00 to 4:00 P.M. Also open Tuesday through Friday, 10:00 A.M. to 4:00 P.M., June through August. Admission: adults $4.00; children $1.00.

Bob Evans has made his mark in two related businesses—as a manufacturer and distributor of his country sausage and as the proprietor of the Bob Evans Restaurants. After World War II, Evans opened a twelve-stool restaurant near Gallipolis. Not satisfied with the sausage available commercially, he started making his own. This blossomed into a sausage business, and he devoted more and more of his time and energy to it. Once Bob Evans Farms Sausage was firmly established in the marketplace, he once again concentrated on the restaurant business, opening a second location in 1962 and coordinating a major expansion in the late 1960s. Today, Bob Evans operates 588 restaurants in nineteen states and is a leading producer of pork sausage under the Bob Evans and Owens brand names.

The Bob Evans Farm is home to the Homestead Museum, the Craft Barn, the original Bob Evans restaurant, and many unique events. The museum reflects the history of the company, and guests sit at the reconstructed counter for the first restaurant owned by Bob Evans. Visitors also browse the thousands of homemade arts and crafts in the Craft Barn. Special events throughout the year include a bluegrass festival, an antique car and power equipment show, and a gospel sing. The most popular event is the Farm Festival, which celebrates the harvest season as it was in rural America of yesteryear.

Bob Evans Farm is on Route 588, 1 mile east of Rio Grande; (740) 245–5305, (800) 944–FARM; www.bobevans.com. The farm is daily April through December, 10:30 A.M. to 5:00 P.M.

Hill Country

The 100-mile-long, 30-mile-wide belt of southern Ohio and northern Kentucky known as the Hanging Rock Iron Region once produced the iron demanded by the booming Industrial Revolution. Eighty charcoal furnaces operated in this region from 1818 to 1916, furnishing iron ingots used to manufacture railroad and farm equipment, heavy machinery, and even the cannons and gunboats used in the Civil War. Abundant quantities of the iron ore, limestone, and timber needed for iron production caused the proliferation of furnaces in the region, and furnace communities sprang up near these facilities.

While many of the region's sandstone stacks today stand in silent memory of this once vital industry, at *Buckeye Furnace,* Ohio's only restored charcoal furnace, all buildings have been reconstructed. Visitors learn the history of the Hanging Rock region and the basics of iron making by reading the many signs along Buckeye's self-guided tour.

The furnace was built into a hillside, and the raw materials (iron ore, limestone, and charcoal) were brought by wagon to the top of the hill, where the

Buckeye Furnace

charcoal was stored under a stock shed to keep it dry, and the limestone and ore were graded and sorted. (The charcoal was produced at a separate location by slowly burning timber under mounds of earth.) Laborers mixed and poured enormous quantities of these materials into the top of the furnace: In a twelve-hour shift, they would measure and load 57,000 pounds of ore, 1,900 pounds of limestone, and 800 bushels of charcoal. As the charcoal burned, temperatures in the furnace reached 600 degrees, causing the impurities in the iron ore to mix with the limestone, forming a waste product called slag. Since molten iron is heavier than slag, the iron could be removed from the bottom of the furnace by opening a stone dam at its base. The liquid iron flowed into sand molds known as pigs. The process of loading raw materials (the "burden") and drawing off the slag and molten iron was continuous—the furnaces operated twenty-four hours a day.

Down the hill from the stock shed and loading area, the Buckeye Furnace general store contains merchandise typical of the nineteenth century. The companies often paid the laborers in scrip, rather than currency, which could only be used at the company store or to pay for company lodging. As a result, some workers were continually in debt to their employers.

moresaltplease

Long before white settlers explored what is today Jackson County, Native Americans came to Salt Creek for its salt. The first whites to take advantage of the creek did so in 1798. They drew water from 30-foot wells and boiled it away in huge kettles. Due to the low salinity of the water, up to fifteen gallons of water were required to produce each pound of salt. Because of the importance of salt in preserving meats, both Congress and the Ohio Legislature passed laws regulating the Jackson saltworks. The discovery of other saltworks both more accessible and with higher salinity led to the decline of Salt Creek's commercial value.

The discovery of richer and more easily transported Lake Superior iron ore caused the decline of the Hanging Rock Iron Region. Buckeye Furnace shut down for the last time in 1894, closing a chapter in the state's industrial history.

Buckeye Furnace is off Route 124, 10 miles east of Jackson, at 123 Buckeye Park Road, Wellston; (614) 297–2457, (800) 686–1534; www .ohiohistory.org/places/buckeye. Open daylight hours year-round.

Northwest of Jackson, the **Lake Katharine State Nature Preserve** contains 1,400 breathtaking acres of rolling wooded hills, dense vegetation, and a cool, clear lake. Stop by the manager's office for maps of the main hiking trails (which are located across the lake from the office) and walk down the path near the office for your first view of tranquil Lake Katharine.

It's a scenic drive to the parking area adjacent to the start of the three main trails on the east side of the lake. The Calico Bush Trail, a favorite in late April and May with wildflower lovers, leads hikers past abundant calico bush (mountain laurel) in full bloom on and between the exposed sandstone formations.

The Pine Ridge Trail crosses Rock Run, a gurgling stream that supplies Lake Katharine's sparkling water, and follows the lakeshore. This 2-mile trail then rises through a ridge of pines to a spectacular overlook.

Ohio's Youth Conservation Corps completed the preserve's newest and most demanding trail in 1979—Salt Creek Trail. Traveling 2 miles through steep hills, wooded ravines, cliffs, and creeks, hikers pass abandoned drift mines, early Native American work sites, and burial pits.

Visitors to this pristine preserve frequently spot varied wildlife, including wild turkey and deer, and occasionally a bobcat or king snake. Because this is a nature preserve, no bank fishing, swimming, or picnicking is allowed, and nonmotorized watercraft are permitted on the winding lake by written permit only, with a maximum of five boats allowed per day.

Lake Katharine State Nature Preserve is 3 miles northwest of Jackson off Route 35 on County Road 59; (614) 286–2487; www.dnr.state.oh.us/dnap/location/lake_katharine.html. Open daylight hours; no admission charge.

Just north of Lake Katharine, under a protective roof, rests a large slab of black hand sandstone with some remarkable Native American carvings—the **Leo Petroglyph.** Probably carved by the Fort Ancient Indians more than 700 years ago, the petroglyph has forty different carved figures, with a fish, a bird, and three human feet plainly visible. The most intriguing carving shows an Indian wearing an elaborate headdress. Nature trails penetrate the deep woods and skirt the upper cliffs of the gorges and forests surrounding the petroglyph.

The Leo Petroglyph is on County Road 28, off Route 35, 4 miles northwest of Jackson; (614) 297–2630, (800) 686–1535 www.ohiohistory.org/places/leopetro. Open daylight hours; no admission charge.

Sue and Jim Maxwell have created a most unusual lodging experience in southeast Ohio: a replica of a twelfth-century Norman castle known as **Ravenwood Castle.** Longtime Anglophiles, the Maxwells have traveled extensively throughout England and Scotland and have always been attracted to castles and the medieval period. Surrounded by the Wayne National Forest and just 7 miles from the Hocking Hills, Ravenwood Castle sits atop a wooded hill. More than 100 acres of forest and large rock formations surround the castle.

Ravenwood's crenelated towers contain the guest rooms and suites. Although the building is new, the couple has been collecting architectural antiques for several years. Each guest room or suite has a stained-glass window, usually in the bathroom, a fireplace with Victorian mantel and gas logs,

TOP ANNUAL EVENTS

Vinton County Wild Turkey Festival,
McArthur, May;
(740) 596–5033;
www.vintoncountytravel.com/Turkey
Festival.htm

Moonshine Festival,
New Straitsville, May;
(740) 394–2838

MSI KAH MI QUI Pow Wow,
Nelsonville, May;
(740) 753–3591;
www.hocking.edu

Oak Hill Village Festival of Flags,
Oak Hill, May;
(740) 682–7292, (740) 682–7057;
www.jacksoncountyohio.org/jw/visit/
events/festival_of_flags.htm

Commercial Point Homecoming,
Commercial Point, June;
(740) 983–4836

Poston Lake Bluegrass Festival,
Guysville, June;
(740) 662–2051;
www.thehartbrothers.com

Appalachian Uprising,
Scottown, June;
(740) 533–7271;
www.appalachianuprising.net

Gallipolis River Recreation Festival,
Gallipolis, July 4th weekend;
(740) 446–0596;
www.galliacounty.org

Lawrence County Fair,
Proctorville, July;
(740) 646–2215;
www.lawrencecountyohio

Fireman's Old Time Festival,
Laurelville, July;
(740) 332–6033;
www.laurelvillevfd.com

Civil War Encampment Days,
Malta and McConnelsville, July;
(740) 962–3200;
www.morgancounty.org/tourism.html

Lancaster Festival,
Lancaster, July;
(740) 687–4808;
www.lanfest.org

Jackson County Fair,
Wellston, July;
(740) 988–2834;
www.jacksonohio.org

Pig Iron Days,
Jackson, August;
(740) 286–2707;
www.jacksonohio.org

All-American Soap Box Derby,
Akron, August;
(330) 733–8723;
www.aasbd.com

Parade of the Hills,
Nelsonville, August;
(740) 753–3525;
www.paradeofthehills.org

Sweet Corn Festival,
Fairborn, August;
(937) 878–7040;
www.sweetcornfest.com

Baltimore Festival–Canal Lock Days,
Baltimore, August;
(740) 438–7881;
www.baltimorefestival.com

Ohio River Sternwheel Festival,
Marietta, September;
(740) 373–5178, (800) 288–2577;
www.mariettaohio.org/sternwheel

Civil War Days,
Somerset, September;
(740) 743–2471, (740) 743–1913;
www.netpluscom.com/~pchs/civilwar.htm

antique light fixtures, and many feature wonderful old doors. The wood moldings around the doors and windows and the castle's five stairways are inspired by centuries-old motifs from Great Britain's stately homes and castles. Each room also has a balcony or private deck overlooking the forest.

Common areas include the Great Hall, with three large stained-glass windows from an old church at one end and a huge arched stone fireplace at the other. Ornate and heavily carved museum-quality Gothic tables and chairs furnish the Great Hall, where guests dine in a convivial "old English" atmosphere. On the lower level is a library stocked with books on a wide variety of topics, a game room, and the charming Rose and Thistle Pub. A small village of medieval-style cottages, each with a whirlpool bath, fireplace, and kitchenette, provides another unique lodging option.

Ravenwood Castle is near the intersection of Routes 56 and 93 at 65666 Bethel Road, New Plymouth; (740) 596–2606, (800) 477–1541; www.ravenwood castle.com. Rates: $65 to $235 per night, double occupancy, including full breakfast. Visa and MasterCard accepted.

Ohio's state parks offer hundreds of cabins throughout the state, most of them modern, two-bedroom deluxe models. For those seeking more rustic and less expensive lodging, *Lake Hope State Park* provides the widest selection of types of cabins in the state park system. In addition to deluxe cabins, Lake Hope has twenty-one standard cabins with wood-burning fireplaces. These cabins, available April through October, accommodate up to six people in four rooms and contain complete kitchens. A third type, the sleeping cabins, have one to four bedrooms, fireplaces, and refrigerators, but no cooking facilities. As with the modern deluxe cabins, the sleeping cabins are available year-round.

The 3,000-acre park includes 120-acre Lake Hope, with its large beach and swimming area, in a heavily wooded section of Vinton County. The park's dining lodge serves meals from May through October, and the park has miles of hiking trails, as does the adjacent state forest. Lake Hope State Park also contains the remains of an old charcoal furnace—Hope Furnace.

Lake Hope State Park is at 27331 Route 278, 5 miles north of Zaleski in McArthur; (740) 596–5253, (866) 644–6727; www.dnr.state.oh.us/parks/parks/lakehope.htm. Cabin rates range from $67 to $77 per night.

Southeast Ohio contains thousands of acres of rugged, hilly countryside covered with thick forests, but the most geologically intriguing area may be the 10,000-acre *Hocking Hills State Park and Forest.* Steep hills, deciduous and evergreen forests, caves, rivers, waterfalls, and abundant plant and animal life provide outstanding recreational opportunities.

A warm, shallow ocean covered Ohio some 300 million years ago and deposited the bedrock of shale and black hand sandstone found in the area.

Black hand sandstone is so named because of a large black hand drawn on a slab of the stone near Newark. Probably drawn by Native Americans, the hand may have served as a marker pointing the way to the outcroppings of flint found at Flint Ridge.

Though primitive man may have used the caves, recesses, and cliffs in the Hocking Hills for shelter as long as 7,000 years ago, pottery fragments confirm the Adena Indians lived here from the time of Christ to A.D. 800. White settlers did not discover the lush forests and flowing streams in these hills until the 1790s.

Old Man's Cave, one of the six major formations in the park, so awed Richard Rowe with its natural beauty in the early 1800s that he decided to live at the cave as a hermit for the rest of his days. Rowe was the "old man" for whom this cave is named. A deep gorge runs along the cave, which is actually a major recess in the sandstone cliff, and water flowing through the bottom of the gorge is hurled over two waterfalls and into the Devil's Bathtub, a large pothole formed in the sandstone by swirling rock and gravel in the stream water. Hiking trails follow the ridges on both sides of the gorge, and a third snakes through the hemlocks, beeches, and yews at the bottom of the gorge.

Decades of erosion have created another spectacular sandstone formation called Ash Cave, a 700-foot horseshoe-shaped rock ledge that forms a recess 100 feet deep. Mounds of ash found here by early settlers indicated that this large rock roof was a popular camping site for Native Americans. Hiking trails run along both ridges and the floor of the gorge, past a 90-foot waterfall.

The Rock House, a massive recess completely enclosed by rock except for the open "windows," is the most cavelike formation in the park—certainly more so than Ash Cave or Old Man's Cave—yet of the three it is the only one not named a cave. Another misnomer is nearby Cedar Falls, a waterfall named by pioneers who mistakenly identified the dense forest as cedar, when, in fact, it is hemlock.

In addition to the six major formations in the park, hiking trails explore thousands of acres in the thickly wooded state forest. The park has forty deluxe cabins in a secluded, peaceful setting and a dining lodge with outdoor swimming pool. The cabins are available year-round but are rented for full weeks only during summer months, with rates ranging from $80 to $95 per night. The dining lodge serves meals from May through October. Other park features include campsites, a seventeen-acre fishing lake, and a summer naturalist program, plus picnic tables, barbecue grills, and shelters scattered throughout the area.

Hocking Hills State Park is 14 miles west of Logan, at 19852 Route 664; (740) 385–6841, (740) 385–6842, (866) 644–6727; www.dnr.state.oh.us/parks/parks/hocking.htm.

The original innkeeper's ambitious goal when he conceived of **Glenlaurel,** his Scottish country inn and cottages, was to build the premier romantic

ALSO WORTH SEEING

Wayne National Forest,
Athens

Burr Oak State Park,
Glouster

Slate Run Living Historical Farm,
Lithopolis

getaway of the Midwest. Situated on 140 wooded acres and backing up to the rocks of Camusfearna Gorge, Glenlaurel welcomed its first guests in 1994.

This full-service resort is a great country escape any time of the year. The eight stone fireplaces of the Manor House and its guest rooms take the chill out of a fall day. A double whirlpool tub in each private bath overlooks the hemlock and trillium. Tucked away in a dense woods, each of the thirteen cottages features an open-air hot tub on a private deck.

Gourmet dining completes this outstanding retreat: The light-as-air Belgian buttermilk waffles topped with maple cream and strawberry-rhubarb sauce are legendary. A "typical" dinner: orange-tomato-basil soup, mixed greens with balsamic vinaigrette, soy-sesame-ginger-marinated salmon over basmati rice with roasted vegetables, finished with a slice of mixed-berry sour cream pie!

Glenlaurel is 5 miles west of U.S. 33, just off Route 180, at 14940 Mt. Olive Road, Rockbridge; (800) 809–7378; www.glenlaurelinn.com. Rates: $119 to $319 per night, double occupancy, including full breakfast. Visa, MasterCard, and American Express accepted.

It took more time and money than its creators ever imagined, but the *Inn at Cedar Falls* was worth the wait. Situated on a hillside meadow, surrounded on three sides by the Hocking Hills State Park, the inn represents two-and-a-half years of work and an investment of a half-million dollars.

First, shingle and plaster were removed from the 1850s-vintage farmhouse, purchased from an eighty-six-year-old woman who was born here, to reveal its original log-and-mud construction. A second log building was moved on site, and the union of these structures now houses a gourmet kitchen and two indoor dining areas. The plank flooring and period pieces give this room a pioneer ambience—it's a place where guests watch culinary artistry in progress. The aromas of American country cooking fill the inn—apple-smoked pork loin, bean soup, bread pudding with whiskey sauce, or chicken with morel sauce.

The inn's garden supplies herbs and edible flowers. Meals are prepared with the local growing season in mind. Guest chefs from Columbus and elsewhere are invited to spend an evening in the kitchen, explaining their technique to guests as they perform their magic. Exceptional breakfasts, lunches, and dinners are then served either in the log house or out on the patio.

The Inn at Cedar Falls offers most unusual accommodations for its overnight guests. Housed in a modern, barn-shaped building are nine guest rooms. Though similar in design to contemporary motel rooms, with individual heating and air-conditioning units, they are furnished with antiques and wood floors. Each has an up-to-date private bath, but no telephone or television. Rocking chairs and tables make the second-floor balcony a delightful spot for reading or just soaking up the hilly landscape. Twelve cozy cottages have been built, each with a gas log stove, a large whirlpool tub, and a private deck. Six log cabins are scattered throughout the inn's 75 acres, each with privacy, cooking facilities, and its own personality.

A section of the prairie meadow that predominates here has been mowed, so guests can stroll down the hill to an outstanding lookout. Here you might encounter deer, fox, or raccoon, while bird-watchers view yellow finches, bluebirds, woodpeckers, ruffed grouse, and wild turkey.

Although the inn occupies a clearing right on Route 374, wooded hiking trails meander nearby. The Buckeye Trail, which connects Old Man's Cave with Ash Cave, is easily joined from here. Or hike to Rose Lake for some trout fishing. Cross-country skiing is a winter favorite.

Innkeepers Ellen Grinsfelder and Terry Lingo want their guests to enjoy the natural wonder of this area as much as they do. And although the kitchen serves overnight guests, others are welcome for dinner if they call ahead and make reservations. Seasonal delights are prepared at mealtime, when visitors come together to share their day's adventures. Lunch is served daily from 11:30 A.M. to 1:30 P.M. Holidays are special times here—the inn provides those without family nearby (or those escaping relatives!) a homey retreat full of holiday spirit.

The Inn at Cedar Falls is located at 21190 Route 374, 10 miles southwest of Logan; (740) 385–7489, (800) 653–2557; www.innatcedarfalls.com. Rates: $99 to $269 per night, double occupancy, including full breakfast. Visa and Master-Card are accepted. Open year-round.

Five cabins nestled in the trees around a spring-fed lake—***Wyandot Woods.*** The cabins are well separated from one another, and each has a private dock on the lake—a perfect spot to fish for largemouth bass, yellow perch, and bluegill, or to launch one of the rowboats provided for guests. Lake swimming is a favorite summer pastime here, or you can loll and sunbathe out on the diving platform floating in the center of the lake. Whatever you choose to do here, the limited number of cabins ensures that you will never encounter a crowd.

Cabins here range from one-bedroom single stories to the bi-level Cedar House with two large decks, an indoor hot tub, and two-plus bedrooms. Each cabin at Wyandot Woods has a deck, porch swing, wood-burning stove with glass front for fire watchers (as well as electric heat), and an outdoor barbecue grill. All are comfortably furnished in pleasing earth tones, and they have plenty of windows looking out on the dense forest. Complete kitchens round out the facilities here.

Wyandot Woods is east of Laurelville; off Route 180; (877) 365–8009, (740) 437–7733; www.wyandotwoods.com. Rates: $135 to $225 per night, depending on the size of the cabin, day of the week, and season. Open year-round. Reservations are required.

Another Hocking Hills lodging option, set on one hundred wooded acres, is *Old Man's Cave Chalets.* These sixteen A-frames, sprinkled on a hillside, are three-room structures, complete with lofts. Each chalet sleeps four and has a deck with a private hot tub, a wood-burning fireplace (plus central heating and air-conditioning), and an efficiency kitchen.

In addition to the A-frames, fifteen larger luxury log homes, sleeping four to eight people, are situated in more secluded locations throughout the hills. These deluxe log homes feature large stone fireplaces, private hot tubs, TVs and VCRs, central air, handmade furniture, and fully equipped kitchens. Four large lodges accommodate groups of up to sixteen guests.

The quiet, isolated location makes this an ideal year-round retreat. Facilities also include a large outdoor swimming pool and recreation area. More than 800 acres of state forest adjoin the property and are available for hiking and exploration.

Old Man's Cave Chalets is at 18905 Route 664, south of Logan; (800) 762–9396; www.oldmanscavechalets.com. Rates: $129 to $405 per night, double occupancy. Reservations required.

In addition to hiking and camping, canoeing and horseback riding are popular in the Hocking Hills. *Hocking Valley Canoe Livery and Fun Center* provides rental equipment along the picturesque Hocking River, with trips ranging from two hours to three days at rates from $20 to $60 per canoe. The livery is at 31251 Chieftain Drive, Logan; (800) 686–0386, (740) 385–8685, 385–2503; www.hockinghillscanoeing.com. Canoe rentals are available April through October; daily between June and August, on weekends or by appointment in April, May, September, and October. Kayaks, rafts, go-carts, miniature golf, and a driving range also are available.

A unique way to experience the natural beauty of the Hocking Hills is riding the rails. *The Hocking Valley Scenic Railway* departs from its Nelsonville Depot for leisurely jaunts through the woods. The route between Nelsonville and Logan was once a part of the original Hocking Valley Railway's Athens Branch. The Hocking Valley was eventually merged into the Chesapeake & Ohio Railway in 1930.

The Hocking Valley Scenic Railway offers diesel-powered rides through the beautiful, rolling hills of Southeastern Ohio aboard vintage equipment. The primary locomotive was built for the Chesapeake & Ohio Railway in October 1952 by the Electro-motive Division of GM. In the 1970s, along with a few other C&O "Geeps," it was transferred to the Chicago, South Shore & South Bend Railroad for use in the C&O subsidiary's freight service. It has been restored and returned to its 1952 as-delivered paint scheme.

The coaches used were built in 1927 by the Standard Steel Car Company for the Chicago, Rock Island & Pacific Railroad. Each coach can seat one hundred passengers and weighs in at 95,200 lbs. They were used for commuter runs between Chicago and Joliet, Illinois. The coaches are heated in the winter, so a comfortable and enjoyable ride is to be had with Santa Claus during the annual Santa trains. Other vintage rolling stock is under restoration and on display.

The Hocking Valley Scenic Railway departs from 33 Canal Street, Nelsonville; (740) 753–9531, (800) 967–7834; www.hvsry.com. Trains depart late April through the first weekend of November, Saturday and Sunday, at noon and 2:30 P.M. Santa specials run the last weekend in November and the first three weekends in December, Saturday and Sunday, at 11:00 A.M. and 2:00 P.M. Rates: adults $11.00 to $15.00; children (ages 3 to 12) $8.00 to $10.00.

If you are traveling through McConnelsville, look for a lovely antebellum mansion dating from 1850. The **Howard House** was first called Rolling Acres and was built as the family home of Ohio Senator Cydnor B. Thompkins. The house is currently home of the Howard House Restaurant. It has been restored and furnished in the style of the 1850s. The elegant meals served at the Howard House feature classic American selections and a range of tasty desserts.

The Howard House is at 507 East Main Street, McConnelsville; (740) 962–5861. Open for dinner Tuesday through Saturday, 4:30 to 10:00 P.M. Lunch is served Monday through Thursday, 11:00 A.M. to 1:30 P.M.

Nature herself has given this site its name, Wahkeena, which is a Native American word meaning "most beautiful." The 150-acre **Wahkeena Nature Preserve,** at the edge of the Hocking Hills, is blessed with so many natural assets that it serves as a center for both outdoor education and nature study.

But the casual visitor won't have to study too hard to see how the preserve got its name. Much of the area is forested with lovely tulip trees as well as oaks. Mountain laurel, brilliant rhododendron, a host of wildflowers, and more than two dozen kinds of fern grace the landscape. While you may not think of Ohio as home to the exotic orchid, Wahkeena boasts eight native varieties of the flower, including the pink lady's slipper.

Visitors can hike three trails into the preserve and may be able to catch glimpses of the permanent residents: white-tailed deer, woodpeckers, maybe even a hawk or an owl. The land itself is noteworthy, with sandstone cliffs part of the preserve's vista, the famous Black Hand sandstone.

Although you can do your own exploring, naturalists also offer guided hikes and walks focusing on wildlife, plant life, or even the ways of the early pioneers in the area. Check in advance for topics, dates, and times.

The Wahkeena Nature Preserve is located at 2200 Pump Station Road, Sugar Grove; (740) 746–8695, (800) 297–1883; www.ohiohistory.org/places/wahkeena. Open April through October, Wednesday through Sunday, 8:00 A.M. to 4:30 P.M. Admission: $7.00 per car.

Square 13, a National Register Historic District, is one of the original blocks of Lancaster, a block noted by architectural historians as one of the finest collections of nineteenth-century architecture in a concentrated area in the nation. Within Square 13 on Lancaster's "Main Hill" is the **Sherman House,** the birthplace and early home of noted Civil War general William Tecumseh Sherman, and his brother, Senator John Sherman, author of the Sherman Anti-Trust Act. This museum is furnished as it would have been when the Sherman family lived there (the home was built between 1811 and 1816) and contains an extensive collection of General Sherman's Civil War memorabilia, mementos, and artifacts. One room is the study of William and John's father, Charles Sherman, who was a justice on the Ohio Supreme Court.

ohio's bulgaria liberator

The man hailed as one of the greatest figures in the history of Bulgaria was born on a farm near New Lexington in 1844. Januarius MacGahan, the "Liberator of Bulgaria," hoped to be a teacher but was unable to land a job with the local school district. Instead, in the early 1870s, he traveled throughout Europe and eventually became a war correspondent in the Balkans, where he filed eyewitness accounts of Turkish atrocities. His reporting shifted British public opinion regarding their support for Turkey and encouraged Russian intervention. MacGahan crossed the Danube with 100,000 Russian soldiers and received a hero's welcome. MacGahan lived out his life in Constantinople and died there in 1878. His body was returned to the United States; he's buried at New Lexington's Maplewood Cemetery.

The Sherman House is at 137 East Main Street, Lancaster; (740) 687–5891; www.shermanhouse.org. Open April through mid-December, Tuesday through Sunday, 1:00 to 4:00 P.M. Admission: adults $6.00; students (ages 6 to 18) $1.00.

The Decorative Arts Center of Ohio is a statewide organization that promotes the appreciation of decorative arts and finds its impressive home in the Reese-Peters House. Within this venue there are permanent and special exhibitions, plenty of art classes and workshops for children and adults, and a gift shop where you can find a souvenir or a book to help you learn more and celebrate decorative arts.

The house itself is a piece of art. The grand, Greek Revival-style home was built around 1835 by William James Reese, the son of a wealthy merchant. After getting a degree in law, Reese came to settle in Lancaster and married into a famous family. His wife, Elisabeth Sherman, was the sister of Secretary of State John Sherman and General William Tecumseh Sherman.

Reese ultimately lost the magnificent house in the financial panic of 1837. Luckily, after a series of owners, the final private owners donated it to Fairfield County. The house was renovated and became the home to the Decorative Arts Center, thanks to the authorization of more than $1 million in capital funds from the Ohio State Legislature.

The Decorative Arts Center is located at 145 East Main Street, Lancaster; (740) 681–1423; www.decartsohio.org. Open Tuesday through Sunday, 1:00 to 4:00 P.M. No admission charge.

After a day of exploring the Sherman House or attending a class at the Decorative Arts Center of Ohio, you may be ready to relax in a charming and relaxing setting. The ***Henry Manor Bed and Breakfast*** is a lovingly restored 1869 Tuscan-Victorian home situated on ten acres of woodlands. Guests can enjoy the outdoors just by sitting in the gazebo or get a little exercise on the woodland trails.

Two guest rooms on the second floor of the home have private baths. The Angel Room's bath is down the hall from the bedroom, and the Yellow Rose Room's bath features the original, old-fashioned claw-foot tub. Both rooms have a romantic feel and are graced with some lovely antiques. A full breakfast is included with the room.

Henry Manor Bed and Breakfast is located at 1755 Cedar Hill Road, Lancaster; (740) 689–8589; www.HenryManor.com. Rate: $95 per night.

The Georgian, an elegant two-story brick mansion, sits on a hill looking down on Lancaster's central business district, just as it has for the past 160 years. Constructed in 1831 for prominent businessman Samuel Maccracken, the Georgian mixes Federal architecture with Regency features and Empire furnishings. The Federal influence can be seen in the symmetrical placement of doors, windows, and fireplaces, while the Regency features are exemplified by the curved bay windows along the west wall. Classic Ionic columns, each containing a complete tree trunk for structural support, form the west portico.

The Georgian

Maccracken came to Lancaster from Big Springs, Pennsylvania, in 1810. Later elected to the state legislature, he introduced the bill funding construction of Ohio's canal system. While serving as Ohio Canal Funds Commissioner, Maccracken raised $6 million in Europe for the project.

This thirteen-room mansion is furnished with handsome pieces dating from the mid-1800s, including some of Maccracken's possessions. The original pine floors and woodwork remain intact, as do the original doors, door frames, and ornate arches. The spiral staircase features a cherry spindle handrail, and a large skylight allows light to spill down the stairs.

Splendid blue marble fireplaces from the quarry in King of Prussia, Pennsylvania, grace the two large parlors, as do matching French chandeliers (ca. 1820). One of the upstairs bedrooms contains a fine Regency bed (ca. 1800)—the type of bed preferred by generals in the Civil War, since it could be assembled and disassembled easily by the troops. One unique item in the museum is a 1792 senility cradle. Similar in design and function to a baby's cradle, cradles such as this were used by old people who were no longer ambulatory.

Hanging on the wall in one of the stairways are original Fairfield County land grants signed by Presidents Jefferson and Madison. Also on display is an American flag with eighteen stars—the flag of the United States from 1816 to 1820. The basement houses the kitchen, equipped as it was in the 1830s, and a unique dry well, where groundwater from the surface drained by way of pipes and was dispersed into the ground beneath the basement.

The Georgian is at 105 East Wheeling Street, on the corner of East Wheeling and North Broad Streets, Lancaster; (740) 654–9923; www.fairfieldheritage .org/georgianmuseum.html. Open April through mid-December, Tuesday through Sunday, 1:00 to 4:00 P.M. Admission: adults $6.00; children (6 to 18) $1.00.

After your tour of the Georgian, be sure to walk up East Wheeling Street for a view of the magnificent restored homes in a hilly, shaded section of Lancaster. If lunch or dinner is the next item on your itinerary, try a 1940s hotel that is making a comeback. Just across the street from the Georgian, *Shaw's Restaurant and Inn* features food, libations, and lodging in a delightful setting. Nine of the inn's twenty-four rooms and suites feature whirlpools and themed decor.

With rich wooden doors and trim, potted greenery, and distinctive floral wall coverings, the main dining room of the hotel has candlelit tables and indirect lighting, creating a cozy atmosphere. The dinner menu changes daily and is known for its sophistication.

Shaw's serves fresh homemade pies and cakes, and the house-made hot fudge sauce is a standout. Due to the popularity of lunch and dinner selections, the dining rooms accept reservations for both meals.

Shaw's has received the prestigious *Wine Spectator* Award of Excellence, noting the depth of the selections of vintage California red wines. In addition to the extensive wine list, a dozen varieties are served by the glass.

Shaw's Restaurant and Inn is at 123 North Broad Street, Lancaster; (740) 654–1842, (800) 654–2477; www.shawsinn.com. Rates: $86 to $218 per night, double occupancy, including full breakfast. Visa and MasterCard accepted.

Abundant clay deposits in eastern Ohio, particularly in Perry and Muskingum Counties, encouraged the manufacture of pottery and ceramic wares in this section of the state. Pottery production in these counties dates to the early nineteenth century, and twenty-two major pottery companies once generated clay products in the area. Only eight of those firms remain in business, but the *Ohio Ceramic Center* preserves the history of the industry and displays samples of the diverse output of those factories.

Set on a hilltop in a cluster of trees, the center consists of five open-air exhibit buildings. Guides provide the background and explain the processes used to produce the assortment of vases, jugs, pots, and pitchers, plus plates, saucers, and other dinnerware—each unique in shape, color, and clay mixture. Some of the older pieces include stoneware jugs and jars from the 1850s, and even older earthenware, which was made from very soft red clay.

The yellow ware, so named because of its yellow hue, came from the East Liverpool, Ohio, area, as did the most unusual brown rockingham pottery. Rockingham (also manufactured in Vermont and Great Britain) can be easily identified by the pitcher handles, which are shaped like a dog—a dog that appears to be looking into the pitcher. The guides also explain the obvious similarity in style of pieces from different companies—the firms frequently hired employees away from one another, and these employees often brought to their new employer the techniques and processes used by competitors.

Modern pottery displays include samples of dinnerware and decorative pottery currently in production at the remaining local companies. The museum also exhibits pottery-making equipment such as molds and old potter's wheels, plus examples of industrial uses of ceramics—drain tubes, shingles, chimney liners, and even filters for air-pollution devices. A resident potter demonstrates the craft of hand-throwing vases, bowls, and jugs, and describes glazing and finishing procedures. Two large shelter houses have been added at the center, where antique pottery is sold on special occasions, the proceeds used to help support this facility.

The Ohio Ceramic Center is on Route 93 between Roseville and Crooksville; (740) 697–7021; www.ohiohistory.org/places/ohceram. The center is open May through mid-October, Monday through Saturday, 9:30 A.M. to 5:00 P.M.; Sunday, noon to 5:00 P.M. Admission: adults $4.00; children $2.00.

Cattle ranch? Ohio? Yep. The **Smoke Rise Ranch Resort** is a working cattle ranch on 2,000 acres in the rolling hills of southeastern Ohio. Visitors can play cowboy or cowgirl, rounding up strays on horseback, doctoring sick calves, checking fences and water tanks, and driving the herd from pasture to pasture. Or you can just enjoy the scenery, exploring it on foot or in the saddle on the more than 100 miles of trails. Other activities include ranch rodeos, team penning, riding lessons, dinner dances, and music festivals.

A wildlife management area and the Wayne National Forest, totaling more than 30,000 acres, border the ranch. The terrain ranges from rock bluffs to lush green bottomland. The abundant ponds provide water for your trail horse and a great place to stop and fish away an afternoon.

Accommodations range from bunk-style cabins and a fully furnished ranch house to picturesque campsites. And you can cook your own grub (ranch talk

all's pottery in crooksville

Given its name, you might suspect Crooksville is notable for the poor character of its citizenry. That is not the case. Instead, Crooksville made its reputation as a center of the pottery business.

The rich clays beneath its soil spawned pottery giants such as Crooksville Pottery Company, the Star Stoneware Company, and the Diamond Stoneware Company in the late nineteenth century. The arrival of rail service in 1890 established Crooksville as "Clay City," and launched a competition with another Ohio pottery town, East Liverpool.

for "food"), or dine with the staff at this family-owned resort. Other amenities include a heated swimming pool, a hot tub, and a clubhouse with a full kitchen.

Smoke Rise Ranch Resort is at 6751 Hunterdon Road, Glouster; (740) 767–2624; www.smokeriseranch.com. Open for trail riding daily, 8:00 A.M. to 6:30 P.M. Lodging is $70 to $175 per night.

moonshinefestival

Legal moonshine? Yes, in New Straitsville in late May you can see demonstrations of moonshine brewing as part of the Moonshine Festival. The character of hill country culture of days past comes back to life in the streets as the music of fiddles and banjos fills the air. There always are plenty of games for the kids, as well as displays and sales of local crafts and plenty of local food specialties. For more information call (740) 394–2838.

It was Harriet and Ora Anderson, she a well-known local artist and he a banker and philanthropist, who decided southeastern Ohio was in need of a cultural arts center. Their quest for a home for their vision led them to an unlikely structure: a historic dairy barn, built in 1914, once part of a large farm minutes from the heart of Athens.

By the time the Andersons discovered the ***Dairy Barn*** in 1977, it was scheduled for demolition in nine days. They rallied area residents and artists and saved it from the wrecking ball. In 1978, the facility was placed on the National Register of Historic Places, protecting it from future demolition.

After a loft renovation, this unique 11,000-square-foot exhibit space today hosts international exhibitions, festivals, performances, and activities for all ages, and all consistent with its mission: to offer exhibitions, events, and educational programs that nurture and promote area artists and artisans, and to draw attention and visitors to Southeast Ohio. In the international arts community, the Dairy Barn is best known for its contemporary art quilt exhibition. The Dairy Barn is at 8000 Dairy Lane, Athens; (740) 592–4981; www.dairy barn.org. Open year-round, Tuesday through Saturday, noon to 5:00 P.M.; Sunday, 1:00 to 5:00 P.M. (until 8:00 P.M. on Thursday). Admission varies by exhibit.

Places to Stay in Southeast Ohio

GLOUSTER

Smoke Rise Ranch Resort
6751 Hunterdon Road
(740) 767–2624,
(800) 292–1732

LANCASTER

Henry Manor Bed and Breakfast
1755 Cedar Hill Road
(740) 689–8589

LOGAN

Inn at Cedar Falls
21190 Route 374
(740) 385–7489,
(800) 653–2557

Old Man's Cave Chalets
18905 Route 664
(800) 762–9396

MARIETTA

Lafayette Hotel
Corner of Front and Greene Streets
(740) 373–5522

NEW PLYMOUTH

Ravenwood Castle
Intersection of Routes 56 and 93
(740) 596–2606,
(800) 477–1541

ROCKBRIDGE

Glenlaurel
14940 Mt. Olive Road
(800) 809–REST

ZALESKI

Lake Hope State Park Cabins
Route 278, 5 miles north of Zaleski
(740) 596–5253,
(800) 282–7275

Places to Eat in Southeast Ohio

LANCASTER

Shaw's Restaurant and Inn
123 North Broad Street
(614) 654–1842,
(800) 654–2477
Lodging is also available.

MARIETTA

Becky Thatcher's Restaurant and Lounge
237 Front Street
(740) 373–4130

Levee House Cafe
127 Ohio Street
(740) 374–2233

McCONNELSVILLE

Howard House
507 East Main
(740) 962–5861

Scioto Ribber
1026 Gallia Street
(740) 353–9329

HELPFUL WEB SITES

Ohio Division of Travel and Tourism:
www.ohiotourism.com

Hocking Hills Tourism:
www.hockinghills.com

Athens County Visitors Bureau:
www.athensohio.com

Marietta Visitors Bureau:
www.rivertowns.org

Southwest Ohio

Native Beauty

Two thousand years ago, along the rivers of what is now southern Ohio, a great civilization arose. The Hopewell culture flourished for more than 500 years, leaving behind extensive burial mounds, earthworks, and artifacts. They are preserved at the Mound City site of the ***Hopewell Culture National Historical Park.*** Excavation and restoration work was conducted by the Ohio State Historical Society in 1920 and 1921, and the site was declared a National Monument in 1923. Additional excavations were conducted in the mid-1960s.

Some of the artifacts discovered and displayed here may have been used to establish trade and diplomatic ties between distant peoples. The territory we now call southern Ohio was the center of a network of peoples extending from Michigan to southern Florida, and from Kansas to the East Coast. The Hopewell included skilled artisans; they fished and hunted, gathered wild foods, and gardened. They lived along river valleys, in permanent or semipermanent villages near the mounds and earthworks they built. By about 500 A.D. the great Hopewell culture ended, perhaps because of social changes. In addition to the Mound City Group, Hopewell Culture National Historical

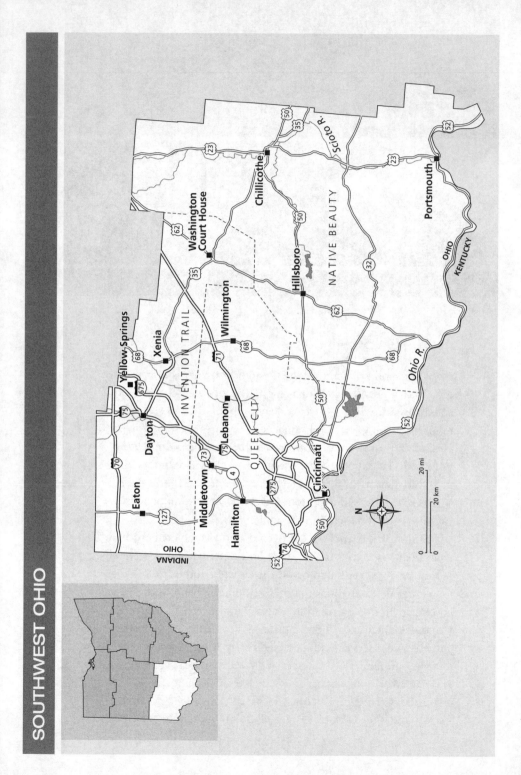

Park preserves four additional Hopewell sites in Ross County: Hopewell Mound Group, Seip Earthworks, High Bank Works, and Hopeton Earthworks.

Hopewell Culture National Historical Park is 3 miles north of Chillicothe on Route 104; (740) 774–1126; www.nps.gov/hocu. Open daily, 8:30 A.M. to 5:00 P.M. (open later in the summer). Admission: adults $3.00; children free.

Thomas Worthington first came to Ohio from Virginia at the age of twenty-three in 1796, when he and a small band of men arrived to claim the land promised their fathers and friends after the Revolutionary War. Worthington permanently moved his family to Ohio in 1798 and quickly became active in the efforts to achieve statehood for the territory. He succeeded in that endeavor and served as a member of Ohio's Constitutional Convention in 1802. After being elected as one of the state's first United States senators, Worthington built his magnificent hilltop estate, *Adena.* Worthington and his wife, Eleanor, raised their ten children at Adena and entertained distinguished guests such as President James Monroe, Henry Clay, Aaron Burr, and the Shawnee Indian chief Tecumseh. After building Adena, Worthington was reelected to the United States Senate in 1811, and later he served two terms as the governor of Ohio.

More than 300 of the estate's original 5,000 acres are now open to the public, and visitors may explore the spacious two-story sandstone home, the barn, the springhouse, and the smokehouse—all located in a rolling meadow above the Scioto River Valley. Self-guided tours of the eighteen-room home allow you to browse at your own pace, appreciating the fine antiques described on the fact sheet, which gives the styles and origins of the furnishings in the home. Although many of the pieces on display did not belong to the Worthingtons, they date from the 1780s to 1820s and are typical of the pieces used at Adena.

AUTHORS' FAVORITES

Hopewell Culture National Historical Park

Adena

7 Caves Nature Preserve

Pike Lake State Park

Lake White Club

Fort Hill State Memorial

Shawnee State Park

Serpent Mound

Rankin House

Signal House

Cohearts Riverhouse

Grant's Boyhood Home

Grant's Birthplace

Valley Vineyards

The large downstairs master bedroom, with its dark ash and oak floors, has a splendid view of the formal gardens. In an adjacent sitting room hangs a most unusual portrait of Thomas Jefferson, created not with paint, but with different colors of wool thread. The enormous state dining room features the actual dining table and chairs used at Adena in 1825. Two large portraits decorate the drawing room; one of Thomas Worthington at age twenty-five and the other of his sister, who married Edward Tiffin, Ohio's first governor.

Two of Adena's most interesting rooms are tucked away down the back stairs: the weaving room, with a large Virginia loom (ca. 1790) and wool and flax wheels, and Worthington's private study. On display in the study is a tomahawk given to Worthington by Chief Tecumseh in 1807. Worthington's musket and his father's sword still hang above the fireplace.

Across the meadow from the home is a scenic overlook of the Scioto River Valley—you can see for miles from this spot. In fact, the splendor of the sunrise over Mount Logan as viewed from Adena is said to have inspired the sunrise design incorporated in the seal of the state of Ohio.

Adena is off Route 104 and Pleasant Valley Road on Adena Road, 3 miles north of Chillicothe; (740) 772–1500, (800) 319–7248; www.ohiohistory.org/places/adena. Open from April through October, Wednesday through Saturday, 9:30 A.M. to 5:00 P.M.; Sunday, noon to 5:00 P.M. Admission: adults $7.00; children (ages 6 to 12) $3.00.

State Motto/Animal

In 1866, the Ohio legislature passed a bill adding a motto to Ohio's Great Seal. The motto, *Imerium in Imperio,* translates from Latin to "an empire within an empire." However, the motto's life span was brief. Critics blasted it as pretentious and feudal, and in 1867 the law authorizing it was repealed. For the next ninety-one years, Ohio had no state motto.

In 1958, Cincinnati sixth-grader Jimmie Mastronardo was disturbed to learn that Ohio was the only state without a motto, and he set about to correct this omission. He decided on a biblical verse from Matthew 19:26: "With God all things are possible." He and his classmates launched a petition drive aimed at the legislature, a drive that succeeded in 1959 when the new motto officially was adopted.

Students also were the driving force behind the designation of the white-tailed deer as Ohio's state animal in 1988. In this case, it was a fourth-grade class at Worthington Estates Elementary School that lobbied lawmakers. The students argued that the white-tailed deer's abundance (there are more deer today in Ohio than there were at the time of settlement) and gracefulness warranted the recognition. The legislators agreed and deemed it so.

Built by Governor Tiffin in 1826, the *Guest House Bed and Breakfast* was a wedding gift from Ohio's first governor to his daughter. Situated 1 block from downtown Chillicothe and listed on the National Register of Historic Places in 1987, the home was "Victorianized" in the 1880s with the addition of a second floor over the east wing of the house with ornate staircases and parquet floors in the hall and dining room. This house was once the home of Edward Tiffin Cook, a gold medalist in pole vault at the 1908 Olympics.

Owners Tom and Kay Binns have traveled extensively—Tom's a retired TWA captain—and have brought the best of the amenities they have enjoyed around the world to the Guest House. The Guest House is a two-story brick building with a guest unit on each floor and a separate entrance for each. Look out the window of either unit and enjoy a view of the Old English garden separating the Guest House from the main building.

The Guest House is at 57 West Fifth Street, Chillicothe; (740) 772–2204; www.guesthousechillicothe.com. Rates: $100 per night, including full breakfast.

Shawnee leader Tecumseh dreamed of banding together 50,000 warriors from all the western Indian tribes in a force that he hoped would end the white man's westward expansion. The plan obviously failed, and the whites eventually conquered the land north and west of the Ohio River and beyond. Tecumseh's story is portrayed nightly, except Sunday, during the summer at Sugarloaf Mountain Amphitheatre in the outdoor drama **Tecumseh!** The Tecumseh Restaurant Terrace serves a buffet dinner each evening prior to the 8:00 P.M. curtain. Backstage tours also are offered daily.

Sugarloaf Mountain Amphitheatre is on Delano Road, east of Route 159, 6 miles northeast of Chillicothe; (740) 775–0700, (866) 775–0700; www.tecumseh drama.com. Performances take place from early June to early September. Admission: adults $16 to $18; children (ages 10 and under) $8.00 to $9.00. Advanced reservations required. MasterCard, American Express, and Visa are accepted.

"Lemonade Lucy" was the nickname Lucy Hayes, the wife of U.S. President Rutherford B. Hayes, was given while she lived at the White House because she

feastofthe floweringmoon

What child hasn't played at being a Native American or a rugged mountain man? The Feast of the Flowering Moon brings reenactment teams together to bring the days of early Ohio back to Yoctangee Park in Chillicothe. During the weekend festival you'll marvel at the skills of artisans and feel the beat of drums that fire the performance of Native American dancers.

The Feast of the Flowering Moon is held in mid- to late May in Yoctangee Park. For more information, write to P.O. Box 879, Chillicothe, Ohio 45601. No admission charge.

would not serve alcohol at parties and receptions. Her birthplace, now the *Lucy Hayes Heritage Center,* is modest compared to the president's official residence, but has much to teach us about the life of Lemonade Lucy and of families of the early 1800s. The two-story Federal-style home houses period furniture as well as memorabilia from the president and the first lady.

The Lucy Hayes Heritage Center is at 90 West Sixth Street, Chillicothe; (740) 775–5829; www.lucyhayes.org. Open April through September, Monday, 10:00 A.M. to 2:00 P.M.; Saturday 1:00 to 4:00 P.M.

In an area once inhabited by Shawnee and Delaware Indians, *7 Caves Nature Preserve* has intrigued visitors since the turn of the century. The park was established as 7 Caves in 1928 and was owned by the Miller family for decades, but is now part of the nonprofit Highlands Nature Sanctuary.

Where's the Capital?

Congress divided the Northwest Territory in 1800 and designated Chillicothe as the capital of the eastern half. The territorial legislature met here in November of 1800 in Abrams's Big House, a two-story log cabin and one of the few buildings in the four-year-old village large enough to accommodate the group. The main floor, where the legislature met, also was used for singing schools, dances, and religious services. Upstairs was a bar. Construction began on a statehouse built of stone taken from neighboring hills.

In 1802, when the population of the eastern division of the territory reached 45,000, Congress authorized the election of delegates to create a state constitution. Thirty-five delegates met in the new Chillicothe statehouse on November 4, 1802, and drafted the document in twenty-five days. Ohio's admission to the Union was in 1803, and the first Ohio General Assembly convened March 1, 1803.

The new constitution called for Chillicothe to remain the capital until 1808, starting an intense competition between towns wanting to be named the permanent capital. Zanesville went as far as building a statehouse and was named the temporary capital in 1809 for its efforts. The brick Zanesville statehouse served as the capital until 1812, when the seat of government was shifted back to Chillicothe.

Meanwhile, Worthington, Lancaster, Newark, Mt. Vernon, Delaware, Dublin, and Pickaway Plains all competed for the permanent site. Dublin was believed to be the front runner, but legend has it that Dublin lost the favored spot as a result of a card game the night before the legislature was to act on the siting of the permanent capital. The winner was a plot of land across the Scioto River from the town of Franklinton.

The new capital site was heavily wooded and did not even have a name. Though Ohio City was the favorite name with many, the legislature designated the future capital as Columbus. State offices moved from Chillicothe to Columbus on October 1, 1816, and the legislature met for the first time in Columbus that December.

Lucy Hayes Heritage Center

Designated as an Ohio Natural Landmark, the 7 Caves Nature Preserve offers a scenic retreat with miles of hiking trails and caves for exploration. The park is home to more than 250 species of plants and more than 60 types of trees, many of which are rare or endangered.

Well-marked trails lead to the 7 Caves, each with its own unique formation: Cave of the Springs, Witches, Phantom, Bear, McKimie, Marble, and Dancing Caves. Rocky Fork Creek flows through the rolling hills of the Paint Valley and is known for its crystal-clear rapids, waterfalls, precipitous cliffs, and canyons. Also, 7 Caves was one of the filming locations for the CBS miniseries *500 Nations,* a Kevin Costner production that celebrated Native American culture.

7 Caves Nature Preserve is 4 miles west of Bainbridge, off U.S. Route 50 at 7660 Cave Road; (937) 365–1935, 1936; www.highlandssanctuary.org. Open April through October, Saturday and Sunday, 10:30 A.M. to 2:30 P.M., plus Friday during the summer. Adults $10.00, children $5.00.

When you're traveling through southern Ohio, you can't help but notice the dozens of lakes in the region—lakes providing boating, fishing, swimming, and other recreational activities. For this reason I heartily recommend that when you travel off the beaten path in southern Ohio, you always pack a swimsuit—particularly on hot summer days.

One of these alluring lakes is thirteen-acre Pike Lake in *Pike Lake State Park,* which offers a delightful spot for swimming, rowing, fishing, or scuba diving. Lifeguards watch over the sandy beach and swimming area during the summer, and rowboats can be rented. Anglers enjoy catching the catfish, large-mouth bass, crappie, and bluegill, and divers take advantage of the remarkably clear water.

thecradleof americandentistry

Bainbridge was a trendsetter in the early 1800s, when Dr. John Harris opened the first school in the United States for teaching dentistry. Thanks to Harris, the town has been recognized as the "Cradle of American Dentistry." Harris founded the first U.S. dental school in 1825 in a modest one-story brick building on Main Street. The building today houses a dental museum.

Although the state park is a modest 600 acres, a densely wooded 10,600-acre state forest surrounds the park. There are numerous hiking trails in the state forest and 7 miles of trails in the park.

Up a shady hill from the lake sit the park's twenty-five rental cabins—twelve deluxe two-bedroom cabins and thirteen standard cabins. All are set in secluded locations, and the deluxe cabins offer completely equipped kitchens, baths, living areas, and screened porches. The standard cabins contain a single large sleeping and living area with four bunks and a fold-out couch, a kitchen, and a bath. Pike Lake also has 112 campsites, and a park naturalist conducts nature programs during summer months.

Pike Lake State Park is at 1847 Pike Lake Road, 7 miles south of Bainbridge; (740) 493–2212, (866) 644–6727; www.dnr.state.oh.us/parks/parks/pikelake.htm. Rates for the cabins range from $50 to $60 per night. Early reservations recommended.

The *Lake White Club* dates back to 1936, but the building housing the club was a log cabin on Pee Pee Creek long before construction of the dam and spillway that created Lake White. The lobby of the restaurant contains the original rough-hewn wooden beams of the cabin, which was built on this spot in the 1820s. The Ohio and Erie Canal could be seen from the windows of that cabin; the canal followed the creek on its way south to Portsmouth. Pee Pee Creek received its name for the initials of Peter Patrick, which he carved in the trunk of a large beech tree beside the stream as a claim on this land in 1785, when this area was still Shawnee country.

The club specializes in down-home country cooking, and the chicken dinners are a house specialty. Other entrees include half a dozen cuts of steak, roast turkey, hickory-smoked ham in raisin sauce, and ham and turkey smothered with a cheese sauce. If the 180-degree view of the lake whets your appetite for seafood, try the broiled or fried pickerel, the lobster tail, the scallops, or the fried shrimp. The club offers prime rib as a special dinner every Saturday night.

The Lake White Club serves generous portions of all its entrees, and the light-wood paneling and bentwood chairs give the dining room a pleasant, not-too-formal atmosphere.

The Lake White Club is at 1166 Route 552, 2 miles south of Waverly; (740) 947–5000, (800) 774–5253. Open Tuesday through Sunday, 4:00 to 8:00 P.M.

Shawnee State Park, with more than 60,000 acres of parkland and adjoining state forest, consists of ridge upon ridge of thick woods in the splendid southern Ohio countryside. To get perspective on the size of this stunningly beautiful acreage, note that the park contains over 130 miles of roads, not to mention miles of hiking and bridle paths. Shawnee is particularly popular in October, when the changing leaves produce hillsides bursting with reds, oranges, and golds. A 5,000-acre section of the park has been set aside as the Shawnee Wilderness Area, preserving the unspoiled natural beauty of the land. The park's two small lakes, Turkey Creek Lake and Roosevelt Lake, both have sandy swimming beaches.

A modern stone-and-timber fifty-room lodge provides overnight accommodations in this peaceful park, as do twenty-five deluxe two-bedroom cabins. Facilities at the lodge include an indoor and outdoor pool, tennis courts, a restaurant, a game room, and an eighteen-hole golf course with putting green, restaurant, and game room. Lodge rates are $79 to $129 per night, double occupancy. The cabins are tucked away in an isolated section of the park and come equipped with all kitchen utensils, linens, and blankets. Cabin rates range from $129 to $199 per night, $699 to $1,050 per week. Numerous campsites are also available.

Shawnee State Park is at 4404 Route 125, 12 miles west of Portsmouth; (740) 858–6621, (800) 282–7275; www.dnr.state.oh.us/parks/parks/shawnee .htm. Open year-round; reservations recommended.

Fort Hill State Memorial offers the traveler a chance to see one of the best preserved Native American earthworks in all of North America. Archaeologists believe that the 1½-mile-long earthen enclosure on the hilltop was constructed by the Hopewell people between 100 B.C. and A.D. 500. Experts believe that this area also contained at least two ceremonial buildings, and probably a village located in the Brush Creek Valley.

This 1,200-acre preserve lies just at the edge of the glacial boundary and has 11 miles of hiking trails. The hilly region is home to a wide variety of flowers and plants. Along with the hiking trails, visitors can take a break at the picnic grounds. A museum also offers information and exhibits on the area's geology and on the archaeological findings around the region.

Fort Hill State Memorial is located at 13614 Fort Hill Road, Hillsboro; (937) 588–3221, (800) 283–8905; www.ohiohistory.org/places/fthill. Open daylight hours. No admission charge.

Impressive but still shrouded in mystery is the **Serpent Mound** in southwest Ohio. This huge snake built of mounded earth stretches for nearly a quarter of a mile. The Serpent Mound is the largest serpent effigy mound in the United States and one of the few effigy mounds in Ohio. Experts believe that the Adena people built this and other mounds, and lived in this area in Ohio from 800 B.C. to A.D. 100. Just what purpose the giant, prehistoric mound played in the life and the culture of the Adena remains a mystery. However, archeologists believe that the uncoiling snake symbolized some mythical or religious principle. Also on this site are smaller, conical mounds that contain artifacts from the Adena people and also appear to serve as burial sites.

birthofthe women'schristian temperanceunion

On Christmas morning 1873, Eliza Jane Thompson and seventy-five other women temperance activists visited every Hillsboro saloon and drugstore that sold alcohol. Thompson, daughter of a former governor and wife of a judge, led the charge into those businesses, where the protestors would kneel, pray aloud, and sing hymns. They informed the shocked owners they'd be back the next day and every day until they stopped selling the devil's brew.

The result: They stopped liquor sales in every Hillsboro store but one. Eliza Jane Thompson's protest movement became the Women's Temperance Crusade, which in turn evolved into the Women's Christian Temperance Union.

The Serpent Mound is located at 3850 Route 73, Peebles; (937) 587–2796, (800) 752–2757; www .ohiohistory.org/places/serpent. Open daily April through October, 10:00 A.M. to 5:00 P.M. Admission: per car, $7.00; bicycles, pedestrians, motorcycles, $2.00; RVs with eight or more people, $9.00.

Rare plants and impressive geological features are waiting to awe the casual hiker or the serious botanist or geologist at the *Davis Memorial Nature Preserve.* This eighty-eight-acre site was donated by Davon Inc. and bears the name of its chairman of the board, Edwin H. Davis.

Visitors enjoy two hiking trails in the preserve. Dolomite cliffs, an impressive geological fault, and a cave are among the geological points of interest. The heavily wooded trails give hikers a chance to see bamboo grass, purple cliff-break ferns, great cane, and a rare plant called Sullivantia, which grew here in preglacial times.

The Davis Memorial Nature Preserve is located at Township Road 126 and 129, 3 miles east of Peebles; (614) 265–6453; www.ohiohistory.org/places/ davis. Open daylight hours. No admission charge.

The redbrick two-story house, with its shake roof and white trim, does not at first appear in any way extraordinary. It does offer a marvelous view down the steep hill to the Ohio River, and across the river into northern Kentucky, but there is no outward evidence of this house's role in history. But 150 years ago, rickety wooden steps led from the river up the hillside to this modest home. Those steps became known as the "stairway to liberation," and on moonless nights slaves escaping from plantations in the South crossed the Ohio River and climbed those weathered steps to the **Rankin House,** home of the Reverend John Rankin.

Rankin and his wife, Jean, were conductors on the Underground Railroad, which transported thousands of slaves to freedom in Canada. Rankin's battle against slavery began with his abolitionist preaching as early as 1815, and a series of his letters on the subject were published in a book in 1826. The home he built on "Liberty Hill" protected runaway slaves from the day it was completed in 1828 until 1863. Rankin used an elaborate set of signals, using lanterns in his windows, to communicate the "all clear" message to Dr. Alexander Campbell and other abolitionists in town.

Designated a National Historic Landmark in September 1997, and now open to the public as a museum, the Rankin House contains some of Rankin's possessions, including his personal Bible, published in 1793. The house has dark hardwood floors and high ceilings typical of the period, as well as completely furnished bedrooms and a kitchen stocked with cooking utensils and equipment used in the mid-1800s.

One upstairs room houses a small abolitionist museum, which tells of the more than 2,000 slaves who stayed at Rankin House (often as many as twelve at a time) on their way to freedom. It was Rankin who told Harriet Beecher Stowe the account of a slave named Eliza who carried her children across the frozen, but thawing, Ohio River. Her bravery was rewarded—the bounty hunters pursuing her found the ice broken up by the time they reached the river the next morning, forcing them to abandon their chase. Stowe immortalized the story of Eliza in her book *Uncle Tom's Cabin*. Because of his influence in the abolitionist movement and his work as a conductor on the Underground Railroad, southern plantation owners offered a bounty for Rankin's life.

The Rankin House is just off U.S. Route 52, west of the central business district in Ripley; (937) 392–1627, (800) 752–2705; www.ohiohistory.org/places/rankin. Open Wednesday through Saturday, 10:00 A.M. to 5:00 P.M.; Sunday, noon to 5:00 P.M., and Tuesday May through December. Admission: adults $3.00; children $1.00.

One of the homes that signaled the Rankin House when the waterfront was clear of bounty hunters, dogs, and slave owners during those Underground Railroad days was on the corner of Locust and Front Streets in Ripley and is today known as **The Signal House.** Built in the 1830s in Greek Italianate style, this home is now a delightful bed-and-breakfast owned by Vic and Betsy Billingsley.

TOP ANNUAL EVENTS

Feast of the Flowering Moon,
Chillicothe, May;
(740) 887–2979;
www.feastoffloweringmoon.com

Yellow Springs Street Fair,
Yellow Springs, June;
(937) 767–2686;
www.yellowsprings.com/events.asp

Summerfair,
Cincinnati, June;
(513) 232–8230;
www.coneyislandpark.com

Roy Rogers Festival,
Portsmouth, June;
(740) 353–0900;
www.sciotocountyohio.com/royrogers.htm

Tecumseh! Outdoor Historical Drama,
Chillicothe, June to September;
(740) 775–0700, (866) 775–0700;
www.tecumsehdrama.com

Blue Jacket,
Xenia, June to August;
(937) 376–4358;
www.bluejacketdrama.com

Black Cultural Festival,
Dayton, July;
(937) 233–0200;
www.blackculturalfestival.org

Wheels of Progress Festival,
Greenfield, July;
www.greenfieldrotary.org/festival.htm

Fayette County Fair,
Washington Court House, July;
(740) 335–5856;
www.fayettecoagsociety.com/fair.html

Cityfolk Festival,
Dayton, July;
(937) 223–3655;
www.cityfolk.org/calendar.htm

Sweet Corn Festival,
Fairborn, August;
(937) 878–7040;
www.greenecountyohio.org/events.html

Ohio Renaissance Festival,
Harveysburg, early September to mid-October;
(513) 897–7000;
www.renfestival.com

The Billingsleys first caught sight of the stately white structure while cruising the Ohio River on their houseboat. When they decided they were ready to leave suburban Cincinnati for a more rural environment, they came to Ripley.

Initially they bought The Signal House to be their home and nothing more. But encouraged by friends enchanted with the place, they decided to share it with others and began operation as a bed-and-breakfast in 1989.

Furnished with family antiques, The Signal House features three porches, twin parlors, and river views from every room. The guest rooms share a bath. Breakfast here can range from homemade breads, muffins, jams, and spreads to sausage and cheese strata.

The Signal House is at 234 North Front Street, Ripley; (937) 392–1640; www.thesignalhouse.com. Rates: $95 to $150 per night, double occupancy, including breakfast.

Highland County Fair,
Hillsboro, September;
(937) 393–9975;
www.ohiofairs.org/highlandcountyfair.html

Montgomery County Fair,
Dayton, September;
(937) 224–1619;
http://montcofair.com/

Circleville Pumpkin Show,
Circleville, October;
(740) 474–7000, (740) 474–8973;
www.pumpkinshow.com

Sauerkraut Festival,
Waynesville, October;
(513) 897–8855;
www.sauerkrautfestival.com

Hallzooween,
Cincinnati, October;
(513) 475–6124, (800) 944–4776;
www.cincinnatizoo.org/VisitorGuide/plan
youradventure/Hallzooween/
hallzooween.html

Fall Festival of Leaves,
Bainbridge, October;
(740) 772–6677;
www.fallfestivalofleaves.com

Springboro Christmas Festival,
Springboro, November;
(937) 748–0074;
www.home.cinci.rr.com/telos/Springboro
Festivals

Historic Clifton Mill Light Display,
Clifton, late November to December;
(937) 767–5501;
www.cliftonmill.com

**Historic Lebanon Horse-Drawn
Carriage Parade & Christmas Festival,**
Lebanon, December;
(513) 932–1100;
www.lebanonchamber.org/

For lunch or dinner in Ripley, stop by *Cohearts Riverhouse.* Sisters Joanne May and Roberta Gaudio, veterans of the Cincinnati restaurant scene, restored this 1840s structure and opened for business in 1989. The second-floor screened porch offers a great view of the river.

Roberta does the cooking, using produce from local farms, handmade pasta, and Amish cheeses. Dinner selections range from pasta and barbecue ribs to chicken, fish, and steaks. Lunch options include soups, salads, and sandwiches.

Cohearts Riverhouse is at 18 North Front Street, Ripley; (937) 392–4819. Open Thursday through Saturday, 11:30 A.M. to 9:00 P.M.; Sunday, 11:30 A.M. to 7:00 P.M. Personal checks accepted.

The modest but solid roots of Ulysses S. Grant (known as Hiram Ulysses Grant as a boy), commander of the Union forces during the Civil War and eighteenth president of the United States, are obvious when you visit *Grant's*

Boyhood Home in rural Georgetown. Built by his father Jesse Grant in 1823, the home is designated a National Historic Landmark. The Grants expanded the home in 1825 and again in 1828. Grant lived here from the age of one until he left to attend West Point at seventeen, the longest period spent at any residence during his lifetime.

Early nineteenth-century furnishings and Grant memorabilia are on display. The white gloves President Grant wore to his inaugural ball and a velvet dress belonging to his wife, Julia Dent Grant, are among the more noteworthy items.

Grant's Boyhood Home is at 219 East Grant Avenue, Georgetown; (937) 378–4222; www.ohiohistory.org/places/grantboy. Open Memorial Day to Labor Day, Wednesday through Sunday, noon to 5:00 P.M., plus weekends in September and October. Rates: adults $3.00; children $1.00.

Queen City

A three-room cottage was the birthplace of a man who would become the highest elected official in the land. The ***Grant Birthplace*** is a simple, one-story home built in 1817. Hiram Ulysses Grant was born in the humble home five years later, on April 27, 1822. (Grant did not become "Ulysses S." until his application to West Point incorrectly identified him as such, a mistake with which he concurred.) Grant's father worked at a tannery, which was next to the Grant home.

Before the home was restored and preserved for all of us to visit, it was loaded on a railroad flatcar and transported on a tour around the United States. Now returned to its original site, it is open to the public and furnished in the style of the early 1800s.

The Grant Birthplace is at 1591 Route 232, Point Pleasant; (513) 553– 4911; www.ohiohistory.org/places/grantbir. Open April through October, Wednesday through Saturday, 9:30 A.M. to noon and 1:00 to 5:00 P.M.; Sunday, noon to 5:00 P.M. Admission: adults $2.00; children (ages 6 to 12) $1.00.

Take time to walk through the historic Milford central business district. Housed in restored commercial buildings, stores on Main Street include early antiques and a cheerful gift shop called 100 Main, which happens to be its address.

On the last Thursday, Friday, and Saturday in September, ***Valley Vineyards*** hosts the annual Ohio Wine Festival, with live entertainment, judging of homemade wines, and other festivities. The rest of the year, Ken Schuchter's Valley Vineyards produces eighteen fine wines from its fifty acres of American and French hybrid and vinifera grapes.

Grape growing and wine making have been popular in southern Ohio for more than 150 years, and the Schuchters planted their first vines at Valley Vineyards in 1969. The winery, in a new chalet-style building, offers a tasting tray with one-ounce servings of nine different wines—the perfect way to investigate and appreciate the vineyard's quality blends. I particularly enjoyed the vidal blanc, the winner of many awards.

The winery has indoor and outdoor seating, with cookout dinners every Friday and Saturday (Sunday also during the summer) on the large patios. Cheese plates and pizzas are always available.

notsogoldrush

You missed the Ohio gold rush of 1868? Well, you didn't miss much. The discovery of what was thought to be gold at Batavia right after the Civil War set off a panic and prompted the establishment of the Batavia Gold Mining Company. Speculators sold shares in this venture for $100 each—big money in those days. Oh, there was gold here, but just minute traces too small to ever be profitably mined. The Batavia gold rush was over as quickly as it started.

Valley Vineyards is on combined Routes 22 and 3, Morrow; (513) 899–2485; www.valley-vineyards.com. Open Monday through Thursday, 11:00 A.M. to 8:00 P.M.; Friday and Saturday, 11:00 A.M. to 11:00 P.M.; and Sunday, 1:00 to 6:00 P.M.

If you are looking for a unique shopping experience or for handcrafted, eighteenth- or nineteenth-century reproduction furniture, then a trip to the **Workshops of David T. Smith** should be on your itinerary. The site actually features many buildings housing woodworking and pottery areas. Visitors are welcome at the showroom and design center.

Each piece of furniture is unique and reflects a period of American furniture building. You can buy a simple table that looks like something the Pilgrims would have used during the first Thanksgiving or a Windsor chair with delicately turned legs. You could come home with a decorative spoon holder or contract to have your entire kitchen renovated with handmade cabinetry.

Pottery is also produced in the workshops. The potters specialize in Redware Pottery, formed from slabs of red clay that is either pressed into molds or thrown on a potter's wheel. Collectors will find a variety of pots, plates, lamps, and sculpture pieces from which to choose.

The Workshops of David T. Smith are at 3600 Shawhan Road, Morrow; (888) 353–9387; www.davidtsmith.com. Open Monday through Saturday, 10:00 A.M. to 5:00 P.M.

On December 23, 1803, Jonas Seaman received a license to operate a "house of public entertainment" at the site today occupied by one of Ohio's premier historic hotels, the **Golden Lamb.** The present building replaced Seaman's cabin in 1815, and the Lamb now provides travelers with fine dining and period accommodations in picturesque Lebanon.

During its nearly two centuries, distinguished guests at the Golden Lamb have included ten American presidents, Henry Clay, Mark Twain (who performed at the Lebanon Opera House in the late nineteenth century), and Charles Dickens, who, it is told, complained vociferously during his visit in 1842 when informed the inn did not serve "spirits." Dickens would maintain his composure if he visited the Golden Lamb today, for the Black Horse Tavern provides complete bar service at the inn. And after some "refreshment," he might well enjoy browsing in the extensive gift shop on the lower level.

With a reputation for serving challenging dishes, the Lamb offers a dinner menu that includes delights such as timbale of filet of sole and salmon mousse with lobster sauce; roast duckling; broiled veal medallion topped with asparagus, crabmeat, and béarnaise sauce; and roast leg of spring lamb with mint jelly. More traditional entrees include steaks, ham, roast pork loin with dressing, and baked salmon. Lunch is also served at the Golden Lamb, with tasty soups, salads, and sandwiches, plus luncheon entrees including broiled petite filet mignon with béarnaise sauce and roasted chicken with dressing.

After eating in one of the four cozy downstairs dining areas, venture past the classy blue-gray lobby and up the stairs to the second floor. There you will discover five opulent private dining rooms. One is the Henry Clay Room (he visited the inn frequently on his trips between Kentucky and Washington, D.C.). Decorated in greens and pinks, this room is furnished with a gorgeous dark hardwood table and matching chairs for ten. With their splendid period pieces, these private dining rooms truly conjure up images of a bygone era.

The second floor also has the most expensive guest room at the inn—the Charles Dickens Room. The massive carved headboard towers 12 feet in the air, as do the mirror and frame on the marble-topped washstand. The third and fourth floors contain the other seventeen guest rooms, each unique in its appointments and named for one of the noteworthy guests who have stayed at the Golden Lamb. The De Witt Clinton Room, for example, is named for the New York governor who traveled to Lebanon in 1825 to attend the opening of the Ohio canal system and is furnished with a canopied four-poster bed and antique maple chests.

The fourth floor of the Lamb also houses the inn's Shaker museum, which is full of pieces collected from the former Shaker community called Union Village. The Shakers migrated to Warren County from New Lebanon, New York, and established a religious communal village. But one of their religious convictions was celibacy, which doomed the sect to a relatively short existence.

Shaker furnishings are simple and functional, devoid of ornamentation. The Shaker Pantry has the characteristic wall pegs for hanging utensils, herbs, and even chairs not in use. The Shaker Retiring Room contains a simple rope-spring bed with trundle, a maple rocker, a pine cupboard, and a very rare Shaker embroidery hoop. Perhaps the most interesting display room—Sarah's Room—belonged to Sarah Stubbs, a young girl who came to live in the hotel with her aunt and uncle after the death of her father in 1883. The room has the furniture that was Sarah's one hundred years ago.

The Golden Lamb is at 27 South Broadway, Lebanon; (513) 932–5065; www.goldenlamb.com. Open daily for lunch and dinner except Christmas Day. Lodging rates: $77 to $103 per night. MasterCard, Visa, and American Express are accepted.

On a bluff overlooking Lebanon just a few blocks south of the Golden Lamb sits one of the best examples of Greek Revival architecture in the Midwest: *Glendower.* Constructed by John Milton Williams, a young attorney, for approximately $5,000 in 1836, the residence was inhabited by the Williams family during Williams's career as county prosecutor and state legislator. Brigadier General Durbin Ward, another influential area politician, purchased Glendower from Williams, and the home remained in the Ward family until the turn of the century.

Knowledgeable guides lead visitors through the home's fourteen rooms and basement, explaining the history and significance of the lavish furnishings, most of which date from the mid-1800s. In the downstairs drawing rooms, the symmetry characteristic of Greek Revival architecture is readily apparent: With matching placement of doors, mirrors, and fireplaces, one side of each room is the mirror image of the other. The original brass deadbolt still secures the front door, and the luxurious ash and walnut floors were installed when the home was built. The formal dining room contains a silver sugar bowl with a lock on it (to keep the servants from pilfering this then-expensive commodity), and the old Regina music box plays flat metal discs, as it has for decades.

In addition to the furnished bedrooms upstairs, one room has a sizable collection of antique dolls and the 1865 sewing machine that won first prize at the Warren County fair. The basement display cases contain pioneer tools such as axes, woodworking equipment, and a carpenter's vise. Other items include old-fashioned irons, candle molds, boot jacks, spectacles, and snuffboxes, plus the compass used to map the village of Lebanon, and a wonderful assortment of fancy hand-turned horseshoes made by Matt Burdett, the village smith in the 1890s.

Glendower is on U.S. Route 42 at 105 Cincinnati Avenue, just south of the business district in Lebanon; (513) 932–1817, (800) 283–8927; www.ohiohistory .org/places/glendowe. Open from June through August, Wednesday through Friday, noon to 4:00 P.M.; Saturday and Sunday, 1:00 to 4:00 P.M.; plus weekends in September and October. Admission: adults $3.00; children (ages 6 to 18) $1.00.

Ohio Renaissance Festival

Once upon a time in a kingdom about 5 miles east of Waynesville there was held the Ohio Renaissance Festival. In some ways, to call this a festival is a great understatement. From humble beginnings, a village of sorts has grown up in a farm field. Several streets of a sixteenth-century English village have and continue to evolve into a real town of make-believe.

A king and queen reign over the town and over amazingly realistic jousting matches. Combatants actually mount horses and, in full armor, race toward each other and attempt to knock the opponent from his mount. One generally ends up bouncing on the ground (although we suspect that they probably decided who was going to take the blow before the match began). No blood is spilled, and no bones are broken, although falling from a galloping horse is a little rough on the body, even with choreography.

Throughout the village are more than 150 costumed shopkeepers and entertainers. Modern times do occasionally intrude in interesting ways. There is something a little odd about seeing a gentleman in tights and tunic holding a crossbow in one hand and a soft drink can in the other. A comical and talented array of performers entertains on several stages scattered throughout the village. Jugglers, tight-rope artists, and a variety of clowns, magicians, and musicians take turns entertaining the crowds.

If you want to participate in medieval activities, you can buy a ticket and try the ax throw or spear chuck, or toss overripe tomatoes at the guy in the medieval equivalent of a dunk tank. There are plenty of unusual craft and artisan shops. Buy a talisman or a fake sword or a pouch to hang at your waist to hold your ducats. More modern souvenirs such as jewelry, glass art, and candles also are plentiful.

The Renaissance Festival is open weekends from late August through early October. Admission is charged. Be prepared to park in a farm field and walk a bit to the "village gates." For specifics, call (513) 897–7000.

If you are fascinated with unraveling the riddles of prehistory, you should visit *Fort Ancient.* This prehistoric settlement is a significant archeological site in North America. Two thousand years ago, Native Americans during the Hopewell culture built a walled enclosure, probably with crude digging tools, such as deer antlers or shoulder bones. The walls, which are earthen, run for 18,000 feet, and consist of 550,000 cubic yards of soil, which was transported in baskets, each capable of holding thirty-five or forty pounds of earth. From the site, archeologists have determined that parts of the walls were actually designed and constructed to align with the sun and the moon to create a calendar for the community. They believe that Fort Ancient served as a ceremonial and social center.

Visitors enjoy hiking the trails not only for the historic value of the site, but also for the beauty of the natural surroundings. The site also features the Museum at Fort Ancient, which has numerous interactive exhibits and highlights 15,000 years of Native American history in the Ohio valley A prehistoric garden demonstrates crops grown 2,000 years ago.

Fort Ancient is at 6123 Route 350, Oregonia; (513) 932–4421, (800) 283–8904; www.ohiohistory.org/places/ftancien. Open April through October, Wednesday through Saturday, 10:00 A.M. to 5:00 P.M.; Sunday, noon to 5:00 P.M.; Admission: adults $7.00; children (ages 6 to 12) $3.00.

With more antiques shops per square mile than any other city or town in Ohio, Waynesville is a browser's paradise. It has more than forty individual shops, plus three large buildings where dozens of dealers display their goods on consignment, and it has become a major antiques marketplace, attracting out-of-state buyers and Ohioans alike. Waynesville's antiques boom started inauspiciously in the mid-1960s with the opening of a handful of shops, but the number has grown steadily ever since. Now, many of the town's commercial buildings, a substantial number of former residences, and even one of the town's churches house antiques stores—in fact, on one block on Main Street, there are nine shops in a row!

Among the many quality shops, one favorite is at 274 South Main Street: *Spencer's Antiques and Imports.* The two-story house with a large front porch and four adjoining buildings hold an impressive inventory. Careful perusal of this 15,000-square-foot shop, with its hundreds of items, takes time, but it will be time enjoyably spent. George and Fay Spencer's inventory includes a large selection of oak furniture—tables, chairs, washstands, chests, wardrobes, and beds—plus many large walnut and poplar pieces. The basement of the main building is filled with old trunks, toys, and stained glass, while the second floor has many antique kitchen gadgets, such as meat and sausage grinders, iron pots, and skillets. Spencer's acquires most of its inventory from southwestern Ohio. Spencer's is open from 11:00 A.M. to 5:00 P.M. Tuesday through Sunday; (866) 897–7775; www.spencersantiques.com.

Caesar Creek Lake and the surrounding recreation area are managed by the Army Corps of Engineers primarily as a flood-control project. However, the 2,830-acre lake provides terrific recreation opportunities. The 1,200-foot-long beach welcomes swimmers, and the lake is a great place for fishing or boating. Remember to bring your fishing license if you want to try your luck at hooking bluegill, saugeye, crappie, largemouth, smallmouth, white, or spotted bass.

The visitor center is a good place to begin your trip to Caesar Creek Lake. It provides an overlook of the park and the dam and has lots of educational information about various features of the lake and the recreation area, including trail maps. The more than 10,000 acres of wildlife area includes forests, meadowlands, and the Caesar Creek Gorge with rushing waters. Visitors enjoy day hikes. Trails range from a 3-mile, easy-to-moderate hike to a 13-mile trek for the serious hiker. Backpacking in the park area is allowed, but you need to stop at the visitor center and get a permit first. The area is also a favorite for bikers and horseback riders.

You can also pick up a free permit and directions to prepare you for a fossil hunt. The fossils here date back to the Ordovician age, when Ohio was covered by a shallow ocean. When a spillway was excavated, the area that was disturbed became a great fossil-hunting zone. Brachiopods (which look like seashells) and the remains of cephalopods (which resemble today's octopi) are chief among the fossils you can discover on your hunt. This is one of the only areas where you can legally remove fossils and keep them as souvenirs of your adventures. If you are planning to bring a group along for picnicking, shelters are available for fees of $25 on weekdays and $50 on weekends. Be sure and call ahead to check availability and to reserve the shelter.

To reach Caesar Creek Lake recreation area, take exit 38 west off Interstate 71 or exit 45 east from Interstate 75. The visitor center is at 4020 North Clarksville Road, Waynesville; (513) 897–1050; www.lrl.usace.army.mil/ccl.

While recreation may be the current focus of the Ceasar Creek Lake area, its history is rich and long. This region was home to the prehistoric Native American tribes, the Hopewell and Adena, and later to the Miami and the Shawnee.

According to local historians, Caesar Creek was named for a black slave, Caesar, who was captured by the Shawnee. The Shawnee must have been favorably impressed by Caesar—they gave him the area around Caesar Creek as his hunting ground. The villages that grew up in the area in the 1700s and 1800s became a Quaker settlement and an important stop on the Underground Railroad, supporting the flight of slaves on their way to freedom in the North.

When the Army Corps of Engineers was clearing land and preparing to dam the river in 1978, log homes dating back to the 1700s were found in the woods. These historic buildings were moved to the **Caesar's Creek Pioneer Village.** Some of the buildings in Pioneer Village were actually erected there and stand on their original sites. Walking through the reconstructed village, visitors can see the log cabins, as well as some of the homes built in the early 1800s, the Quaker meeting house, and the toll house. The grounds are open daily, but the houses are only open on special occasions or if you prearrange a tour. Pioneer Village is in Waynesville, on the southeast side of Ceasar Creek Lake. From Waynesville, go east on Route 73 for about 1 mile. Turn right on Clarksville Road, then left on Oregonia Road, then left again on Pioneer Village

Road. The Village is at 3999 Pioneer Village Road, Waynesville; (513) 897–1120; www.caesarscreekvillage.org.

It will take a little effort to visit the **Harveysburg Free Black School.** The school is not open to the public on a regular basis, but tours can be arranged by calling (513) 897–6195.

This unassuming one-room schoolhouse has a special place in Ohio history. It was the first free school for black children in the state. Jesse and Elizabeth Harvey, the founders of Harveysburg, founded the school in 1831 after finding out there were no educational opportunities for black children. The Quaker community supported the school that allowed black and Native American children the then-rare opportunity to enter elementary school and continue in that tiny schoolhouse until they received a high school diploma.

The schoolhouse is a simple, brick structure with a modest cupola on the roof to house the school bell. The school was acquired by the Harveysburg bicentennial committee in 1976 with a mission to preserve it as a part of the community's history. Primers, historical documents and slate blackboards remain for the visitor from this important chapter in the history of education and the search for freedom in Ohio.

The school is at 23 North Street in Harveysburg; (513) 897–6195. Open by appointment.

Many visitors to Warren County are attracted to the area because of southern Ohio's most popular amusement park complex: **Paramount's Kings Island.** Its seven themed areas, dozens of rides including nine coasters (the Beast is rated by the *Guinness Book of World Records* as the longest wooden rollercoaster on earth), live shows, international shops, and restaurants delight the millions who visit the park during its April-through-October season. Other favorites include WaterWorks, a fifteen-acre waterpark, and the Nickelodeon-themed area. Paramount's Kings Island is on I–71 at Kings Mill's; (800) 288–0808; www.pki.com.

A seventy-year-old train station that houses three superior museums and an OMNIMAX theater? That's the incomparable **Cincinnati Museum Center.** This magnificent, 500,000-square-foot art deco railroad station, built in 1933 as a center of regional travel, is now a center of fine exhibits and spectacular film showings. During its heyday as a rail hub, hundreds of trains arrived and departed from here each day. And while it is still an Amtrak station (one eastbound and one westbound daily, both in the middle of the night), the crowds gather now not to greet passengers, but rather to discover the past.

One attraction at the Cincinnati History Museum is the world's largest S-scale city model, called "Cincinnati in Motion." It combines model trains with trolleys, homes, and city buildings. Interpreters help take the visitor back in time and tell the story of Cincinnati and its early days as a bustling river town. Children will find their own kind of fun at the Cinergy Children's Museum, where they can explore interactive exhibits that use simple machines, balls, and a water play area to stimulate young imaginations. The Museum of Natural History and Science has walk-through re-creations of limestone caves and an Ice Age exhibit, as well as a Fossil Prep Lab that lets visitors observe scientists at work.

The Robert D. Linder Family OMNIMAX Theater wraps you in sight and sound, highlighted by a multistory, 72-foot, domed screen. Dramatic films that depict flight and rapid travel appear to pull you into the action, while spectacular landscapes completely surround you.

Cincinnati Museum Center is at 1301 Western Avenue, Cincinnati; (513) 287–7000, (800) 733–2077; www.cincymuseum.org. Open Monday through Saturday, 10:00 A.M. to 5:00 P.M.; Sunday, 11:00 A.M. to 6:00 P.M. Admission is charged. Call for OMNIMAX show times and ticket prices.

Ready for a museum experience in which your ears are just as dazzled as your eyes? The ***American Classical Music Hall of Fame and Museum*** will fit the bill. For those who already love classical music, this institution is a natural choice. For those who are not as familiar with the genre, the museum is a particularly comfortable and intriguing way to become acquainted. Even children will be entranced by the music cones that encircle visitors with sound and by the interactive displays. The Hall of Fame gives you insights into the life and work of the inductees, who are some of the greatest contributors to the current world of classical music and include such artists as Leontyne Price and Isaac Stern. In addition, there are special collections of bugles and stained-glass portraits from a nineteenth-century opera house.

The American Classical Music Hall of Fame and Museum is at 4 West Fourth Street, Cincinnati; (513) 621–3263; www.americanclassicalmusic.org. Open weekdays, 10:00 A.M. to 4:00 P.M.

European elegance with a musical backdrop graces the intimate ***Symphony Hotel.*** The full-service bed-and-breakfast welcomes guests into a graceful 1871 building, furnished in turn-of-the-century antiques but modernized to provide private baths, telephones, televisions, and air-conditioning. A European-style breakfast also is included in the room rate.

The Symphony Hotel is across the street from the Cincinnati Music Hall, which was constructed in 1878. The musical theme continues into the hotel. Every guest room is dedicated to a composer, including Mozart, Brahms, Bach, and Beethoven. The dining room serves a special fixed-price, four-course meal prior to performances at the music hall. Dinner guests must make reservations in advance. Reservations can also be made for special events such as parties, meetings, or luncheons.

ALSO WORTH SEEING

| Cincinnati Art Museum | Irwin M. Krohn Conservatory, Cincinnati |
| Cincinnati Zoo and Botanical Gardens | Dayton Art Institute |

The Symphony Hotel is at 210 West Fourteenth Street, Cincinnati; (513) 721–3353; www.symphonyhotel.com. Rates: $69 to $99 per night.

One of the finest small art museums in the United States, the *Taft Museum of Art* is a National Historic Landmark. Built in 1820, this Federal-period building is home to nearly 700 works of art, including the work of European and American Masters. However, this stunning building served first as a residence for Martin Baum. During his ownership of the property from 1829 to 1863, Nicholas Longworth began a tradition of artistic patronage that was expanded by the last private owners of the house, Charles Phelps Taft and Anna Sinton Taft. They acquired and decorated their home with treasures ranging from French Renaissance enamels and Italian decorative arts to Chinese porcelains and European and American oils.

The home and collections were donated as a gift to the people of Cincinnati in 1927, and the house opened as a museum in November 1932. With its slender Tuscan columns, the Taft Museum is a Federal-period country villa. The central section of the structure features delicate elliptical windows, while the southeast façade has a distinctive upper and lower columned porch.

The collection includes works by such masters as Rembrandt, Hals, Gainsborough, Sargent, Ruisdael, Turner, and Corot. There's an extensive presentation of French Renaissance Limoges enamels and watches of the seventeenth and eighteenth centuries.

The Taft Museum of Art is at 316 Pike Street, Cincinnati; (513) 241–0343; www.taftmuseum.org. Open Tuesday, Wednesday and Friday, 11:00 A.M. to 5:00 P.M.; Thursday, 11:00 A.M. to 8:00 P.M.; Saturday, 10:00 A.M. to 5:00 P.M.; Sunday noon to 5:00 P.M. Admission: adults $7.00; college students and seniors $5.00; children (under 18) no charge.

Letters from President William Howard Taft's mother to her relatives in the East proved invaluable in the restoration of Taft's childhood home. *The William Howard Taft National Historic Site* was the childhood home of the twenty-seventh president of the United States. It is Greek Revival in design; square and symmetrical with decorative trim. The home has been restored and is much as it must have been in the mid-1800s. The Taft family has provided many personal effects, including portraits and books, that would have been in the Taft household when the young William was growing up.

Congress designated the house a National Historic Site and monument to the president in 1969, and placed it under the administration of the National Park Service. The William Howard Taft National Historic Site is at 2038 Auburn Avenue, Cincinnati; (513) 684–3262; www.nps.gov/wiho. Open daily 8:00 A.M. to 4:00 P.M.

In 1833, the daughter of the new president of Lane Seminary moved into a stately residence on the campus. This house, the **Harriet Beecher Stowe House,** has now been renamed to acknowledge the legacy of the former resident.

Harriet Beecher Stowe wrote the landmark story *Uncle Tom's Cabin,* which dramatically portrayed the cruel and dehumanizing effects of slavery. The Stowe House is now a Black history, education, and cultural center.

The Harriet Beecher Stowe House is located at 2950 Gilbert Avenue, Cincinnati; (513) 751–0651, (513) 324–2218; www.ohiohistory.org/places/stowe. Open May through Labor Day, Tuesday through Thursday, 10:00 A.M. to 3:00 P.M., Saturday, 10:00 A.M. to 3:00 P.M., plus Tuesday and Wednesday in April, September, and October. No admission charge.

If you're in the mood for mouth-watering barbecued ribs and chicken, plus ice-cold beer, try Ted Gregory's **Montgomery Inn.** This popular restaurant claims to serve the "world's greatest ribs," a designation with which few customers would argue. Although the menu at the Montgomery Inn does include selections such as steaks, pork chops, and filet of sole, the restaurant is known for tender ribs and chicken dripping with a zesty sauce.

While waiting in the bar for your table, you'll see photographs of the likes of Tommy Lasorda and Billy Carter displayed on the wall, each autographed and extolling the virtues of Ted Gregory's barbecue. On the rough wood paneling in the comfortable dining rooms are photos and paintings of Gregory's other passion—horse racing. You'll even find some bridles and jockeys' shirts displayed throughout the inn.

For those unable to decide between barbecued ribs and barbecued chicken, try some of each with the half-and-half dinner, which is served with crisp tossed salad and the inn's famous Saratoga chip potatoes. The management thoughtfully provides bibs for those partaking of the sauce-laden barbecue.

If you're not hungry for barbecue (which seems inconceivable once you experience the aroma in this restaurant), other menu selections include Cantonese-style fried Oriental shrimp with sweet 'n' hot sauce, Wisconsin's Pride duckling, and a number of sandwiches (including a barbecued beef sandwich).

The Montgomery Inn is at 9440 Montgomery Road (exit 12 off I–71), Montgomery; (513) 791–3482; www.montgomeryinnribs.com. Open Monday through

Thursday, 11:00 A.M. to 11:00 P.M.; Friday, 11:00 A.M. to midnight; Saturday, 3:00 P.M. to midnight; Sunday, 3:00 to 10:00 P.M. MasterCard and Visa are accepted.

Founded in 2003, the **Tri-State Warbird Museum** set lofty goals for itself, including being recognized as one of the most-admired museums dedicated to military and historic aviation. This museum honors both the pilots and planes that defended America during wartime, particularly during World War II. The planes and exhibits on display pay tribute to our rich military aviation history, recognizing the creativity, commitment, and sacrifice of so many during the crucial conflict in the 1940s.

Among the collection are such treasures as the P-51D Mustang, *Cincinnati Miss*. Smartly painted with a black and yellow checkered nose and yellow tail sections, she represents the definitive version of the P-51 single-seat fighter. Powered by a supercharged Merlin engine to a single prop, the D version delivered 1,695 horsepower, had a maximum speed of 437 miles per hour, a service ceiling of 41,800 feet, and a combat range of 1,000 miles. This long-range fighter aircraft entered service in 1943, featured six .50-caliber machine guns and is still regarded as one of the best piston-engine fighters ever built. Nearly 8,000 P-51 D/K Mustangs were built.

Another mid-war entrant was the TBM-3 Avenger. Aptly named, the Avenger was designed and built to retaliate against the Japanese Navy after its attack on Pearl Harbor. Grumman and General Motors produced 9,836 Avengers, equipping them with a power-operated gun turret, heavy 22-inch torpedoes, bombs, rockets, and depth charges. The Wright Cyclone 14 engine delivered 1,726 horsepower, giving the Avenger a maximum speed of 276 miles per hour, a ceiling of 30,100 feet, and a range of more than 1000 miles. It was a torpedo attack by British-flown Avengers which sank two of the world's largest battleships, the Japanese *Musashi* and *Yamato* in October 1944 and April 1945 respectively.

An equally proud member of the museum's collection is its twin-engine B-25 Mitchell bomber. Approximately 10,000 of these bombers were built by North American Aviation. Although designed for bombing runs at medium altitudes, they frequently were used for treetop-level missions against Japanese airfields and shipping in the Pacific. Powered by twin Wright Cyclone engines, each producing 1,850 horsepower, the B-25 had a top speed of 275 miles per hour, a combat range of 1,350 miles, and a ceiling of 25,000 feet. The most famous wartime use of B-25s was the 1942 Doolittle Raid, where pilots flew off the aircraft carrier USS *Hornet,* bombed Tokyo and then crashed in China. It was also a B-25 which collided with the Empire State Building in New York City in 1945.

Many pilots in the U.S. Navy, Air Force, and Marines and the British Royal Air Force learned to fly at the controls of a T-6 Texan. A total of 15,495 Texans, a single-engine, advanced trainer aircraft designed by North American Aviation, trained tens of thousands of wartime pilots. The museum's yellow and red Marine AT-6D version—*Tweety*—features a 600-horsepower radial engine, with a maximum speed of 208 miles per hour and a range of 730 miles.

Another common trainer was the Stearman Model 75 biplane. The museum's bright blue and yellow one is an excellent example of this popular trainer, originally built during the 1930s. Its rugged construction and open-air dual cockpit seating made it a popular crop duster and leisure aircraft once the war concluded.

One of the most intriguing exhibits at the 20,000 square-foot Tri-State Warbird Museum is not an even an airplane. It's the ANT-18 Link Trainer. This was the first flight simulator trainer, built of wood in 1932 by Edwin A Link who used bellows and other parts from his father's Link Piano and Organ Company. World War II produced a tremendous demand for new pilots, and cadet pilots could become proficient in instrument flying in 50 hours using the ANT-18. By war's end, 10,000 of the trainers had been built, teaching many of the 190,000 pilots trained in the U.S. during World War II.

The museum also honors Cincinnati-area military aviation veterans, such as Tom Griffin, who flew with Lt. Col. Jimmy Doolittle, and Russell B. Witte, Jr., a B-25 bomber pilot with more than fifty missions flying from North Africa over Sicily and Italy. He was awarded the Distinguished Flying Cross and nine Air Medals. Many of the museum's aircraft are still airworthy and can often be found at regional air shows and similar events.

The Tri-State Warbird Museum is at 4021 Borman Drive, Batavia; (513) 735–4500; www.tri-statewarbirdmuseum.org. Open Wednesdays, 4:00 to 7:00 P.M.; Saturdays, 10:00 A.M. to 3:00 P.M.

The founders of the Mariemont Company designed and constructed the village of Mariemont as a totally planned community modeled after the "garden city" villages in England. In the 1920s, they envisioned Mariemont as a rural alternative to bustling Cincinnati nearby.

Although it's no longer in the country (Mariemont is now in the suburban ring surrounding Cincinnati), this quaint village, with its Tudor commercial buildings and peaceful, tree-lined residential neighborhoods, does provide the tranquil existence sought by its founders. The entire village is listed on the National Register of Historic Places.

The *Mariemont Inn,* a member of Historic Hotels of America, offers visitors a charming place to imbibe, dine, and spend the night. It is set facing the circle in the center of the commercial business district, and the striking Tudor exterior is rivaled by the interior decor in this classic structure. Each of the sixty guest rooms contains the dark, heavy woods and rich colors typical of the

Mariemont Inn

Tudor period; the spacious suites come furnished with ornate canopy beds, and there are antiques throughout the inn. Your day starts off with complimentary coffee or juice, delivered to your room at your convenience.

Visitors unwind in the cozy old-English pub, and the popularity of the dining room for breakfast, lunch, and dinner with area residents and business-people speaks for the excellent food. An innovative breakfast-brunch-lunch menu featuring omelets, homemade soups, fine salads, and a wide selection of sandwiches is served from 6:30 A.M. until 2:00 P.M. The varied dinner selections include fresh seafood, pasta, veal, and many great steaks, with appetizers and desserts to accompany these dishes. The inn is now part of the Best Western hotel group.

The Mariemont Inn is at 6880 Wooster Pike (U.S. Route 50), Cincinnati; (513) 271–2100, (800) 780–7234; www.bestwestern.com/mariemontinn. Lodging rates: $76 to $94 per night. MasterCard, Visa, and American Express accepted.

After your meal, enjoy a stroll, jog, or bike ride in the picturesque village, or stop by the gift shop, bookstore, ice-cream parlor, or other shops adjacent to the inn. Though downtown Cincinnati is only fifteen minutes from Mariemont, when you're walking through this peaceful community, the big city seems worlds away.

Looking for a very different food festival? How about celebrating the wonders of the zucchini? In Eldorado each July, residents and nearby farmers host the Zucchini Festival. Those who appreciate this nutritious and flexible member of the squash family will have a terrific time tasting various zucchini dishes. Games, craft displays, and music are all part of the activities.

The Zucchini Festival is free and held in mid-July in Eldorado. Call (937) 273–2092 for information.

It is the last of its kind in Clermont County. The ***Stonelick Covered Bridge*** has become not just an icon of a bygone era, but magnet for tourists and the

mt.healthy

In 1817, John La Boiteaux and Samuel Hill founded Mt. Pleasant in Hamilton County. Although the town was known as Mt. Pleasant for years, the post office urged the residents to rename it, to avoid confusion with the "other Mt. Pleasant." They did, choosing Mt. Healthy as the new name in gratitude for being spared the cholera epidemic that struck Cincinnati in the late 1840s.

Cincinnati lost 7 percent of its population to cholera in 1849, during the nineteenth century's second global epidemic of this once-terrifying disease. Ohio had become vulnerable for the first time due to increased contact with travelers from other parts of the United States and the world.

inspiration for local artists. This covered bridge, also known as the Perintown Covered Bridge, was built in 1878, restored in 1971, and was placed on the National Register of Historic Places in 1974. The 140-foot-long bridge is supported by an impressive twelve panel Howe Truss system, a system patented by William Howe in 1840. This system uses vertical iron rods, instead of vertical timber posts, and crossed timber members forming the familiar X-shaped supports. The bridge spans Stonelick Creek and is open to traffic.

The Stonelick Covered Bridge in on Stone-Williams Corner Road (County Road 116) in Clermont County, two-tenths of a mile west of the junction of U.S. Route 50 and Route 222 (go north on Stone-Williams Road.)

The Benninghofens were an affluent family in the late 1800s. Their Italianate home was built in 1861. The *Benninghofen House* has 13-foot ceilings beautifully painted and adorned with heavy moldings. Cherry woodwork, parquet floors, and chandeliers are original to the home, which was placed on the National Register of Historic Homes in 1973.

The home itself is a wonderful reflection of the times, but the visitor also will find various collections in the home noteworthy. Civil War enthusiasts will want to note the field desk, sword, and flag from the Ohio Volunteer Infantry. Dolls, surveying equipment, pottery, and vintage furniture all provide color and life to this slice of Ohio history.

The Benninghofen House is at 327 North Second Street, Hamilton; (513) 896–9930. Open Tuesday through Saturday, 11:00 A.M. to 4:00 P.M. Admission: $3.00.

When most of us think of a museum of sculpture, we don't even begin to imagine what awaits us on a visit to the *Pyramid Hill Sculpture Park and Museum.* Yes, there are thirty-five interesting pieces to view and ponder, but they are set in a 265-acre arboretum. This is one of the four largest sculpture gardens in the United States. Your leisurely walk down three well-marked trails takes you past gardens, seven lakes, and a wide variety of trees. There is even the remains of a nineteenth-century stone pioneer home.

These outdoor features provide a backdrop for the nearly three dozen sculptures. Some, like *Eve* by Marc Mellon, are traditional. *Age of Stone* by Jon Isherwood evokes the feeling of a mystic place filled with ancient druids. The park also features a series of one-way roads that allow visitors to view the art from their private cars. The park provides bus tours, but you need to make a reservation for this guided tour. Pyramid Hill offers many special children's programs in the summer months, as well as music programs that provide a blending of arts that will enchant the entire family.

The Pyramid Hill Sculpture Park and Museum is 3 miles southwest of Hamilton on Route 128 at 1763 Hamilton-Cleves Road; (513) 887–9514, (513) 868–8336; www.pyramidhill.org. Open April through October, Tuesday through Sunday, 10:00 A.M. to 6:00 P.M., November through March, Saturday and Sunday, 10:00 A.M. to 4:00 P.M. Admission: weekdays $3.00; weekends $4.00; children (ages 5 to 12) $1.50.

Sorg Opera House Ghost

Since 1891, the Sorg Opera House has been a place where the starstruck come and linger. More than one hundred years ago, a wealthy entrepreneur, Paul Sorg, built the theater. Famous actors and grand productions were invited to the Middletown stage to perform with Jeannie Sorg, Paul's wife and a great fan of the performing arts.

Over the life of the theater the likes of George M. Cohan and Bob Hope have taken their place on center stage. It became a movie house in the 1920s and hosted the first "talkie" shown in town. A fire damaged the building in 1935, but it was renovated and reopened four years later.

The legend of the theater centers on Paul Sorg. As owner, the well-dressed business baron is reported to have always claimed the best seat in the house when he attended performances. In the 1890s those seated in the orchestra or the first balcony arrived at the opera house in full evening dress. Paul Sorg was a fixture at his theater, dressed in fashionable garb and seated in his favorite seat in the first row of the first balcony.

Through the years and even today, staff and patrons sometimes claim they catch a glimpse of the nattily attired Sorg taking his place in the first balcony. When asked to describe the man, many ghost spotters have described him as he appears in his portrait, which hangs in the theater lobby. Sometimes only his footsteps are heard crossing the stage or walking overhead on the catwalks. So, while actors and actresses have come and gone, the first owner maintains his star status as the legend of the Sorg Opera House.

The Sorg Opera House is located at 63 South Main Street, Middletown.

Picture a thoroughfare of pumpkins. In the autumn you can walk past hundreds of pumpkins at the ***Barn 'n' Bunk Farm Market.*** In warmer weather, the market is filled with bedding plants, hanging baskets, and Amish-made lawn furniture, as well as farm-fresh produce. The market grew out of the family farm of Bev and Tom Theobald.

The century-old barns now house a variety of shops. More than fifty local crafters provide items from candles and baskets to birdhouses and furniture pieces. On the sweeter side, you can also indulge in honeys, jellies, candies, Amish baked goods, and even ice cream. Weekends in September and October feature special fall displays and events, and the market puts on its finest for visitors in the days before Christmas.

The Barn 'n' Bunk Farm Market is on Route 73 and Wayne-Madison Road in Trenton; (513) 988–9211; www.barnnbunk.com. Open April through December 23, Monday through Friday, 10:00 A.M. to 6:00 P.M.; Saturday, noon to 6:00 P.M.; Sunday, noon to 5:00 P.M.

Invention Trail

The community of Miamisburg has the largest conical burial mound in Ohio—the ***Miamisburg Mound.*** Artifacts excavated from this 68-foot-high mound, which contains 54,000 cubic yards of earth, indicate the Adena Indians built it sometime between 1000 B.C. and A.D. 100. With a circumference of nearly 900 feet at the base, the mound had two burial vaults: one 8 feet from the top of the mound containing a bark-covered skeleton, the other 36 feet down and surrounded by logs but without any skeletal remains.

Visitors to the mound, which today is overgrown with brush and trees, can climb 116 steps to the top of this impressive earthwork for a splendid view of the Miami Valley. A thirty-six-acre park encircles the mound, with picnic tables, barbecue grills, and shelter houses.

The Miamisburg Mound is 1 mile south of Route 725 on East Mound Avenue, Miamisburg; (937) 866–4532; www.ohiohistory.org/places/miamisbg. Open daylight hours, no admission charge.

After climbing the mound, you may want to stop for cocktails or dinner at Miamisburg's ***Peerless Mill Inn.*** A huge waterwheel and the flowing Miami and Erie Canal once powered a former lumber mill (built in 1828). The building was converted into a restaurant called the Peerless Pantry one hundred years later, but that historic structure was destroyed by fire in 2003 and has since been rebuilt.

Country favorites, including roast turkey with celery dressing and steaks, dominate the menu, along with classy seafood and sophisticated dishes such as veal Gruyère—veal topped with cheese, tomato, and a light brown sauce. The house specialty is roast duckling, served with wild rice, orange sauce, and corn fritters. If you're having trouble deciding on an entree, pick two or three from six selections and create your own Peerless Mill combination plate. Diners receive a delicious house seven-layer salad with their meals. Be sure to try the homemade chowder before your dinner, and the daily fresh cobbler for dessert.

The Peerless Mill Inn is at 319 South Second Street, Miamisburg; (937) 866–5968; www.peerlessmillinn.net. Open for brunch, Sunday, 10:00 A.M. to 2:00 P.M.; and dinner, Tuesday through Thursday, 5:00 to 9:00 P.M.; Friday and Saturday, 5:00 to 10:00 P.M.; Sunday, 3:00 to 9:00 P.M. MasterCard and Visa are accepted.

Just south of downtown Dayton, along the Great Miami River, is the landmark Deeds Carillon, a 151-foot-high, fifty-seven-bell carillon that stands at the entrance to *Carillon Historical Park.* Dedicated in 1942, the carillon was given to the people of Dayton by Colonel Edward Deeds and his wife Edith. Concerts delight audiences from May through October.

In addition to the bells, this sixty-five-acre park has an outstanding group of exhibit buildings, primarily dedicated to Dayton's invention, transportation, and settlement history. The museum's crown jewel has to be the 1905 Wright Flyer III in Wright Hall, a National Historic Landmark and part of the Dayton Aviation Heritage National Historic Park. Weighing 855 pounds, this plane was the world's first practical aircraft and was described by Orville Wright as the plane in which he and Wilbur learned to fly. Two years after their historic 1903 flights at Kitty Hawk, Wilbur stayed aloft in the Flyer III for thirty-nine minutes at an average speed of 38 miles per hour. Orville Wright later supervised the initial restoration of this aircraft.

Deeds Barn, a replica of the carriage house that stood behind Colonel Deeds's home, houses exhibits that underscore the contributions of Deeds and his friend and contemporary Charles F. Kettering. It was on the second floor of the original barn that Kettering and his "barn gang" revolutionized automobile ignition and lighting systems, and the barn contains a 1912 Cadillac, the first production auto to feature these innovations. Kettering and Deeds went on to found Dayton Engineering Laboratories Company (later called Delco). Kettering's early inventions at National Cash Register Company and Deeds's later accomplishments in developing the Liberty aircraft engine also are displayed.

The two-story log building called *Newcom Tavern,* Dayton's oldest existing building, was the home of George Newcom. It also served as Dayton's first courtroom. The tavern includes many of its original items, such as the china used by Colonel and Mrs. Newcom, and the colonel's favorite rocking chair.

Newcom Tavern

Other displays in Carillon Historical Park include locomotives and railroad cars, a restored canal lock and covered bridge, a working 1930s print shop, and a replica of the Wright brothers' bicycle shop. The Dayton Sales Company automobile showroom has a 1910 Speedwell, a 1923 Maxwell, and a very rare 1908 Stoddard-Dayton.

Carillon Historical Park is at the intersection of Patterson and Carillon Boulevards, east of I–75 at the Edwin Moses/Nicholas Road exit, Dayton; (937) 293–2841; www.carillonpark.org/index.html. The park is open Monday through Saturday, 9:30 A.M. to 5:00 P.M.; Sunday, noon to 5:00 P.M. Admission: adults $8.00; children (ages 3 to 17) $5.00.

Dayton's historical sites provide interesting glimpses into the lives and work of some of its most famous citizens. The final resting place of some of these notables, ***Woodland Cemetery and Arboretum,*** is also a quiet spot to reflect on their contributions. This cemetery is one of the five oldest rural garden cemeteries in the country. The 100-acre arboretum and cemetery was planned as the city of Dayton grew, and opened in the 1840s. Such places provided a peaceful alternative to burial in highly populated urban centers. In this cemetery are the graves of poet Paul Laurence Dunbar, both Orville and Wilbur Wright, Ohio Governor James Cox, and writer and humorist Erma Bombeck.

Visitors enter the cemetery through the impressive Romanesque gateway and chapel. This imposing structure was built in 1889, has an original Tiffany stained-glass window, and is listed on the National Register of Historic Places. This structure also houses the administrative offices where visitors can find walking tour maps or borrow a cassette player and headset that provides an audio tour of Woodland's highlights. Special tours can be arranged by calling ahead; special events are listed on the Web site. More than 3,000 trees and 10,000 monuments are found on the grounds. Some memorials are modern in design, such as the 29,000-pound structure forming the monument for writer Erma Bombeck. Others are more traditional, with statuary of angels, cherubs, and urns or replicas of Greek or Egyptian temples. Some, like the grave of the child Johnny Morehouse, reflect poignant stories. This memorial pictures the faithful dog that pulled the child from a river after he had fallen in, but too late to save him.

Woodlawn Cemetery and Arboretum is located at 118 Woodland Avenue, Dayton; (937) 228–3221; www.woodlandcemetery.org/Intro.htm. Open Monday through Friday, 8:00 A.M. to 3:00 P.M. and Saturday, 8:00 A.M. to noon. No admission charge.

Art lovers, families, art historians, and those just looking for a glimpse of the unusual can find just what they're looking for at *The Dayton Art Institute.* Located in downtown Dayton, overlooking the Great Miami River, the impressive Italian Renaissance–style museum features an impressive collection of more than 12,000 objects spanning 5,000 years of art history. Highlights include an outstanding Asian collection, seventeenth-century Baroque paintings, and

Victoria Theater

Some of the attractions of the historic Victoria Theater in Dayton are easy for the visitor to see and appreciate. The turn-of-the-twentieth-century building is graced by lavish period touches, such as gilt trim and green marble pillars. But another attraction is a bit more elusive.

According to legend the ghost of a young actress occasionally makes an appearance behind the glass and bronze doors of the Victoria. The young lady is winsome, wearing a 1900s black taffeta dress nipped in at the waist and draped softly to the floor. She has a penchant for appearing in the mirror of one of the third-floor dressing rooms.

It is from that dressing room, the legend says, that the ghost, nicknamed Vickie, made her final dramatic exit. In the middle of a production, Vickie is supposed to have forgotten a fan she needed in the next scene and so told the other actors she was returning to the dressing room to get it. She was last seen climbing the stairs. She never returned to the stage. She just vanished.

Did Vickie sneak out of the theater to join a lover? Did she meet with foul play? No one knows for sure, but theatergoers and staff say that she still remains, in spirit. The door to the fabled dressing room seems to have a mind of its own, and feminine footsteps sometimes can be heard tripping lightly on the stairway. If you hear the rustle of taffeta, detect the scent of rose perfume, or feel the light brush of a young lady passing close to you, then you, too, have experienced the continuing performance of Vickie.

eighteenth- and nineteenth-century American art collections. In addition, the institute features innovative exhibits, including a hands-on family "Experien-center," which let visitors experience art in a new and participatory manner.

The Dayton Art Institute also exhibits some objects never before seen in galleries dedicated to Native-American and Oceanic art forms. In addition to the extensive permanent collections, the institute hosts world-class special and traveling exhibits, and art-related educational and cultural events. The historic building also houses an education resource center and an art reference library.

The Dayton Art Institute is located at 456 Belmonte Park North, Dayton; (937) 223–5277; www.daytonartinstitute.org. Open daily 10:00 A.M. to 4:00 P.M.; Thursday and Friday until 8:00 P.M. No admission charge.

The *Dunbar House State Memorial* was the first state memorial in Ohio dedicated to an African American. This distinction seems fitting, since Paul Laurence Dunbar is often referred to as the poet laureate of African Americans. The turn-of-the-twentieth-century home of Italianate design was the poet's final residence.

The son of former slaves, Dunbar used his writing to portray the dilemmas faced by a recently freed but still disenfranchised people. Dunbar died at age thirty-four in 1906, but his mother lived in the Dunbar House until 1934. Thanks to her care in preserving her son's belongings, visitors can view many of his original works and personal items as well as many of the family furnishings.

The Dunbar House State Memorial is located at 219 Paul Laurence Dunbar Street, Dayton; (937) 224–7061, (800) 860–0148; www.ohiohistory.org/places/dunbar. Open Memorial Day to Labor Day, Wednesday through Saturday, 9:00 A.M. to 5:00 P.M.; Sunday, noon to 5:00 P.M., plus weekends in April, May, September, and October. Admission: adults $6.00; children (ages 6 to 12) $3.00.

Making science fun is the mission of the *Boonshoft Museum of Discovery* in Dayton. Formerly the Dayton Museum of Natural History, today Boonshoft uses a hands-on, interactive environment to foster interest in and understanding of all things scientific.

Travel through time and space at the Caryl D. Phillips Space Theater, where an advanced computer graphics system projects stunning skylines and impressive galaxies. On stage at the Oscar Boonshoft Science Central's Science Theater are live performances showcasing mind-boggling scientific stunts. The Boonshoft also houses an extensive collection of 1.4 million real animal specimens and artifacts, including live animals at the indoor Charles Exley Jr. Wild Ohio Zoo, complete with a variety of native Ohio wildlife such as coyotes, river otters, and bobcats. Other favorite exhibits include the Mastodon Dig and the Sonoran Desert. For a birds-eye view of the museum's outdoor amphitheater and lush woodland trails, kids climb the Mead Treehouse.

The Boonshoft Museum of Discovery is at 2600 DeWeese Parkway, Dayton; (937) 275–7431; www.boonshoftmuseum.org. Open Monday through Friday, 9:00 A.M. to 5:00 P.M.; Saturday, 11:00 A.M. to 5:00 P.M.; Sunday, noon to 5:00 P.M. Admission: adults $8.50; children (ages 2 to 12) $7.00.

For a look at more modern modes of transportation, be sure to see the more than 300 aircraft and missiles displayed at the impressive *U.S. Air Force Museum.* With seventeen acres of exhibit space in the three main hangar-type buildings, plus the Presidential and Research/Development Galleries, this may be the world's most complete aviation museum. From a Wright Brothers original to an Apollo space capsule, the museum contains an incredibly comprehensive collection of flying machines. Spads, Camels, Spitfires, Mustangs, the B-29 that dropped the atomic bomb on Nagasaki in 1945, and the enormous Strategic Air Command B-36 bomber—all of these are in one museum.

Located only 3 miles from the place where the Wright Brothers tested their early designs, the museum, in addition to the aircraft, balloons, and missiles, has hundreds of exhibits that chronicle the history and milestones of military aviation. The newest hangar focuses on the Cold War era to the present day, and features a B-1B bomber, an F-117 Stealth fighter, and a B-2 Spirit stealth bomber. Also new is the Hall of Missiles, including a collection of intercontinental ballistic missiles. And there is an outstanding IMAX theater, which shows spectacular aviation-related films.

The U.S. Air Force Museum is at Wright-Patterson Air Force Base, off Route 4 northeast of Dayton at 1100 Spaatz Street; (937) 255–3286; www.wpafb .af.mil/museum. Open daily except Christmas, Thanksgiving, and New Year's Day, 9:00 A.M. to 5:00 P.M. No admission charge except for the IMAX theater.

The newest addition to the National Park System's Dayton Aviation Heritage History Park is the *Huffman Prairie Flying Field.* While the Wright Brothers may have taken that first flight at Kitty Hawk, this field was where they tested and perfected their flying machines and their flying skills. The experimental planes, the Flyer II, built in 1904, and the Flyer III, built in 1905, were tested on this prairie land. Along with testing airplanes, this plot of land was also home to the Wright Company flying school from 1910 to 1916, the first flight school in the world. A hanger, similar to the one you would have seen if you visited the Wright brothers, has been erected on the site. In addition to the historic value of the field to flight buffs, this area is also the largest remaining remnant of prairie land in Ohio.

Huffman Prairie Flying Field is located at Gate 16A of Wright Patterson Air Force Base off Route 444; (937) 425–0008; www.nps.gov/daav. Open daily except Wednesday 8:30 A.M. to 5:00 P.M. Closed Thanksgiving, Christmas, and New Year's Day. Admission: free.

The Dayton area is celebrated for innovations in transportation, and its fleet of MetroDucks is carrying on this worthy tradition. If you've never ridden in this type of restored World War II amphibious vehicle, it is worth the trip if only to be able to brag that you rode in one of the few remaining, functional ducks that can still motor across the river and lumber right onto land. The real acronym for the vehicle is DUKW, military shorthand for a utility vehicle with front-wheel drive and a tandem axle. D signifies the first year of production, 1942. U is the code for an amphibious utility truck. K specifies front-wheel drive, and W means two rear axles. However, since the somewhat less-than-sleek boat on wheels looked like a duck and performed like a duck, the sound-alike nickname stuck. While some of these amphibious crafts remained in service during the Korean War, helicopters fast replaced these stout supply vehicles, which carried cargo and supplies from ship to shore and back. One DUKW has retired to the Dayton area as a tour vehicle for **MetroDucks.** This company offers one-hour park and river tours in the summer season. There is just something about the feeling of motoring along a path in something that feels like a cross between a school bus and a tank, heading toward the Great Miami River and plunging right in.

MetroDucks provide tours from the Dayton MetroPark's RiverScape, 111 East Monument Avenue, Dayton; (937) 278–2607; www.metroducks.com/dayton.htm. Open Memorial Day through Labor Day, Tuesday through Sunday, with tours at 1:30, 3:00, and 4:30 P.M. and Thursday through Sunday at 7:00 P.M. Admission: adults $15.00; children (ages 4 to 12) $10.00; children (3 and under) $1.00.

Ohio is rich in ancient cultures. One of the best ways to learn more about one of these cultures is to visit **SunWatch Indian Village/Archaeological Park,** a reconstructed Native American village. This twelfth-century village was rebuilt based on the archeological findings discovered on this site. You'll see pottery and other artifacts typical of the village's era.

The village is named SunWatch because of the advanced system of charting time developed by the village's original inhaitants. During summer months, reconstruction continues at the site, in search of more clues to the past. In season, you'll observe planting, harvesting, house construction, and the manufacture of various artifacts.

SunWatch Indian Village/Archaeological Park is at 2301 West River Road, Dayton; (937) 268–8199; www.sunwatch.org. Open Tuesday through Saturday, 9:00 A.M. to 5:00 P.M.; Sunday, noon to 5:00 P.M. Admission: adults $5.00; children (ages 6 to 17) $3.00.

Daniel Arnold established his 158-acre family farm in 1830 and constructed a farmhouse six years later. The Arnold family worked the farm until 1910, and today this entire farmstead is being restored to its appearance in the 1880s. It's called *Carriage Hill Farm Museum,* and it's part of Carriage Hill MetroPark.

The farmhouse contains furnishings typical of a nineteenth-century conservative farm family—quilting frame, wood-burning cook stove, and firebox—while bubbles and imperfections in the house's window glass identify it as original. During hot weather, the Arnolds prepared their meals at the outdoor "summer kitchen" to avoid further heating the farmhouse; on many weekends, volunteers now use the cookstove in the summer kitchen to bake fresh bread.

Other demonstrations at Carriage Hill include a blacksmith who operates the old blower, and a woodworker who shapes furniture on a foot-powered lathe. Like any 1880s farm, Carriage Hill has a variety of farm animals: cattle, chickens, horses, sheep, and pigs. The horses are used to giving hayrides through the reserve's lush meadows and woods. Hiking and bridle trails also wind through the park's acreage. Special events such as square dances, cider pressing, and old-fashioned wheat threshing take place throughout the year at Carriage Hill.

Carriage Hill MetroPark is at 7800 East Shull Road, north of Interstate 70 off Route 201, Dayton; (937) 278–2609; www.metroparks.org/_carriagehill/carriage hill.aspx. The park is open daily except Christmas and New Year's Day, 8:00 A.M. to dusk. The farm museum is open weekdays, 10:00 A.M. to 5:00 P.M.; weekends, 1:00 to 5:00 P.M. No admission charge.

You have to give *Clifton Mill* credit—it has burned down twice, but it has always come back. The first water-powered gristmill at this site on the Little Miami River was built in 1802. Called Davis Mill for its founder Owen Davis, this first mill prospered until destroyed by fire in the 1840s. But a year or two later, a second mill was erected here, a mill that did its part for the Union Army by providing cornmeal and flour to Federal troops during the Civil War.

This mill, however, burned down about the time the Confederacy was defeated. In 1869, the Armstrong family built a third mill on this site, which they sold to Isaac Preston twenty years later.

Three generations of Prestons operated the mill until 1948. And although it avoided catching fire again, Clifton Mill did sit idle, deteriorating for fifteen years, until Robert Heller bought it and breathed life into it once again. The Satariano family acquired the mill in the mid 1980s, expanding it. A covered bridge now spans the gorge, providing spectacular views.

Today visitors enjoy self-guided tours of this impressive six-story power plant. The huge James Leffel Company turbine on the lowest level, installed in 1908, once provided electricity for farms, homes, and businesses in Clifton, Cedarville, and Yellow Springs at a very modest $1.00 per month per customer.

Clifton Mill grinds flour, cornmeal, and pancake mix as it has for decades, a process you observe during your tour. And meal and flour, along with homemade breads, pies, and other pastries, are available for purchase, as are fine jams, jellies, syrups, teas, spices, and other specialties. Clifton Mill also serves breakfast, soups, sandwiches, and salads, plus ice cream. On a nice day, take your meal or snack out on the Millrace Deck, and listen to water rushing under your feet on its way to the turbines. At Christmastime, the mill is radiant with 2.6 million lights. There's an enormous collection of Santa Clauses and a 100-foot waterfall of lights.

Clifton Mill is at 75 Water Street (Route 72), Clifton; (937) 767–5501; www .cliftonmill.com. Mill tours: $2.00. Open Monday through Friday, 9:00 A.M. to 4:00 P.M.; Saturday and Sunday, 8:00 A.M. to 5:00 P.M. (closes earlier late November through January).

Designated a National Natural Landmark by the National Park Service, the *Clifton Gorge Nature Preserve* rates as some of Ohio's most beautiful public land. Over the years, the swift Little Miami River has carved a deep gorge through the thick forest, a process started by the raging meltwaters of the last retreating glacier. The power of the river once turned the wheels of two gristmills in the area—Clifton Mill (described above) and a second mill, the remains of which are still visible in the gorge.

Given the clean vertical drops of the limestone cliffs, Clifton Gorge ranked high with rock climbers until that activity was banned in 1982. Concern for the nearly 350 different wildflowers in the park, which provide an unparalleled spring wildflower display, prompted the rock-climbing prohibition.

The preserve has miles of hiking trails along both rims of the gorge and following the river at the floor of the canyon. The adjacent John Bryan State Park contains twelve additional hiking trails, campsites, and picnic areas.

Clifton Gorge Nature Preserve is on Route 343, just west of Clifton. The entrance to John Bryan State Park is on Route 370, near Clifton; (937) 767–1274; www.dnr.state.oh.us/dnap/location/clifton.html. Open daylight hours; no admission charge.

Another fabulous natural area is Antioch College's *Glen Helen,* a 1,000-acre preserve and outdoor education center adjacent to the college's Yellow Springs campus. Designated a National Natural Landmark by the National Park Service in 1965, Glen Helen has a thick regrown forest canopy, a full array of woodland wildflowers, and undisturbed native wildlife. Scenic features include valleys carved by glacial meltwater, ledges, potholes, cascades, and the Yellow Spring, from which the village gets its name. Flowing at seventy gallons per minute, the spring has built a distinctive hill of travertine deposits that extends from the cliff line down to the valley floor. Numerous hiking trails permeate the landscape.

Nearly two-thirds of Glen Helen is thickly wooded, and the balance is mowed meadow and planted prairie—a diversity that creates varied habitats for many species of animals and birds. A 2½-mile stretch of the beautiful, free-flowing Little Miami River courses through the glen.

One unique feature of this preserve is its Raptor Center. Here injured birds of prey—hawks, owls, falcons, eagles, osprey, and vultures—are nursed back to health for their return to the wild. The center also serves as a public education facility, permitting visitors to view and better understand these marvelous creatures.

Glen Helen is accessible from Route 343 just east of Yellow Springs, or from the Trailside Museum, 505 Corry Street, Yellow Springs; (937) 767–7375; www.ghei.org. Open year-round, daylight hours. No admission charge.

Known as a hotbed of antiwar and counterculture activity in the sixties and early seventies, Yellow Springs remains slightly eccentric. The marchers and demonstrators have been replaced by potters and shopkeepers, but Antioch College still provides the youthful emphasis of this uncommon community.

If you've decided you need more time to explore the Yellow Springs area, spend the night at the historic **Arthur Morgan House.** No Ohio town seems more suited to the bed-and-breakfast concept than this one, and the Arthur Morgan House fits the bill perfectly. Built in 1921 for the president of Antioch College, Arthur Morgan, this substantial three-story structure has a huge screened porch—a perfect spot to enjoy a morning cup of coffee or the evening breeze.

The innkeeper has created an appropriately peaceful setting with cozy furnishings, including Ohio antiques. Located on a quiet residential street just a half block from the business district, the Arthur Morgan House features four guest rooms.

Arthur Morgan House is at 120 West Limestone Street, Yellow Springs; (937) 767–1761; www.arthurmorganhouse.com. Rates: $95 to $115 per night, double occupancy; includes continental breakfast.

Ohio is home to the **National Afro-American Museum and Cultural Center,** a repository for preservation, study, and interpretation of the traditions, values, social customs, and experiences of African Americans. The museum's permanent exhibit, From Victory to Freedom, chronicles the period from 1945 to 1965—from victory in World War II to freedom through the passage of federal civil rights legislation. Photographs and artifacts re-create a period of social struggle and dramatic change. Particularly impressive is the award-winning film *Music As Metaphor,* which presents the inspiring Black music of the period and features artists such as Paul Robeson, Fats Domino, Dizzy Gillespie, and many others.

The first phase of this museum opened in 1988, and it is bordered by a scenic wooded area. Three additional phases of development are planned.

The National Afro-American Museum and Cultural Center is at 1350 Brush Row Road, Wilberforce; (937) 376–4944, (800) 752–2603; www.ohiohistory

.org/places/afroam. The museum is open Tuesday through Saturday, 9:00 A.M. to 5:00 P.M. Admission: adults $4.00; children and students $1.50.

What qualifies a theater performance as "an epic drama"? How about a three-acre stage alive with eighteen horses, fifty actors, flaming arrows, and musket and cannon fire? **Blue Jacket** brings Ohio frontier times to life. This is a dramatization about the life of Blue Jacket, a white man adopted by the Shawnee Indians, and his struggle to help his adopted people protect their homeland from frontiersmen, such as the legendary Daniel Boone and Simon Kenton, who were determined to establish settlements in Ohio.

The performance takes place in a tiered outdoor amphitheater. Dinner and backstage tours also are available, as well as souvenirs and pictures from the gift shop. Reserving tickets in advance is a good idea. When you call you can also find out about other special events that take place throughout the summer season.

Blue Jacket is performed at 530 South Stringtown Road, just east of Xenia; (937) 376–4358; www.bluejacketdrama.com. Performances are given Monday through Saturday, mid-June through August, 8:00 P.M. Admission: adults $16.00 to $18.00; children $8.00 to $9.00.

Places to Stay in Southwest Ohio

CHILLICOTHE

Guest House
57 West Fifth Street
(740) 772–2204

CINCINNATI

The Mariemont Inn
6880 Wooster Pike
(513) 271–2100

The Symphony Hotel
210 West Fourteenth Street
(513) 721–3353,
(888) 281–8032

PORTSMOUTH

Shawnee State Park
Route 125, 12 miles
west of Portsmouth
(740) 858–6621,
(800) 282–7275

RIPLEY

The Signal House
234 North Fourth Street
(937) 392–1640

YELLOW SPRINGS

Arthur Morgan House
120 West Limestone
(437) 767–7509

Places to Eat in Southwest Ohio

LEBANON

The Golden Lamb
27 South Broadway
(513) 932–5065
Lodging is also available.

MIAMISBURG

The Peerless Mill Inn
319 South Second Street
(937) 866–5968

MONTGOMERY

Montgomery Inn
9440 Montgomery Road
(513) 791–3482

RIPLEY

Cohearts Riverhouse
18 North Front Street
(937) 392–4819

WAVERLY

Lake White Club
Route 552, 2 miles south
of Waverly
(740) 947–5000,
(800) 774–5253

HELPFUL WEB SITES

Ohio Division of Travel and Tourism:
www.ohiotourism.com

Cincinnati Convention and
Visitors Bureau:
www.cincyusa.com

Cincinnati Enquirer:
http://enquirer.com

Dayton Convention and
Visitors Bureau:
www.daytoncvb.com

Paramount's Kings Island:
www.pki.com

West Central Ohio

Rural Roots

Just up the road from Yellow Springs' Antioch College (and across the Greene County–Clark County line) is a most remarkable store—***Young's Jersey Dairy Farm Store***. Located at a working dairy, Young's caters to the nearby college crowd and the area's year-round residents with fresh breads and pastries, fountain service, and homemade ice cream.

Young's bakes from scratch its vast selection of doughnuts and pastries—turnovers, brownies, pies, cream horns, pecan rolls, coffee cake, fudge, and cookies, plus glazed, whole-wheat, powdered, jelly-filled, and cinnamon doughnuts. The fountain offers shakes, splits, sundaes, and ice-cream sodas created with Young's homemade ice cream. The shakes are particularly good—made in every flavor imaginable. Served regular or extra thick, the calf shake has two scoops of ice cream, the cow shake comes loaded with four scoops, and the diet-busting bull shake contains five scoops.

The Golden Jersey Inn, an authentic frame barn with giant oak timbers fastened with wood pegs, serves country meat-loaf, chicken and dumplings, and bacon-wrapped pork chops. They also serve country breakfasts and a full lunch menu of

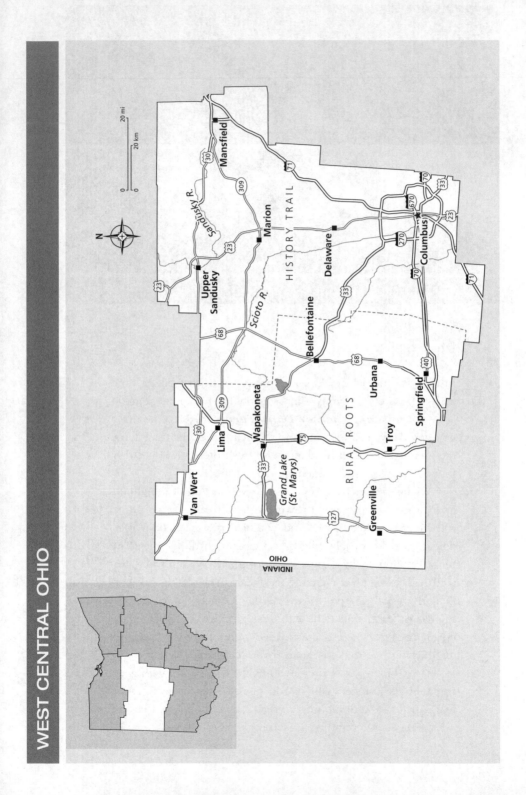

sandwiches and side orders. After you eat, check out the farm animal petting zoo, wagon rides (Saturday and Sunday during warmer months), and Young's farm-themed miniature golf course, Udders and Putters.

Young's Jersey Dairy Farm Store is on U.S. Route 68 just north of the Greene County–Clark County line at 6880 Springfield-Xenia Road, Yellow Springs; (937) 325–0629; www.youngsdairy.com. Open daily, 6:00 A.M. to 10:00 P.M.

The 6,000-square-foot home that today houses the *Willowtree Inn* has seen its share of both good times and bad. The original section of the home, built in 1830, was constructed in the Federal style as a manor house for a family of means and influence. This home and its 160-acre farm were purchased in 1853 by Captain Newell Kerr for $13,000. The Kerrs greatly expanded the place, and an innovative running-water system was installed.

At the turn of the century, however, the Kerrs moved out and began renting the farm and house, which eventually fell into disrepair. After numerous tenants and vacancies, and several interim owners, the Debold family purchased the house, outbuildings, and five acres in 1973. They transformed the structure to its former glory. They dredged and enlarged the property's spring-fed pond,

AUTHORS' FAVORITES

Young's Jersey Dairy Farm Store	Fort Recovery
Willowtree Inn	Allen County Museum
Brukner Nature Center	Harding Home
H. W. Allen Villa	Stengel-True Museum
Piqua Historical Area	Indian Trail Centers
Fort Jefferson State Memorial	Indian Mill State Memorial
Bear's Mill	Malabar Farm
Oak Island	Kingwood Center
Zane Shawnee Caverns	Richland Carousel Park
Mad River Mountain	Living Bible Museum
Piatt Castles	Ohio Statehouse
Ohio Caverns	Columbus *Santa Maria*
Neil Armstrong Air and Space Museum	North Market

which had filled with silt and been choked with watercress. And they restored the springhouse-smokehouse, which had been described as one of the county's finest.

Today Chuck and Jolene Sell own this historic structure and share it with guests as a bed-and-breakfast. Furnished with antiques, the Willowtree Inn offers rooms or a suite, some with private baths. Visitors sit by the pond and watch the ducks paddle by, or guests can pull up in front of one of the home's four fireplaces.

The Willowtree Inn is at 1900 West Route 571, Tipp City; (937) 667–2957. Rates: $60 to $85 per night, which includes a full breakfast. Reservations and a deposit required.

With 165 acres and more than 6 miles of trails, the **Brukner Nature Center**'s mission is to preserve and present to the public the splendor of the outdoors. Hardwood and pine forests, ridges, and ravines—all are accessible by the center's nature trails. Visitors observe the flora and fauna while hiking by Cattail and Catface Ponds and while following the banks of the Stillwater River.

The spring woodland flora delights visitors with displays of bluebells, trillium, Dutchman's breeches, and delphinium. In summer, Queen Anne's lace, thin-leaved coneflowers, butterfly milkweed, and prairie roses flourish along the trails. Occasional glimpses of hawks, garter snakes, cottontail rabbits, white-tailed deer, and chipmunks give visitors a sample of Brukner's diverse native fauna.

The wildlife rehabilitation unit nurses back to health injured animals brought to Brukner. Those unable to survive in the wild are kept in the animal room on display for visitors to the center. Brukner also hosts a variety of classes and seminars on topics such as quilting, woodcarving, gems and minerals, stargazing, beekeeping, and natural history.

Brukner Nature Center is at 5995 Horseshoe Bend Road, off Route 55 west of Troy; (937) 698–6493; www.bruknernaturecenter.com. Trails are open during daylight hours. The exhibit building is open Monday through Saturday, 9:00 A.M. to 5:00 P.M.; Sunday, 12:30 to 5:00 P.M. Admission charged only on Sundays: adults $1.00; children 25 cents; or $2.00 per family.

In 1804, for $5.00 an acre, John Johnston bought the 235 acres he called Upper Pickaway Farms. John and Rachel Johnston, along with their eleven children, lived in the family farmhouse from its completion in 1815 to the 1860s. This historic farm has been restored to its appearance in 1829 and is now part of the **Piqua Historical Area.**

The farmhouse is completely furnished with pieces dating from the early 1800s. The Johnstons used the outdoor fruit kiln to dry apple slices from the farm's two orchards. One feature that attracted Johnston to this property was the flowing spring, and he built a springhouse to utilize the cool spring water to refrigerate meats, milk, and produce. Inside the two-story structure, the clear water circles a stone island in the center of the floor. Items requiring cooling were placed either on the stones or in the flowing water. The spring also provided fresh drinking water for the family. When Johnston advertised the farm for sale in 1857, he estimated the spring's output at ten gallons per minute. The second floor of the springhouse originally contained accommodations for the farm's hired help, but today holds an oak loom (ca. 1750) on which rug making is demonstrated.

The Johnstons' enormous double-pen log barn, constructed in 1808, is the largest log barn in Ohio. Johnston used it for his flock of one hundred sheep, and the original pens and beams are still plainly visible. Other attractions at the Piqua Historical Area include canalboat rides on a restored section of the Miami and Erie Canal and an Indian museum dedicated to the tribes prevalent in Ohio from the seventeenth to mid-nineteenth centuries.

The Piqua Historical Area is at 9845 North Hardin Road east of Route 66, north of Piqua; (937) 773–2522, (800) 752–2619; www.ohiohistory.org/places/piqua. Open from April through October, Wednesday through Saturday, 9:30 A.M. to 5:00 P.M.; Sunday, noon to 5:00 P.M. Admission: adults $7.00; children (ages 6 to 12) $3.00.

In October 1791, the forces of General Arthur St. Clair built Fort Jefferson as an outpost, one of the chain of defensive forts constructed to protect army supplies from Indians. Named for Thomas Jefferson, then secretary of state, the fort served as a supply base for the campaigns of General St. Clair and General "Mad" Anthony Wayne. It was abandoned in 1796, its location too accessible to the enemy and its water supply too vulnerable.

Today, visitors to the **Fort Jefferson State Memorial** find a monument 6 feet square and 20 feet tall made of granite field boulders. The fort only exists in the imagination of those who travel here; none of the structure survived.

Fort Jefferson State Memorial is on County Road 24 at Route 121, Fort Jefferson; (614) 297–2630, (800) 686–1535; www.ohiohistory.org-places/ftjeffer. Open daylight hours; no admission charge.

The water of Greenville Creek meanders around a bend in the stream and pushes into a lake surrounded by lily pads. It then cascades over a dam or is forced into the millrace leading to historic **Bear's Mill.**

In 1824, President James Monroe granted the site of the mill, as well as water rights, to Major George Adams. In 1849, Gabriel Bear constructed Bear's Mill. One hundred and thirty years later, Terry and Julie Clark, a local family, discovered the mill for sale while taking a leisurely drive in the country. Terry, having a fascination for anything old, immediately was drawn to the property.

Bear's Mill

They decided this noble, rustic building and its adjoining property were perfect for them. After two years of renovation, the Clarks reopened Bear's Mill in 1981.

Today, Bear's Mill is listed on the National Register of Historic Places and is an operating, water-powered, stone-grinding flour mill. It is owned by the Clarks and run by a nonprofit organization, the Friends of Bear's Mill.

Terry oversees the milling of cornmeal, rye, cracked-wheat, and whole-wheat cake flour. All of these are stone ground on the original 1849 French buhr-stones, which have a porous and abrasive quality favored by old-world millers. The grinding process is slow and cool, which preserves the nutrients in the flour.

Julie makes wheel-thrown and hand-built pottery, both functional and decorative, which is available for purchase. The rustic specialty shop offers whole-some stone-ground flour, as well as a selection of home, gift, and gourmet items. These include organic grain products and cereals, pancake and soup mixes, gourmet coffees, preserves, and sauces. Handcrafted wood items, garden accessories, tableware, handmade jewelry, soaps, and candles are also available. Visitors are welcome to take a self-guided tour of the four-story mill.

Bear's Mill is off Route 36 at 6450 Arcanum-Bear's Mill Road, 5 miles east of Greenville; (937) 548–5112; www.bearsmill.com. Open January through March, Thursday, Friday, and Sunday, 11:00 A.M. to 5:00 P.M.; Saturday, 9:00 A.M. to 5:00 P.M.; plus Wednesdays, 11:00 A.M. to 5:00 P.M., April through November; and Mondays, 11:00 A.M. to 5:00 P.M., in December.

General Anthony Wayne arrived in Greene Ville in 1793 and built the largest fortification on the western frontier. After the signing of the Treaty of Greene Ville between Wayne and representatives of the Wyandot, Delaware, Miami, Shawnee, Pottawatomi, Chippewa, Ottawa, Kickapoo, Kaskasia, Piankeshaw, Eel River, and Wea nations on August 3, 1795, the area opened for settlement.

At the end of the War of 1812, and with the defeat of Indian chiefs Tecumseh and The Prophet in 1813, a second treaty was signed with the Indians August 20, 1814, by William Henry Harrison, who served as Wayne's aide in 1795.

The buildings which constitute the *Garst Museum* preserve and present this region's rich history. In 1852, George Coover built the Garst House as an inn for travelers on the Dayton and Union Railroad. John Hufnagle purchased the property in 1861 as a gift to his daughter Miranda Garst. It remained in the Garst family until 1946 when it was converted into a museum. It is on the National Register of Historic Sites.

Another son of Darke County is Lowell Thomas, one of the twentieth century's most notable newsmen, known for his wondrous tales of exotic lands. Built in the 1880s, the Lowell Thomas birthplace, a two-story in Gothic Victorian style, was moved from Woodington to the Garst Museum grounds and completely restored.

The museum's Coppock Wing houses its Lowell Thomas and Annie Oakley collections, including the largest known collection of Annie Oakley memorabilia. The Village Wing features items from Buffalo Bill Cody, Anna Bier paintings, as well as an old school room, a post office, a print shop, a barber shop, and a doctor's office, among others.

The Garst Museum is at 205 North Broadway, Greenville; (937) 548–5250; www.garstmuseum.org. Open March through November, Tuesday through Saturday, 11:00 A.M. to 5:00 P.M.; Sunday, 1:00 to 5:00 P.M.; December and February, Friday and Saturday, 11:00 A.M. to 5:00 P.M.; Sunday, 1:00 to 5:00 P.M. Admission: adults $3.00; school-age children $1.00.

Cedar Bog Nature Preserve has seen it all since its glacial upbringing—mastodons probably fed here and all of Ohio's Native American cultures lived in the area. The bog is the largest and best example of a boreal and prairie fen complex in the state, and as such it supports many rare plants as

annieoakley

A teenager with a gun? Today that phrase provokes anxiety, but it was a different story back in 1875. That's when fifteen-year-old Phoebe Ann Moses, born in a log cabin near North Star, challenged champion marksman and showman Frank Butler to a shooting match and won. Annie, as she was called, prevailed over Butler at a place called Oakley near Cincinnati, and hence the legend of Annie Oakley was born.

Annie married Frank Butler a year later, and they began touring together and eventually were featured in Buffalo Bill's Wild West Show. Annie died on November 3, 1926, and she and Frank are still together, in North Star's Brock Cemetery.

well as excellent orchid, prairie, and woodland wildflower displays. It is the artesian flow of cool water filtered through limestone gravel that makes this place environmentally unique. Spotted turtles and swamp rattlesnakes also call the bog home.

Cedar Bog Nature Preserve is at 980 Woodburn Road, Urbana; (937) 484–3744, (800) 860–0147; www.ohiohistory.org/places/cedarbog. Open April through October, Wednesday through Sunday, 9:00 A.M. to 4:30 P.M.; by appointment the rest of the year. Rates: adults $4.00; children (ages 6 to 12) $3.00.

In 2000, the Westcott House Foundation was established to renovate a home designed by noted architect, Frank Lloyd Wright. The **Westcott House,** the only Prairie-style home in Ohio designed by Lloyd Wright, was fully restored and opened as a museum and educational center in 2005. Construction on the home began in 1904 and ended four years later. Wright designed the home for the Ohio manufacturer Burton J. Westcott and his wife Orpha. The home was converted into an apartment building in the 1940s, so the effort to return it to its original configuration took a great deal of research, effort, and millions of dollars.

The house was quite a break from the traditional architecture of the time. Wright focused on the horizontal lines of the land on the American prairie and replicated the flat, horizontal plains in the lines of this and other prairie-style designs. Rather than following the rising, skyscraping designs popular in U.S. cities prior to World War I, Wright created these low-rising structures, which gave a feeling of security and harmony with the land. To ground the home, he created a central hearth area. Surrounding benches create an inner room of sorts and a place of comfort. Rooms blend one into another, with a feeling of openness, and were designed as multipurpose areas. The building materials and the design of the home reflect Wright's desire to blur the lines between interior and exterior, between nature and human construction. He built the home of wood and stucco, and he created connections with the surrounding landscape via a terrace, a pool, and gardens. Some have compared the home to a Shinto temple. A bank of divided windows stretches across an entire side of the house, creating an impressive vista, reminiscent of a shoji screen, perhaps inspired by Wright's trip to Japan shortly before he designed the home. These expanses of windows and skylights flood the entry and common areas with natural light. In addition, Japanese-inspired elements include sleeping porches, many restored lanterns, and a clay-tiled roof.

The Westcott House is at 1340 East High Street, Springfield; (937) 327–9291; www.westcotthouse.org. Tours: Wednesday through Saturday at 11:00 A.M., 1:00 P.M., and 3:00 P.M.; Sunday 1:00 P.M. and 3:00 P.M. Admission: adults $8.50, students $6.00.

To get a peek at what earned the Westcotts enough money to build this great home, head over to the center of the city of Springfield to the **Heritage**

Center. The center has a rare Westcott automobile on display. The center has permanent exhibits highlighting Ohio and regional history in its 13,000 square feet of permanent gallery space and uses an additional 3,000 square feet for a variety of temporary and traveling exhibits. The Heritage Center building itself is impressive. The massive 53,000-square-foot brick and stone edifice is an imposing structure in the middle of downtown and is listed on the National Register of Historic Sites. The structure was constructed in 1890 to house city offices and a farmers market. Along with the Heritage Center, the history society maintains an archive and library resource center for students, researchers, or those attempting to hunt down their family history.

The Heritage Center is at 117 South Fountain Avenue, Springfield; (937) 324–0657; www.heritagecenter.us/museum. Open: Tuesday through Saturday, 9:00 A.M. to 5:00 P.M. Admission: free, but donations are accepted.

Ready to sail away to your own private island? *Oak Island at Indian Lake* could be the place to live out that fantasy. This cottage getaway is a solitary retreat on Oak Island. You'll have to take a boat to reach your private sanctuary.

Whether you are looking for a romantic vacation, family reunion, or family getaway, you can relax at the private beach or on the cottage's covered patios. The cottage has one and one-half baths and three bedrooms, each with a double bed; two rollaway beds are also available. The kitchen comes equipped with a range, oven, refrigerator, and freezer, as well as cooking and serving utensils.

Around the area of Indian Lake you'll find restaurants, sailing, waterskiing, golf, and plenty of natural areas for walks, hikes, and exploring. At the close of summer, generally in the first week of September, the residents around the lake set off flares around the rim of the lake to create a "Ring of Fire." This is a reenactment of a Native American tradition that welcomed the coming of autumn.

Oak Island at Indian Lake is accessible only by boat from Russells Point; (614) 560–3859, (866) 236–7350; indianlake.com/island.htm. Open May through September. Rates vary by season, day of the week, and length of stay.

The 6,000-acre Indian Lake, with its shady islands, peninsulas, and lakefront homes, attracts recreation seekers for fishing, boating, and waterskiing.

Fifteen miles southeast of Indian Lake, a private park, *Zane Shawnee Caverns,* offers a fascinating cavern, camping, and unique accommodations. A swift underground river eroded the 11-million-year-old cavern from the limestone, leaving a labyrinth of caves and tunnels and unusual crystal formations. Water seeping through the rock and dripping down on limestone boulders has created distinctive beehive crystals and, in one case, rare cave pearls. These pure white crystal balls formed in a small pool of water around tiny pieces of rock and dust. The only other set of similar pearls in existence is in a cave in Switzerland.

Zane Shawnee Caverns, with its many "rooms," splendid colors, and clear pools of forty-degree water, was discovered by a young boy in 1892 when his dog fell in a hole and dropped down into the cavern. Early visitors entered through that same hole (which is still visible from inside the cavern); they were lowered in a basket and given a kerosene lamp. In the early 1900s, these self-guided tours cost 10 cents. The Shawnee Nation United Remnant Band of Ohio purchased the caverns in 1996.

Today it takes about forty minutes for guides to lead a group from one end of the cavern to the other. The tour reaches a depth of 132 feet below the surface, but various tunnels and crevasses shoot off from the main cavern to even greater depths.

america'sfirst concretestreet

Once the site of a Native American settlement, Bellefontaine (pronounced "bell-fountain") is most famous for something we take for granted today— paved roads. It was here in 1891 that the Buckeye Cement Company laid an 8-foot strip of concrete on Main Street, America's first concrete street. The company later paved around the courthouse, and this innovation attracted engineers from across the country. A section of the street was displayed at the 1893 Chicago World's Fair, winning a gold medal. We've been pouring concrete ever since.

The park's 200 acres of woods, ridges, and ravines also offer camping and lodging for overnight guests. If you're not a tent camper, Zane Shawnee Caverns has a covered wagon fitted out with seats, carpeting, screens, electric lights, and a double bed for rustic sleeping outdoors. Another delightful place to rest one's head is the Eagles' Nest. Set on stilts in a heavily wooded ravine, this screened sleeping shelter contains a double bed, with a picnic table and barbecue grill adjacent. Two more summer cabins offer accommodations, each with electricity, a table and chairs, a screened porch, and a fire ring in front. Owl's Nest has bunked double beds; Hawk's Nest has one double bed and single bunk beds. Camping and lodging are $14 to $120 per night.

Zane Shawnee Caverns is on Route 540, 5 miles east of Bellefontaine; (937) 592–9592; www zaneshawneecaverns .org. Open April through October. Reservations and a deposit are required for accommodations.

Winter recreation in Logan County is centered at ***Mad River Mountain*** ski resort, with twenty slopes and trails for skiers and snowboarders, and four runs for snowtubing. The 120 hilly acres of the resort are open during the December through March season. Ski instruction and rental equipment are offered. Mad River Mountain is on U.S. Route 33 at 1000 Snow Valley Road,

5 miles east of Bellefontaine; (937) 599–1015, (800) 231–7669; www.skimad river.com.

Rural Logan County might seem an unusual place for two brothers to build a pair of castles, but that is precisely what Colonel Donn Piatt and General Abram Sanders Piatt did during the mid-1800s. Members of the Piatt family came to America in the 1670s from southeastern France. Donn and Abram's grandfather, Jacob Piatt, served on George Washington's staff during the Revolutionary War. Jacob's son Benjamin, after fighting in the War of 1812, acquired 1,700 acres in the Mac-A-Cheek Valley, named after a local Shawnee settlement. It was Benjamin's sons, Donn and Abram, who built the two stone castles a mile apart in what is today Logan County.

Abram Sanders Piatt built the first of the *Piatt Castles,* Castle Piatt Mac-A-Cheek, using an architectural style which blends Gothic Revival and Second Empire. The three-story home (with five-story watchtower) has walls 2 feet thick made of locally quarried limestone, which was hand-chiseled on the site.

The castle has remained in the Piatt family since its construction, and all furnishings in the castle are family originals. The first stop on guided tours of Castle Piatt Mac-A-Cheek is the spacious drawing room, with its intricate oak, walnut, and cherry floors and splendid ash, pine, and walnut walls. Fine woodwork graces the entire castle, as do frescoed ceilings painted by French artist Oliver Frey in 1880. These ceilings have survived a century surprisingly well, without so much as a touch-up.

The castle's furnishings include horsehair-stuffed couches and chairs, massive carved beds, and wardrobes—some dating as far back as the Revolutionary War period—plus a collection of Native-American artifacts. The family's historic firearms collection and a private chapel, complete with altar and kneeler, are upstairs.

Down the road, Donn Piatt's Flemish-style *Mac-O-Chee Castle* (a variation of the name Mac-A-Cheek) contains impressive woodworking and ornately painted walls and ceilings throughout. The castle was completed in 1881, but the Piatt family lost ownership of this three-story, twin-spired structure in the mid-1890s, when Ella Piatt, Colonel Donn Piatt's widow, sold it. It served briefly as a health spa, but eventually stood empty and even was used as a barn for more than a decade. Now it's back in the Piatt family and open to visitors. It is an excellent example of a late-nineteenth-century estate.

The Piatt Castles are on State Route 245, 1 and 2 miles east of West Liberty; (937) 465–2821; www.piattcastles.org. Both castles are open daily May through October 11:00 A.M. to 4:00 P.M. (to 5:00 P.M. in summer); Friday, Saturday, and Sunday mid-March through April. Castle "Mac-A-Cheek" is open daily late November through early January. Admission: adults $9.00; children (ages 5 to 12) $6.00.

Mac-O-Chee Castle

Caves and caverns are scattered across (and under) Ohio, but the largest of such caverns open to the public are at **Ohio Caverns.** With a fifty-four-degree temperature, a visit to Ohio Caverns can be enjoyed any time of year, no matter what the weather on the "outside."

Inside, you'll discover exquisite crystal-white stalactite and stalagmite formations. Unique coloring and ever-changing shapes make this cave tour a treat. Like many such caverns, the more unusual formations have been named—the "Crystal King" and "Pathway through the Palace of the Gods." The real intrigue is not the clever designations, but rather the strange and natural beauty underground. Bring your camera and enjoy.

Ohio Caverns is at 2210 East Route 245, 4 miles east of West Liberty; (937) 465–4017; www.ohiocaverns.com. Open daily 9:00 A.M. to 4:00 P.M. (until 5:00 P.M. April through October). Admission: adults, $10.50; children (ages 5 to 12) $5.50.

On the afternoon of July 6, 1901, the town of Versailles suffered a disastrous fire. The epicenter of the blaze was the old Sheffel Mill, which had stood unused for many years and now burned like tinder as a fierce west wind pushed the flames into the heart of town. Six blocks of local businesses and thirty-eight homes were destroyed.

The **Inn at Versailles** now occupies several of the structures built after the fire of 1901. The upstairs had been The Snyder Hotel, while the kitchen once housed the Beare's Coffee Shop. The lobby was the W.C. Beare Grocery Company, the Alsace Room was a drug store, and the Lorraine and Versailles rooms were a hardware store.

The inn's modern life began in 1992, when, after sitting vacant for years, it was completely renovated in the style of a French country inn. There are twenty rooms, including a master suite with fireplace, several two-bedroom suites and rooms with kitchenettes and a full-service restaurant. Be sure to visit the nearby Winery at Versailles, for tastings, events, and winery tours.

The Inn at Versailles is at 21 West Main Street, Versailles; (937) 526–3020; www.innatversailles.com. Rates: $45 to $189 per night.

At 10:56:20 Eastern Daylight Time on July 20, 1969, Neil Armstrong became the first man to step onto the lunar surface. "That's one small step for a man—one giant leap for mankind," crackled Armstrong's first radio transmission from Tranquility Base, as he accomplished the goal set by John Kennedy in the early 1960s. It was less than seventy years earlier that Dayton's Wright Brothers had conquered powered flight over the sands of Kitty Hawk—from the first successful aircraft to lunar exploration in a little more than six decades.

The *Neil Armstrong Air and Space Museum* in Wapakoneta celebrates the achievements of local boy Armstrong and other Ohioans who contributed to the field of aviation. A NASA F5D Skylancer aircraft flown by Armstrong in the early 1960s greets visitors, and from the Skylancer you simply follow the runway lights to the entrance of the futuristic exhibit building.

Sketches, models, and photographs trace the history of manned flight, from the earliest use of balloons to powered aircraft and space travel. The bright yel-

america'sfirst gasolinepowered automobile

It could have happened anywhere, but it happened here, in 1891. America's first gasoline-powered automobile chugged out of John Lambert's implement store and hit the roads in Ohio City, such as they were. No doubt this caused a stir, as the strange, noisy contraption tooled along, dodging trees and potholes. Lambert reportedly ran into a hitching post on one of his early forays, and this very first car was destroyed in a fire later that same year. Lambert continued to tinker with automobiles and held 600 patents related to the invention.

grandlakest.mary's

Stretching from Lake Erie to the Ohio River in western Ohio, the construction of the Miami & Erie Canal was a major catalyst in the state's development. For the canal to succeed, it needed a reliable water source at its high point, near Celina. Some 1,700 men, paid 30 cents a day, labored for years to create Grand Lake St. Mary's, the largest man-made lake in the world when it was completed in 1845. Today, with the canal long gone, the lake is a haven for recreation.

low, single-engine Aeronca propeller plane flown by Armstrong at age sixteen, and his Gemini Eight space capsule, span his accomplishments as an aviator. Other exhibits include spacesuits from the Gemini and Apollo missions, a Jupiter rocket engine, and not particularly tempting packets of astronaut space food. One video projection room continuously shows marvelous footage of American astronauts from various Apollo missions walking, hopping, jumping, and driving on the lunar surface.

The Neil Armstrong Air and Space Museum is at Interstate 75 and Bellefontaine Street, Wapakoneta; (419) 738–8811, (800) 860–0142; www.ohiohistory .org/places/armstron. Open Monday through Saturday, 9:30 A.M. to 5:00 P.M.; Sunday noon to 5:00 P.M. Admission: adults $7.00, children (ages 6 to 12) $3.00.

One location on the Wabash River was the site of both one of the worst defeats and one of the most important victories for American troops battling the Native Americans in the 1790s. Native warriors led by Little Turtle and Blue Jacket caught General Arthur St. Clair's forces in a surprise attack on November 4, 1791, killing or wounding three-quarters of the soldiers.

But two years after St. Clair's defeat, General "Mad" Anthony Wayne picked that spot on the Wabash to construct a fort consisting of four blockhouses connected by log stockade walls. Each blockhouse measured 20 feet square, and Wayne's troops finished ***Fort Recovery*** in less than a week. When the Native Americans attacked on the morning of June 30, 1794, Wayne's forces prevailed, setting the stage for the general's final victory over the natives at Fallen Timbers on August 20, 1794, and the signing of the Treaty of Greeneville in 1795.

treatyofgreenville

In the summer of 1795, fresh from his victory at the Battle of Fallen Timbers, General "Mad" Anthony Wayne returned to Fort Greenville and waited. By July, twelve tribes with more than 1,300 braves arrived to hammer out a peace treaty with the whites.

On August 3, 1795, the Treaty of Greenville was signed, opening most of Ohio to white settlement. Outgunned, the Native Americans took cash and gave up two-thirds of what is today Ohio. For the native peoples, this was yet another sad chapter in their forced migration west.

Visitors to Fort Recovery inspect the two reconstructed blockhouses and view artifacts from the original fort in the two-story stone museum. These artifacts include an army-issue felling ax, bottles, a skillet handle, and bone-handled knives and forks. The museum has other items used in battle here two centuries ago, such as howitzer shells, cannon balls, grapeshot, and parts of muskets and pistols.

One exhibit explains the construction of Fort Recovery, describing how 13-foot logs with one end axed to a point were placed on end in 3-foot-deep trenches to form the stockade walls. A gap approximately every 6 feet allowed the fort's defenders to point their rifles through the wall and fire on attackers. Other displays in-clude mannequins of an army sergeant and a Native American brave clothed in their respective 1794 battle uniforms, a collection of muskets and military swords from the 1860s, plus Native American artifacts from Mercer County such as tomahawks, leather goods, and arrowheads.

Fort Recovery State Memorial is near the intersection of Routes 49 and 119, Fort Recovery; (419) 375–4649, (800) 283–8920; www.ohiohistory.org/places/ftrecov. Open daily June 1 to Labor Day, noon to 5:00 P.M., plus weekends in May and September. Admission: adults $3.00; children $1.00.

Lima residents boast of having one of the best county museums in the state—the *Allen County Museum*—and it is. Two floors in a modern brick building contain hundreds of items. Its pioneer kitchen contains old-fashioned butter stamps, molds, and churns, while the pioneer bedroom has a corn-husk mattress on a primitive wooden bed. The mother of the Haller twins (Kathern and Sophie) rocked her infants on the rare double cradle bench during their first year in 1852.

The museum has collected a variety of wagons and buggies, including a covered wagon and a hearse, as well as antique cars such as a magnificent 1909 Locomobile Sports Roadster. Downstairs features a number of muskets and pistols and all manner of Native American items including arrowheads, beads, ornate Hopi dolls and masks, pottery, blankets, and a large ribbed canoe. A nineteenth-century doctor's office and a general store are completely stocked with items typical of the era.

One unusual item is the 1903 Kodak "mugging" camera, used by the Lima police department at the turn of the century (plus sample mugshots demonstrating the policemen's photographic abilities). Other collections include rocks, fossils, and minerals found in the county, and a group of antique farm implements.

Next to the museum is the Log House, furnished with primitive pioneer possessions, and the MacDonell House, a Victorian mansion renowned for its handsome woodwork, big game trophies, and period pieces.

The Allen County Museum is at 620 West Market Street, Lima; (419) 222–9426; www.allencountymuseum.org. Open Tuesday through Sunday, 1:00 to 5:00 P.M. No admission charge.

History Trail

In 1890 Warren G. Harding, then twenty-five years old, and his fiancée planned and had built the dark-green home at 380 Mount Vernon Avenue, Marion. From the *Harding Home,* he conducted his famous "front porch" campaign in 1920 and won the presidency. The Harding years in the White House were turbulent ones—his administration was rocked by scandals, including the infamous Teapot Dome incident. Harding died in San Francisco in 1923, without completing his term of office.

The eldest son of a doctor, Harding was born in Blooming Grove, Ohio, on November 2, 1865. After working as a printer's apprentice, he bought the *Marion Daily Star* at the age of nineteen. In 1891, he married Florence Kling DeWolfe, daughter of one of Marion's wealthiest and most prominent Republicans, on the stairway of the home they had designed. Harding's election to the Ohio Senate in 1899, as lieutenant governor of Ohio in 1903, and to the United States Senate in 1914 laid the groundwork for his successful presidential campaign in 1920. He used the large front porch of his home—the porch he had expanded in 1900—to speak to the 600,000 voters who traveled to Marion in the summer of 1920 to hear the acclaimed oratory of the Republican candidate.

Inside the entryway sits the small wooden desk where Harding sat on election night reading the latest telegraphed election returns. Nearly all the furnishings and accessories in the Harding home are exactly as the Hardings left them when they went to Washington in 1921. Many of the art objects collected by the Hardings on their three trips to Europe are there, and so is the hat worn by the twenty-ninth president at his inauguration. The small building behind the Harding residence, which served as the press headquarters during the 1920 campaign, now is a museum.

porkrind, anyone?

It may not be exactly a celebration of health food, but Harrod festivities honoring pork rinds reflect the local popularity of this legendary snack. Of course, the Pork Rind Heritage Festival features this lip-smacking treat, but it also includes a hog roast and a variety of other food fare. And no pork rind fan could leave without cheering on the Pork Rind Parade or staying to enjoy the live entertainment.

The festival is held on Main Street mid-June, Harrod; call (419) 648–2063 for more information.

The Harding Home is at 380 Mount Vernon Avenue, Marion; (740) 387–9630, (800) 600–6894; www.ohiohistory.org/places/harding. Open Memorial Day to Labor Day, Wednesday through Saturday, 9:30 A.M. to 5:00 P.M.; Sunday, noon to 5:00 P.M., plus weekends in September and October. Admission: adults $6.00; children (ages 6 to 12) $3.00.

Not far from the Harding Home are the ten-acre grounds containing the *Harding Tomb.* Constructed in 1927 of Georgia white marble, the 52-foot-tall memorial surrounds the graves of President and Mrs. Harding (she died in 1924, a year after her husband). Labrador granite tombstones cover the graves of the Hardings, who were buried here on December 21, 1927. The careful rows of maple trees on the grounds form the shape of a Latin cross.

The Harding Tomb is at the corner of Route 423 and Vernon Heights Boulevard, Marion; (740) 387–9630; www.ohiohistory.org/places/hardtomb. Open daylight hours; no admission charge.

Marion offers visitors another intriguing museum: the **Stengel-True Museum.** Judge Ozias Bowen built this three-story mansion in 1864 at a cost of $20,000. Bowen arrived in Marion from New York in 1828 and married Miss Lydia Baker, the daughter of Eber Baker, the founder of Marion. Judge Bowen's grandson, Henry A. True, made a provision in his will establishing the museum, and a local optometrist, Dr. Frederick Stengel, contributed many of the collections displayed at Stengel-True.

A wonderful old Regina music box plays waltzes (for a nickel). The front parlor contains a grand piano that once belonged to Florence Kling Harding and one of the ornate marble fireplaces found throughout the museum. Displays include collections of rare and antique guns, all types of early lamps and lighting instruments (from candles to kerosene fixtures), and a wall full of antique clocks (next to a case loaded with old pocket watches).

Pioneer antiques dominate the upper floors—spinning wheels, yarn winders, dough pans, hay forks, and a butter churn. A small staircase on the third floor leads up to the rooftop cupola, which offers a splendid 360-degree view of Marion.

The Stengel-True Museum is at 504 South State Street, on the corner of South State Street and Washington Avenue, Marion; (740) 382–2826. Open Saturday and Sunday, 1:00 to 4:30 P.M. No admission charge.

Richard Hendricks purchased his dream in 1963—the 10,000-foot **Indian Trail Caverns** he had first visited as a child. Once called the Wyandot Indian Caverns, this bit of underground history first opened in 1927 but closed ten years

thecrawford incident

Ohio was the site of many conflicts between white settlers and Native Americans. One of the most gruesome was the execution of Colonel William Crawford by Delaware and Wyandot Indians. In 1782, Crawford, a friend of George Washington, led a force of 480 men bent on attacking Native American villages along the Sandusky River.

Not only did his campaign fail, but Crawford was captured and held responsible for the atrocities committed by whites at Gnadenhutten. Crawford literally was burned alive at the stake after being beaten and tortured. Today, Crawford County bears his name as a reminder of this incident.

later. Hendricks, the postmaster in nearby Vanlue, worked nights and weekends whenever the weather would permit, clearing glacial debris from the floor of the caverns, and reopened them in 1973.

TOP ANNUAL EVENTS

Columbus Arts Festival,
Columbus, June;
(614) 224–2606;
www.gcac.org/fest

Peony Festival,
Van Wert, June;
(419) 238–6223;
http://vanwert.com/peony

Strawberry Festival,
Troy, June;
(800) 348–8993;
www.troyohio.gov/SF2006/SF2005
home.html

Pork Rind Heritage Festival,
Harrod, June;
(419) 648–3427

Rose Festival,
Columbus, June;
(614) 645–6640;
http://recparks.columbus.gov/events/
RecParks_30.asp

National Threshers Annual Reunion,
Fulton County Fairgrounds,
Wauseon, June;
www.nationalthreshers.com/main.html

London Strawberry Festival,
London, June;
(740) 852–1582;
www.londonstrawberryfestival.com

Miami Valley Steam Threshers Show,
Plain City, July;
(614) 296–5814;
www.miamivalleysteamshow.org

Wacky Boat Race,
Russells Point, August;
(937) 843–4557;
http://indianlake.com/bulletin.htm#year

Bucyrus Bratwurst Festival,
Bucyrus, August;
(419) 562–2728;
www.bratfest.org

All Ohio Balloon Rally,
Marysville, August;
(614) 875–4335;
http://centralohioballoonclub.org

Dublin Irish Festival,
Dublin, August;
www.dublinirishfestival.org

Acidic water seeping through the 400-million-year-old rock created the caverns. The formation of the caverns was particularly rapid (in geological time), occurring when this part of Ohio was under a warm, shallow ocean. In fact, Indian Trail was part of a reef millions of years ago. Advancing glaciers dumped sandy debris on the floor of the caverns, and Hendricks removed much of it to increase the height of the caverns. In addition to the 650 feet originally open to the public, the Hendricks family is continually opening new sections as the excavation continues.

One section of the caverns opened in 1990 in what is called the Sheridan Pit. A number of universities and museums of natural history have been excavating this site since 1992. In it were discovered 9,000- to 13,000-year-old bones of Ice Age animals, such as the short-faced bear. This bear was as tall

Farmer Merchant Days,
Union City, August;
(317) 964–5409;
www.darkecountyohio.com/
communities/unioncity.htm

Ohio State Fair,
Columbus, August;
(888) 646–3976;
www.ohioexpocenter.com

Miami County Fair,
Troy, August;
(937) 335–7492;
www.miamicountyohiofair.com

Darke County Fair,
Greenville, August;
(937) 548–5044, (800) 736–3671;
http://darkecountyfair.com

Reynoldsburg Tomato Festival,
Reynoldsburg. September;
(614) 866–2861;
www.reynoldsburgtomatofestival.org

Marion Popcorn Festival,
Marion, September;
(740) 387–3378;
www.popcornfestival.com

Crestline Harvest – Antique Festival,
Crestline, September;
(419) 683–3800

Harvest and Herb Festival,
Ada, September;
(419) 634–0936;
www2.wcoil.com/~adanet/hhf.html

Heritage Days Festival,
Lucas, September;
(419) 892–2784;
www.malabarfarm.org

Ohio Gourd Show,
Greenville, late September, October;
(937) 547–0025;
http://ohiogourdsociety.org/history/
history.htm

as a quarter horse, could run 40 miles per hour, and was one of the fiercest predators in North America. Other bones found in this pit were from a prehistoric elk-moose, a giant beaver as large as a bear, and an ancient wild boar. In 1995, an 11,000-year-old spear point made from an antler was unearthed, the oldest known artifact in Ohio.

The Hendricks family has learned a great deal about the caverns from the many geologists and archeologists who have studied the formation, and they share this knowledge with those who tour the caves. Smoke-stained walls and ceilings, in addition to artifacts discovered here, indicate that prehistoric humans lived in the caverns, taking advantage of the year-round fifty-two degree temperature. Indian Trail has six skylights open to the surface and a natural stone ladder that Indians may have used to go in and out of this unique geological formation. Tour guides point out dozens of natural rock sculptures that seem to form shapes such as Abe Lincoln's face and a wolf's head.

Indian Trail Caverns is on Route 568, 4 miles northwest of Carey; (419) 387–7773; www.indian-trail-caverns.com. Open Memorial Day to Labor Day, Saturday and Sunday, 1:00 to 5:00 P.M., or by appointment. Admission: adults $7.00; children $5.00.

The United States government constructed a saw- and gristmill for Ohio's Wyandot Indians in 1820 in gratitude for their support during the War of 1812. The mill was on the Sandusky River, and government-appointed millers ground flour and cornmeal for the Wyandot reservation until the Indians were relocated to Kansas in 1843, putting the mill out of operation.

A second mill was built 300 feet downstream from the first in 1861 and operated until 1941. This mill had a reputation for particularly good stone-ground buckwheat and cornmeal, and has since become the country's first museum of milling—***Indian Mill State Memorial.***

The museum includes a detailed explanation of the four types of mill waterwheels: the overshot, undershot, breast, and horizontal wheels. Exhibits explain the history of gristmills and sawmills and their importance to early Ohio settlements. Perhaps the most intriguing feature of the museum is the working model of a water turbine mill. This model demonstrates the complex system of "flights" that transported grain and milled meal from floor to floor in the mill—from its entry down a chute to the grinding stones on the lower level to the upper floors for sifting, separating, and sacking. Outside the mill, a three-acre park across the river bridge is a tranquil and picturesque spot for a picnic or just relaxing.

Indian Mill State Memorial is at 7417 County Road 47, off Route 67 or U.S. Route 23 northeast of Upper Sandusky; (419) 294–3349, (800) 600–7147; www .ohiohistory.org/places/indian. Open Memorial Day through Labor Day, Friday and Saturday, 9:30 A.M. to 5:00 P.M.; Sunday, 1:00 to 6:00 P.M., plus weekends in September and October. Admission: adults $1.00; children (ages 6 to 12) 50 cents.

Humphrey Bogart and Lauren Bacall married and honeymooned on a farm near Lucas, Ohio? Unlikely as that might seem, it did happen on May 21, 1945, at ***Malabar Farm,*** the 914-acre farm of Pulitzer Prize-winning novelist Louis Bromfield. Bromfield was born in nearby Mansfield in 1896 and graduated from Mansfield Senior High School. Though he studied agriculture at Cornell and journalism at Columbia, this prominent author and screenplay writer never received a college degree.

After driving ambulances in World War I, Bromfield remained in Europe and published his first novel, *The Green Bay Tree,* in 1925, launching a literary career that would produce thirty-three books over the next thirty-three years, as well as a number of screenplays. Although dedicated to his writing, Bromfield never lost his interest in agriculture. In 1939, when the outbreak of World War II forced Bromfield and his family to flee France, he began searching Ohio for suitable farm acreage to practice the conservation techniques he had learned from his grandfather and French farmers. He found Malabar—

salesday

Talk about a tradition. London has held a livestock auction the first Tuesday of every month since 1856. In all those years, only four sales have been canceled: two in 1863, one in 1865, and one in 1868. Farmers bring their herds in for the 10:00 A.M. sale, and then spend the day "in town." Crowds often number two to three thousand people on Public Square for a "sales day."

or, more accurately, created Malabar (which means "beautiful valley" in a Native American dialect) by purchasing four adjacent farms in the lush, rolling hills of Richland County. Saving only four rooms of the original farmhouse, Bromfield added twenty-eight others, including nine bedrooms, six full baths, and four half baths, producing the airy rambling estate where he entertained family and friends.

Among the many visitors to Malabar were Hollywood celebrities such as William Powell, Errol Flynn, Dorothy Lamour, and Shirley Temple—all friends of Bromfield's his work in motion pictures. Bromfield explained his innovative "grass farming" method of agriculture to them, a system of planting grasses in critical areas to arrest soil erosion and reinvigorate the earth. Bromfield distrusted the effects on the soil of using every available acre for grain production; instead he cultivated only enough acreage to support his dairy operation.

The Bromfield home is furnished exactly as it was when the family lived here, with many of the pieces brought back from France in 1939. Bromfield also imported the bright wallpapers from France, and all the oak floors and walnut doors are original. Two Grandma Moses paintings hang in the house, and, because of Bromfield's love of the outdoors, every room on the first floor has an outside door. Bromfield had the twenty-nine-drawer desk in his study custom built, only to discover he was unhappy with the way it "felt." He actually worked at a card table behind the desk.

The family's boxer dogs were important members of the household, and the doors of the house were equipped with special latches that the dogs could open, giving them free run of Malabar. In addition to guided tours of the house, self-guided tours of the barns, chicken coop, smokehouse, and the farm's active dairy operation are also offered. Cross-country skiing is popular at the farm in the winter, with rental equipment available.

Malabar Farm is at 4050 Bromfield Road, west of Route 603 off Pleasant Valley Road, south of Lucas; (419) 892–2784; www.dnr.state.oh.us/parks/parks/malabar.htm. Open daily year-round, except major holidays. Tours of the house are $3.00 for adults, $1.00 for children ages 6 to 18; wagon tours of the farm are $1.00 for adults, children under 12 free.

Just down the road from Malabar Farm is a former stagecoach stop on the old Cleveland-Marietta line called the *Malabar Inn.* David Schrack and his sons, attracted to this location because of the rapidly flowing spring (later called Niman Spring), built the inn in 1820. The inn had deteriorated badly when Louis Bromfield acquired it in the late 1930s, but he renovated the structure and used it to house the overflow of guests visiting Malabar. Bromfield also took advantage of the springhouse next to the inn, using the cold water flowing through the sandstone troughs to cool the organic produce sold at his roadside market.

The Malabar Inn serves fine country fare in the brick two-story building, which has a large deck on three sides. Dinner selections include rainbow trout, smoked Ohio ham, steaks, roast top round of beef, and pan-fried calves' liver with bacon. For lunch, there are salads, sandwiches, homemade soups, and specialty entrees. One dining room is elegantly paneled and trimmed in white; the other features bright wallpaper. Both have a Williamsburg flair, potted plants, and plenty of windows for enjoying the tall trees around the inn. The breads and desserts at Malabar are made from scratch, and the rich cheesecake is particularly good.

keene'sfireproof house

Fred Sharby was afraid of fire. Two of the theaters he owned burned flat, and he had a terror of dying in a fire. So he tore down his house on the north side of Roxbury Street in Keene and built a new one, all of fireproof materials. Steel girders, stucco, plaster, and fireproof floor tiles, doors of solid metal, and a furnace enclosed in cement walls have indeed lasted to this day without a fire. Fred wasn't so lucky. He chose the night of November 28, 1942, to go to the Cocoanut Grove in Boston and died in that fire.

The Malabar Inn is at 3645 Pleasant Valley Road, just west of Route 603, south of Lucas; (419) 938–5205. Open weekends in March and April; Tuesday through Thursday, 11:00 A.M. to 2:30 P.M.; Friday and Saturday, 11:00 A.M. to 8:00 P.M.; Sunday, 11:00 A.M. to 7:00 P.M. May through October. MasterCard and Visa are accepted.

The late Charles Kelley King, chairman of the board of Mansfield's Ohio Brass Company, spent $400,000 building and furnishing his palatial French Provincial estate in 1926—an estate now dedicated to the study and display of gardening, horticulture, birds, and related subjects, and called *Kingwood Center.*

ALSO WORTH SEEING

Franklin Park Conservatory and Botanical Gardens, Columbus	**COSI, Center of Science and Industry,** Columbus
German Village, Columbus	**Ohio Historical Society and Ohio Village,** Columbus
Short North arts and entertainment district, Columbus	**Wexner Center for the Arts,** Columbus
Columbus Zoo	**Wyandot Lake,** Columbus
Columbus Museum of Art	

King joined Ohio Brass in 1893, working his way through the ranks from chief engineer to sales manager, and later from vice president and president to chairman. After his death at age eighty-four in 1952, his will established an endowment for the development and perpetual maintenance of Kingwood. Two of the three floors of the mansion are open to the public. Perhaps the most impressive room is the formal dining room, with its hand-painted French wallpaper, delicate crystal chandelier, and antique chairs and table—a room that any monarch would proudly claim. The mansion also houses an extensive library on horticulture, landscaping, and related topics.

The grounds of the estate include twelve distinct gardens, each designed and arranged by the staff. The center plants 55,000 tulips each year, with the peak blooming season for these during the first two weeks in May. The tulips are replaced with 35,000 annuals to create a summer display. The paths also take you past Kingwood's collections of trees, shrubs, and ferns, and nature trails allow you to enjoy the abundant wildflowers. A variety of ducks and ornamental birds freely roam the grounds, and 130 species of native birds have been sighted on the premises. The greenhouse and orangery feature displays of seasonal flowering plants, cacti, orchids, and tropical plants.

Kingwood Center is at 900 Park Avenue West (Route 430), in Mansfield; (419) 522-0211; www.kingwoodcenter.org. Grounds and greenhouse are open daily, 8:00 A.M. to sundown (closing at 5:00 P.M. November through March). Kingwood Hall is open Tuesday through Saturday, 9:00 A.M. to 5:00 P.M.; Sunday (April through October only), 1:00 to 5:00 P.M. No admission charge.

The modern carousel emerged in the 1870s, when an English engineer-manufacturer named Frederick Savage applied steam power to these marvelous devices. Within a few years of this enhancement, Robert Tidman, an amusement ride manufacturer from England, designed one of the first up-and-down cranking devices that gave the horses their now-familiar galloping motion. Machines could now support two and three (eventually up to five) concentric rows of elaborately carved wooden horses and various other menagerie figures, as well as the many decorative panels and trimmings which were used to give the carousel a grand appearance by hiding its mechanicals. Musical accompaniment also evolved, from the simplicity of a drum or set of bells to the rich sounds of a band organ.

Consequently, public demand for carousels reached new heights in much of Europe and America, rising steadily in the years approaching the turn of the century and then truly booming in the two decades following 1900. This demand was further driven by the increased number of amusement parks built on both continents. Wherever it was, the carousel became a central part of a magnificent social event, as crowds of people in their Sunday best would climb aboard a favorite steed or just sit and listen to the lively music while enjoying the breeze generated by the machine.

Unique carving styles emerged from each of three separate regions producing carousels. English carousel figures were the easiest to identify because their "romance" side (the side which faced out and thus received more detailed carving) was on the left, unlike most other European and all American figures, whose outer side was on the right. This difference stemmed from the clockwise direction of English carousels, which encouraged riders to mount their horse properly from the left and was a result of the fact that the ring-catching game so popular in continental Europe and America never caught on in England. Conversely, carousels in the United States and the rest of Europe rotated counter-clockwise to leave the right hand free to reach for the ring.

With tools in hand, gifted craftsmen gave us what has come to be known as the "golden age" of the wooden carousel in America, which extended from around 1880 to the early 1930s. During this time, carousels became evermore artistically grand and technologically advanced, with electricity replacing steam and the development of an overhead cranking mechanism, still in use today, that produced a smoother galloping motion.

Carousel Magic! is a working carousel factory, where skilled craftspeople use time-honored techniques of carving, finishing, and painting to transform hardwood blocks to prancing ponies and magical menagerie figures. Here new figures are created, old ones are restored, and brand new carousels are built. Visitors enjoy a tour that features the history, styles, and construction of carousels. Carving classes also are available.

Carousel Magic! is at 44 West Fourth Street, Mansfield; (419) 526–4009, (888) 213–2829; www.carouselmagic.com. Factory tours are available April through December, Tuesday through Saturday, 10:00 A.M. to 4:00 P.M. Admission: adults $5.00; children (ages 5 to 12) $1.50.

Mansfield also is home to the first new hand-carved wooden carousel built since the 1930s. Reminiscent of a turn-of-the-century Philadelphia-style carousel, the main attraction at *Richland Carrousel Park* features fifty-two distinctive wooden animals and two chariots. These colorful figures were hand carved and painted in Mansfield. Guarding the entrance to the carousel are two large bronze horses, cast from antique molds.

Music is provided by a Stinson organ, which helps conjure up childhood memories for many of the carousel's riders. Eighteen hand-painted scenery

Lincoln's Last Journey

Abraham Lincoln journeyed across Ohio in life and death, and some say the slain president still travels Ohio's railways. Between the time of the popular vote and the formal vote of the Electoral College in 1860, Lincoln visited Ohio. It was, we are told, in the office of Ohio Governor William Dennison that Lincoln actually heard he had won the presidency. Visitors to the newly renovated Ohio Statehouse can see the very desk at which the governor and President-elect Lincoln sat that day. The desk has been preserved and the current governor uses it as part of his working office. The rest of the rooms and chambers have also been restored to the style, color, and furnishings that Mr. Lincoln saw during that happy visit.

Lincoln journeyed back across Ohio on the trip that marked the close of his presidency and the end of his life. The funeral train for the slain president stopped in Columbus, and the body of Lincoln lay in state in the statehouse rotunda. The educational center in the lower level of the building documents that sad event, describing the crowds that packed the statehouse and grounds to pay their respects to the fallen leader.

The Lincoln funeral train also gave people in farming and rural regions the chance of a glimpse of their assassinated president. A special lead engine, or pilot car, steamed down the rails in advance of the funeral train. People came to the tracks to wait in sad tribute. As the train, draped in black, passed by, some could see the ornate coffin and the men on guard around it.

The image of that somber journey burned itself into the memories of the adults and children who stood in a final tribute along the rail line. But some say that moment was also somehow burned into the fabric of time. Each April 27, legend has it that Lincoln's train again rolls down the track. The muffled sound of the steam locomotive passes through the quiet Ohio countryside. Those who tell the tale of the recurring trip say that the dim light from the funeral train illuminates the ever-vigilant guards who will forever stand over the last journey of their fallen leader.

panels adorn the top of the carousel, depicting Mansfield past and present.

Richland Carrousel Park is at 75 North Main Street, Mansfield; (419) 522–4223; www.richlandcarrousel.com. Open daily, 11:00 A.M. to 5:00 P.M. (extended hours in the summer). No admission charge; rides are 75 cents.

A walk through the Bible? That's what you'll find at the *Living Bible Museum,* dedicated to "bringing God's word to life." The vision for this unique museum—Ohio's only wax museum—dates back to the early 1970s, when pastor Richard Diamond and his wife, Alwilda, toured a museum in Georgia that depicted the Ascension of Christ. Moved by the exhibit, the Diamonds started planning for a Bible museum. After years of work, the museum opened its doors for the first time on August 15, 1987.

The Living Bible Museum has forty-one vivid life-size re-creations of favorite Old and New Testament stories, including a wax re-creation of the Last Supper. From the Creation of Man to the Judgment of Man, these scenes are complete with narrative and special effects. A second museum—Miracles of the Old Testament—opened in August 1994.

The Living Bible Museum is at 500 Tingley Avenue, Mansfield; (419) 524–0139, (800) 222–0139; www.livingbiblemuseum.org. Open Monday through

The Lady in Gray

If you take a moment to stroll through the historic Camp Chase Confederate Cemetery in Columbus, some say the Lady in Gray may join you. A grieving young woman with her hair tied back in a bun and dressed in an 1860s-style gray traveling suit is fabled to walk among the gravestones there. Visitors to the site, which rests on what was Camp Chase Union Military Camp during the Civil War, have reported seeing this sad woman, always looking down and weeping.

Adding to the legend, flowers have been placed on the grave of the Unknown Soldier and on the grave of Benjamin Allen, a Confederate soldier in the 50th Tennessee regiment. Since the site is also home to Civil War reenactments and commemorations, the legend grows. Those participating in the reenactments and dressed in period garb or uniform have reported either being joined by the Lady in Gray, hearing an otherworldly weeping, or having their commemorations disrupted by violent gusts of wind

So as you stroll among the tombstones, the Lady in Gray could be floating nearby, still grieving for a loved one lost in the great Civil War. The annual Camp Chase Memorial Service for fallen Confederate Soldiers is held at the cemetery at 2900 Sullivant Avenue, Columbus. This commemoration has been held at this site since 1895. For more information call (614) 276–0060.

Saturday, 9:00 A.M. to 6:00 P.M.; Sunday, 3:00 to 7:00 P.M. Admission: adults $4.50 for each museum, students $3.50 for each museum, age 5 and under free.

During the Civil War, the grounds were used as a Union Army training facility because of a healthy spring located near the site. In the 1880s, Mansfield donated the land to the state of Ohio for a state reformatory. Work began on the **Ohio State Reformatory** (OSR) in 1885.

"Mansfield's Greatest Day," proclaimed the *Richland Shield* with a banner headline on November 4, 1886. The cornerstone laid that day evolved into a magnificent chateauesque structure. Noted architect Levi T. Scofield designed the Ohio State Reformatory to resemble medieval chateaux and castles. Spiritual and uplifting architecture was intended to provide a transcendent religious experience to help reform the behavior of young male prisoners. The East Cell Block houses the world's largest free-standing steel cell block, rising six tiers. After numerous delays, the first prisoners arrived at this turn-of century prison in 1896, and inmates passed time there for nearly 100 years, until its closing in 1990.

The Ohio State Reformatory is listed on the National Register of Historic Places and today welcomes visitors. It also welcomes film crews. *The Shawshank Redemption* with Tim Robbins and Morgan Freeman was shot here, and so were scenes from *Air Force One* with Harrison Ford, *Tango and Cash,* and *Harry and Walter go to New York.* Special events at OSR include the always popular Ghost Hunts and the Haunted Prison Experience around Halloween.

The Ohio State Reformatory is at 100 Reformatory Road, Mansfield; (419) 522–2644; www.mrps.org. There is one tour daily June through August, Tuesday through Friday at 2:00 P.M. Sunday tours are at 1:00 P.M., mid-May to late September. Admission: adults $8.00; children (6 to 17) $6.00.

If you are hungry for a superb meal in an elegant setting, **Doc Henderson's** may be just the prescription. This upscale restaurant is located in a lovely, historic home. The former residence of a local doctor—hence the name—was built around 1884 and is on the National Registry. An extensive remodeling project has created a bistro-style main dining room with a creative menu and a good, if not extensive, wine list. Appetizers, main dishes, and desserts range from the traditional to the exotic. There are fish and chips for the mainstream palate, but look for the specials that may feature calamari with a Thai curry mayonnaise, or try the chicken saltimbocca. Make sure to leave a little room for the special Oreo cream puff to top off your meal.

Doc Henderson's restaurant is located at 318 East Fifth Street in Marysville; (937) 642–6661. Open Monday through Thursday, 11:00 A.M. to 9:00 P.M.; Friday and Saturday, 11:00 A.M. to 10:00 P.M.

Between 1839 and 1861, Ohio inmates constructed the foundation and ground floor of the **Ohio Statehouse.** Built in the Greek Revival style, the statehouse is situated on a ten-acre site donated by four prominent Columbus landowners. Greek Revival was the architecture of choice in nineteenth-century America, with Greece representing one of the world's earliest democracies. The statehouse, with its center rotunda and cupola, mimics the stature of the Greek Parthenon. The large Doric colonnades are typical of Greek Revival structures.

Construction of this significant building did not happen easily; it took seven different architects more than twenty-two years, encompassing a cholera epidemic and an eight-year work stoppage. One of the most important architects on the project was Nathan B. Kelly. He added many flourishes to the building, though his thanks was to be fired because the commissioners overseeing the project viewed these same flourishes as both too expensive and too lavish. To Kelly's credit, it was he who realized that the design contained no heating or ventilation system, an oversight he corrected.

During the twentieth century, growth in state government resulted in the building being continuously remodeled, with its magnificent high-ceilinged rooms slowly chopped up and subdivided with new walls and drop ceiling after drop ceiling. Heating and cooling systems produced a ground floor most notable for its exposed (and occasionally leaking) steam pipes and wiring.

A comprehensive restoration of the statehouse and adjoining Senate Building in the 1990s was long overdue. This massive project, which required the Ohio house and senate to meet outside the statehouse complex for two years, restored Ohio's most significant government buildings to their earlier grandeur. The Capitol Atrium, which connects the two buildings, was added as well. It was on this site in 1859 that Abraham Lincoln spoke to a small group of Ohioans about the just-completed Lincoln-Douglas debates. The ground floor today hosts a museum and visitor center, with guided tours available.

The Ohio Statehouse is at the corner of Broad and High Streets, Columbus; (614) 752–6350, (614) 728–2695, (888) 644–6123; www.ohio.history.org/places/statehse. Open Monday through Friday, 7:00 A.M. to 7:00 P.M.; Saturday and Sunday, 10:00 A.M. to 5:00 P.M. No admission charge.

Moored in the Scioto River downtown in Ohio's capital city is a unique attraction, the *Columbus* **Santa Maria.** Built to commemorate the 500th anniversary of Christopher Columbus's historic voyage, this is the world's most authentic representation of Columbus's flagship. Tours of this historic vessel give one a new appreciation for the hardships endured by early mariners who spent months at sea on crafts such as these.

The *Santa Maria* was constructed from plans provided by the King of Spain in 1990. She measures 98 feet in length, and her 65-foot mainmast was carved from a single Douglas fir tree. Her sails cover 2,700 square feet and her rigging requires 4,000 feet of line.

The Columbus *Santa Maria* is moored just north of West Broad Street at Marconi Boulevard, Columbus; (614) 645–8760; www.santamaria.org. Open April through December, Monday through Friday, 10:00 A.M. to 3:00 P.M.; Saturday and Sunday, noon to 5:00 P.M.; extended hours during the summer. Admission: adults $3.50; children $2.00.

Looking for fresh food or just a fresh shopping experience? Try the **North Market** in Columbus. In operation since 1876, the market is a celebration of food and fun. During the summer months, there is an outdoor market showcasing the best from neighboring farms, as well as entertainment and children's activities. Gourmet cooks can find the freshest eggs, poultry, meats, seafood, cheeses, vegetables, and fruits. A Touch of Earth offers a large assortment of spices and herbs.

The Ohio State Fair

Perhaps the carnival rides on the midway aren't your idea of getting away from the crowds and onto the road less traveled. But visitors to the Ohio State Fair, as well as many of Ohio's county fairs, can find the simple pleasures of yesteryear if they look beyond the glare of the midway.

Visiting the animal exhibits takes you back to the time when fairs were truly a celebration of rural life. Here's an example: One of the most charming and whimsical animal competitions is found in the rabbit barn. There is something comical about a judge walking down a row of fluffy bunnies, noses wiggling, whiskers twitching, and tall rabbit ears standing up on alert. You may be amazed at just how many kinds of rabbits are shown at the fairs, from tiny dwarfs to those the size of the average dog, and some with ears that droop like those of a basset hound.

The more traditional farm animals also are a treat for all members of the family to observe. Check the daily schedule for the children's competitions. You'll be charmed by the spunk of a 3-foot-tall girl or boy showing a cow, goat, or pig that has to be twice the child's weight.

Just a trip through the barns can bring a smile to your face. The goats will greet you with grumpy bleats, and the sheep are forever being groomed and fluffed by their owners. In order to keep the animals clean and fresh looking, some owners will wrap them in blankets, often with a signature color and the name of the family farm. It looks, to the city dweller, as if they are uniformed and suited up for some kind of sheep football game.

The modern fair is awash with food wagons featuring fried just about anything. But if you want something that will keep you in that bygone, farm feeling, just keep walking past the wagons to the Dairy Barn. Not only can you see a huge sculpture of something (it changes every year) made out of pounds and pounds of butter, but you can get a scoop or a cone of some dairy-fresh ice cream, or a cheese sandwich that doesn't taste like it came out of a plastic wrapper.

wherethetomato isking

Tomato juice, tomato soup, tomato sauce—they all are standard fare at the annual Tomato Festival in Reynoldsburg. But you'll find some surprising and different tomato dishes, too, from fried-green tomatoes to tomato brownies.

Reynoldsburg takes special pride in the red fruit—or vegetable, depending on your point of view. You'll see the lovely red round tomato on city signs proclaiming Reynoldsburg "The Tomato Capital."

It's certain that the tomato is king during the yearly celebration as the city welcomes farmers, cooks, and tomato lovers to town to eat and compete.

The festival is generally held in the early part of September. Call (614) 866–2861 for a tomato festival update.

Fresh herbs are also available at North Market Produce.

If you want to add specialty baked goods to your table, or just nibble on a delicious snack while you shop, stop in at Benevolence, Omega Artisan Baking, or Mozart's. You can even complete your table with fresh flowers from Market Blooms or a bottle of that special wine from Grapes of Mirth.

International specialties are also within easy reach at the North Market. Flavors of India stocks a full line of Indian foods and spices. Firdous Express serves Mediterranean foods, including a line of fresh-baked goods. Sushi and Japanese groceries can be found at Nida's Sushi. China Market serves more than forty prepared Asian dishes and offers ingredients for preparing Asian at home, while Sabor Mexicano has an extensive line of Mexican spices, sauces, tortillas, and other south-of-the-border delights.

The North Market is located at 59 Spruce Street, Columbus; (614) 463–9664; www.northmarket.com. Open Monday, 9:00 A.M. to 5:00 P.M. (optional merchant day, not all businesses are open); Tuesday to Friday, 9:00 A.M. to 7:00 P.M.; Saturday, 8:00 A.M. to 5:00 P.M.; Sunday, noon to 5:00 P.M.

The North Market sits in the midst of two of Columbus's best entertainment areas, the Arena District (named for Nationwide Arena, home of the Columbus Blue Jackets NFL hockey team) and the Short North. These commercial areas and residential neighborhoods just north of the heart of downtown are loaded with great restaurants, bars, clubs, and other entertainment venues. Similarly, if you take High Street south of downtown, visitors find two other popular gathering areas, the Brewery District and German Village.

One of the city's most storied restaurants is in the heart of the Brewery District, **Handke's Cuisine.** Chef Harmut Handke uses his experience at world-class kitchens around the world—including Germany, Switzerland, Holland, Jamaica, and Barbados—to create out-of-this-world epicurean delights. The winner of thirty-eight gold medals at international culinary competitions, Handke serves up dishes such as roasted Alaskan sablefish in shiso broth with shrimp dumplings, baby bok choy, carrots, leeks, and shiitake mushrooms; sautéed free-range chicken breast with pan gravy, garnished with sautéed shiitake mushrooms, pearl onions, calamata olives, and tomato Julienne; and herb-crusted roasted rack of lamb on sautéed polenta, and beluga lentil and white bean ragout.

Handke's is set in the nineteenth-century former home of the Schlee Bavarian Brewery. The solid stone walls and rounded stone ceiling of the downstairs dining area create a unique and sophisticated environment for fine dining.

Handke's Cuisine is at 520 South Front Street, Columbus; (614) 621–2500; www.chefhandke.com. Open Monday through Friday, 5:30 to 10:00 P.M., Saturday, 5:00 to 10:00 P.M. Reservations recommended.

Columbus has more than its share of quirky and unusual museums. Offerings include the **Early Television Museum,** which features hundreds of pre-World War II American and British TV's, including mechanical televisions from the 1920s and 1930s. Other displays include a collection of antique picture tubes and early television studio production equipment and a 1930s sixty-line flying spot TV scanner camera. Visitors can see themselves as they would have appeared on a 1930s mechanical television system.

Kelton House

Your tours in the Columbus area may take you to the lovely Kelton House. This grand and charming mansion was built in 1852 and is a fine example of Greek Revival architecture. The home and its lovely Victorian garden at 586 East Town Street are now a favorite spot, not just for tours, but for special events such as wedding and anniversary celebrations.

The Junior League operates the mansion, but legend has it that the home still feels the touch of the Kelton family. Fernando Kelton built the home in the mid-1800s, and it remained in the family until 1975. The last of the Keltons to occupy the home was Fernando Kelton's granddaughter, Grace Bird Kelton. She was nationally known in her own right as an interior designer. She preserved the lovely old home's furnishing in the graceful style of her grandfather's era.

The legend surrounding Kelton House is that though Ms. Kelton passed from this world on Christmas Eve 1975, she just couldn't leave the care of the family manse to outsiders. Tales tell of the former owner returning to rearrange the furniture or move objects or just walk through the house to make sure that the current caretakers don't forget who is really in charge of this piece of Kelton family history.

The Early Television Museum is at 5396 Franklin Street, Hilliard (a suburb northwest of Columbus); (614) 771–0510; www.earlytelevision.org. Open Saturdays, 10:00 A.M. to 6:00 P.M. and Sundays, noon to 5:00 P.M. No admission charge, but donations welcome.

Ed Jeffers is Mr. Ohio Barber, with more than four decades of experience trimming locks, as well as decades of service on the Ohio Barber Board and the National Association of Barber Boards of America. In 1988, his interest in barbering history, artifacts, and memorabilia spawned the *Ed Jeffers Barber Museum,* which opened with just ten pieces. Today, it has grown to several thousand pieces dating back to the 1700s, including more than a dozen whirling barber poles, historic barber chairs, recreated barbers shops from various eras, and hundreds of centuries-old mugs and razors. Also on display are some of the gory tools of the trade from the days when barbers also served as surgeons and dentists.

The Ed Jeffers Barber Museum is at 2/12 South High Street, Canal Winchester, (614) 833–9931; www.edjeffersbarbermuseum.com. Call to schedule a tour.

Another intriguing small museum is the *Motts Military Museum* in suburban Groveport, which is dedicated to preserving the memory of all who have served in the United States military. Exhibits and artifacts span from the Revolutionary War to modern times, many associated with a particular soldier or group of soldiers. For example, the Civil War Union Coat on display was worn by a Major Thomas Henry at Gettysburg in 1863. And the Civil War Colt .44 revolver was donated to the museum by a relative of the soldier who carried it in 1860. Other exhibits include one of Columbus native Eddie Rickenbacker's medals, a World War II Landing Craft, and a corncob pipe owned by General Douglas MacArthur.

The Motts Military Museum is at 5075 South Hamilton Road, Groveport; (614) 836–1500; www.mottsmilitarymuseum.org. Open Tuesday through Saturday, 9:00 A.M. to 5:00 P.M.; Sunday, 1:00 to 5:00 P.M. Adults $5.00, students $3.00.

Gahanna has become part of the Columbus metropolitan area, but the city also has been able to preserve some of its historic structures and with them, a unique identity. Original log homes and Victorian-influenced homes and shops still grace this city core. One way to enjoy this history on a nice day is to take a walking tour around the *historic district of Gahanna.* The area was settled just after the Revolutionary War. The federal government gave away plots of land as payment to Union soldiers. John Clark formally founded the city in 1849.

You could start your tour at the *Lily Stone Bed & Breakfast* at 106 S. High Street. This building began its life as the Stone family home and was built around the year 1900. The Stone family that settled here were descendents of Thomas Stone, one of the signers of the Declaration of Independence. The

Gahanna Historical Association owns the B&B, and volunteers keep the three-guest room operation going. Almost directly across the street is the home of the city's founder, John Clark. Just to the north of the John Clark House is one of the original log homes build in the Gahanna area. This house was originally built in 1840 and was relocated to this spot by the Historical Society in 1968. If you head further north on High Street, you will find the Sanctuary. This late Gothic Revival–style building is on the National Register of Historic Places. Built as a Lutheran church in 1895, the impressive brick structure has become a popular place for wedding receptions. If you do not see a bride and groom posing for wedding photos there, you may see them at Creekside Park. Walk west on Town Street toward the river and turn south or left on Mill Street. Town Street and Granville Street bound the park, where an old mill once labored. Now a waterfall graces the former millrace. This park is one of the centerpieces of an effort to preserve and rejuvenate the historic district. Along your walk through the historic district you will find shops offering handicrafts, antiques, and other collectibles.

If you are still hankering for a little more Gahanna history, take a little drive down Johnstown road to what the locals call the "Moosesonian." While scarcely displaying the wealth or breadth of collections of the Smithsonian, the **Ohio State Moose Association Museum** will be of special interest if you, or a family

Roses Are for Romance

Romance off the beaten path could mean treating your special someone to—not a dozen roses—but hundreds of dozens! You can't pick them and take them home, but the two of you can share the sweet smell of romance as you stroll through the rose gardens of Whetstone Park in Columbus.

The park is home to ball fields and to wooded paths and ponds, but the highlight of the area is the impressive display of rose bushes, especially during the month of June, when the park hosts the rose festival. Rose fanciers love to walk among the varieties and see their favorite flowers. The casual gardener will appreciate the rows and rows of roses just for their broad spectrum of colors and light, inviting fragrance.

If you wander the Park of Roses on summer weekends, don't be surprised to see a wedding party using this as a floral background for their most romantic day. The park also hosts many concerts and poetry readings in the spring and summer months.

The poet Robert Burns wrote, " My love is like a red, red, rose . . ." The park can't guarantee love, but a romantic ramble through the roses could be a good beginning.

The rose festival is held in early to mid-June at Whetstone Park, 3293 North High Street, Columbus. Call (614) 645–6640 for information.

member, belong to the Loyal Order of Moose or the Women of the Moose. While modest, this collection of pictures, documents, and moose memorabilia is one of only two such collections in the county. Hours are limited, so plan ahead.

The Ohio State Moose Association Museum is at 335 West Johnstown Road, Gahanna; (614) 337–2200. Open Monday through Thursday, 3:00 to 6:00 P.M.; Friday and Saturday, 1:00 to 6:00 P.M. Admission: free.

The Hanby family and the work done at the **Hanby House** touched the lives of many Americans during the mid-1800s. This house, built in 1846, served as a stop on the Underground Railroad, helping slaves in their flight from the South to freedom. Benjamin Hanby was a minister, teacher, and an abolitionist.

Hanby also was famous as a composer. Among his works are "Darling Nellie Gray" and "Up on the Housetop." The Hanby House contains many family belongings, including the original printing plates for "Darling Nellie Gray" and the composer's flute.

Bishop William Hanby, Benjamin Hanby's father, was a United Brethren minister and co-founder of Otterbein College. Hanby House has been designated a United Methodist shrine.

The Hanby House is located at 160 West Main Street, Westerville; (614) 891–6289, (800) 600-6834; www.ohiohistory.org/places/hanby. Open May through September, Saturday and Sunday, 1:00 to 4:00 P.M. Admission: adults $1.50; children (ages 6 to 12) 50 cents.

Gentlemen, start your engines. That's what visitors to the **Motorcycle Hall of Fame Museum** no doubt would like to do. . . start up the many powerful and exotic bikes on display. Enshrined in the Hall of Fame are more than 200 motorcyclists who have made major contributions to the sport—from early twentieth-century racing champ Ralph Hepburn to modern-day enthusiast Jay

Hanby House

Leno. In addition to the Hall of Fame, the museum consists of three large exhibit areas.

One favorite exhibit is the Heroes of Harley-Davidson, which features many great Harley bikes. But the focus of this exhibit is the people who have built Harley-Davidson into one of the world's great commercial brands. For example, you will see a painstaking recreation of the famous Milwaukee backyard shed where William Harley and Arthur Davidson created their first motorcycle in 1903. And you'll learn about Bessie Stringfield, the 1940s African-American "Motorcycle Queen of Miami" who broke color and gender barriers as a competitive rider. Whether your interest is racing or cruising, any motor-cycle enthusiast will be in hog heaven here.

The Motorcycle Hall of Fame Museum is at 13515 Yarmouth Drive, Picker-ington; (614) 856–2222; www.motorcylemuseum.org. Open daily 9:00 A.M. to 5:00 P.M. Admission: adults $5.00; children (ages 12 to 17) $3.00.

Places to Stay in West Central Ohio

RUSSELLS POINT
Oak Island at Indian Lake
accessible only by boat from
Russells Point
(937) 843–4653

TIPP CITY
Willowtree Inn
1900 West State Route 571
(937) 667–2957

VERSAILLES
Inn at Versailles
21 West Main Street
(937) 526–3020

Places to Eat in West Central Ohio

BELLVILLE
Der Dutchman
720 State Route 97
(419) 886–7070

COLUMBUS
Handke's Cuisine
520 South Front Street
(614) 621–2500

Figlio
1369 Grandview Avenue
(614) 481–8850

Rigby's
698 High Street
(614) 461–7888

LUCAS
Malabar Inn
3645 Pleasant Valley Road
(419) 938–5205

HELPFUL WEB SITES

Northwest Ohio

Historic Plain

Surrounded by cornfields in the plains of northwest Ohio is a unique historical village—***AuGlaize Village.*** Seventeen recon-structed or restored buildings (ca. 1860 to 1920) have been gathered from the surrounding area and provide visitors with a glimpse of life a century ago in this flat farming region of the state. Self-guided tours of AuGlaize allow you to explore at your own pace.

In Dr. Cameron's office, built in 1874 in Jewell, there are old medical journals and catalogs advertising medical products such as foot and ankle braces and the "Harvard Physician's Chair" that rural doctors used for surgery, adjusting it to one of dozens of positions depending on the particular procedure to be performed. Dr. Cameron owned one of these chairs, and it is in the back room of his office.

The Chapel of Crosses Church, which the congregation of Saint John's Lutheran Church in Sherwood built in 1875, is a one-room frame structure containing an antique wooden pump organ. The Story and Clark Company of Chicago manufactured this ornately carved instrument in 1892.

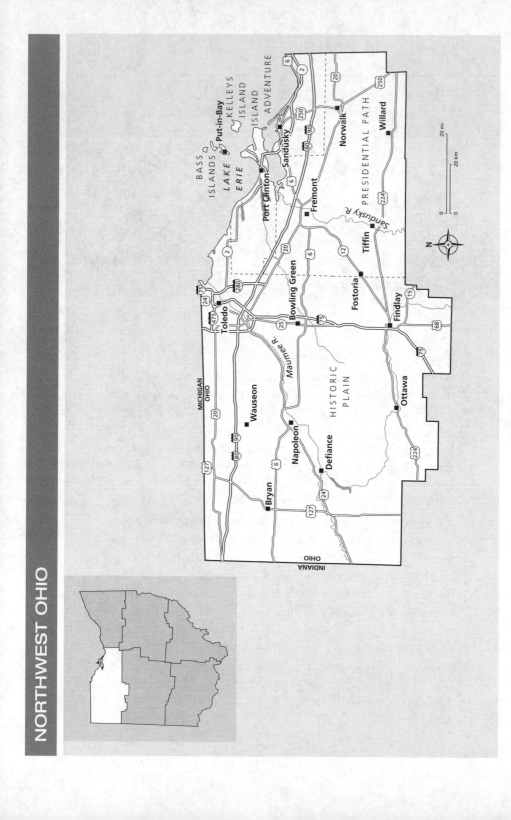

The Sherry School has textbooks from the mid-1800s, including McGuffey's *Eclectic Spelling Book,* teacher Mable Carroll's attendance records from the 1882 school year, and a student's certificate of promotion from 1896. The mailboxes in the front room of the old post office from Mark Centre still have mail in them—a 1906 copy of the *Saturday Evening Post* and a postcard dated 1899 notifying a Defiance man that he owes the Farmer Mutual Fire Protection Association another 25 cents on his insurance policy.

Other restored buildings include a completely equipped 1903 dentist's office (containing some grisly looking instruments), the Ayersville Telephone Company with its old-fashioned switchboard and telephones, a blacksmith's shop, the Minsel Barber Shop, a sawmill, a gas station, a railroad station, an operating smokehouse, and a broom factory.

AUTHORS' FAVORITES

AuGlaize Village

Fort Defiance

Independence Dam State Park

Historic Sauder Village

Barn Restaurant

Columbian House

Bluebird Passenger Train

Toledo Museum of Art

Tony Packo's Cafe

Wildwood Preserve Metropark

Fallen Timbers State Memorial

Isaac Ludwig Mill

LaRoe's Restaurant

Fort Meigs

Schedel Arboretum and Gardens

Heineman's Winery and Crystal Cave

Perry's Cave

Island House

Mon Ami Winery

Hotel Lakeside

Marblehead Lighthouse

Glacial Grooves

Cedar Point

Merry-Go-Round Museum

Wagner's 1844 Inn

Captain Montague's

Edison Birthplace Museum

Old Prague Restaurant

Inland Seas Maritime Museum

Rutherford B. Hayes Presidential Center

Crystal Traditions of Tiffin

Firelands Museum

Historic Lyme Village

Mad River & NKP Railroad Society Museum

Seneca Caverns

AuGlaize Village's two museums hold a varied collection of pioneer items. One building has an extensive assortment of antique farm implements, such as an elaborate, horse-drawn straw baler, and numerous fruit and tobacco presses.

fountaincity

Bryan was known as "Fountain City" because of its artesian wells. It all started in 1841 when Daniel Wyatt was digging a well next to his log cabin. He stopped digging at the end of one day; when he awoke the next morning, water was pouring out of the hole. Water would flow from just about any hole dug in the area, and this liquid abundance attracted settlers to Bryan.

But the spouting water was not completely a blessing. In the 1880s a New Yorker claimed the fountains violated a patent he held, and he demanded $10 from each well owner, a claim described locally as the "Great Swindle." And some of the fountains resulted in litigation, as neighbors were flooded out by the spewing discharge. The flow gradually subsided, with the last fountain petering out in 1971.

Also in the museum is a 1936 farm tractor, a 1937 four-wheel-drive tractor, and a rare 1919 Defiance Motor Company truck. This local auto and truck manufacturer assembled vehicles for six years until the company failed in 1925. For military buffs, a separate building contains military equipment and hardware, including Civil War uniforms, cannons and mortars, and a variety of pistols and muskets (including a 1763 "Brown Bess" flintlock). Model railroad enthusiasts will enjoy the building filled with small trains.

Throughout its season, AuGlaize Village hosts special events days, such as the annual Harvest Demonstration and the Johnny Appleseed Festival. Craft experts show the old-fashioned way to dip candles and weave rugs, and demonstrate other pioneer skills.

AuGlaize Village is south of U.S. Route 24 on Krouse Road, 3 miles west of Defiance; (419) 784–0107, (419) 782–7255; www.defiance-online.com/auglaize. The village is open on seven event weekends May through October 11:00 A.M. to 4:00 P.M. Admission: adults $3.00; children $1.00.

A quiet residential neighborhood in nearby Defiance is the site of a former fortification that played a significant role in this region's history. The bluff at the confluence of the Maumee and Auglaize Rivers was where General "Mad" Anthony Wayne's American troops built *Fort Defiance* in 1794. Wayne launched his campaign against the Native Americans and British in the area from this fort, which consisted of four blockhouses and a tall stockade fence around the perimeter. It was erected in five weeks, and General Wayne, admiring the completed fortification, is reported to have said, "I defy the British, the Indians, and all the devils in hell to take it!" Upon hearing that, a fellow officer suggested, "Then call it Fort Defiance."

It was from here that Wayne's forces marched against the Native Americans, defeating them at the Battle of Fallen Timbers. Two cannons, one facing each river, are all that remain of the fort today. When you stand on that hill, however, at the junction of these great rivers, the strategic importance of this spot is readily apparent.

The Fort Defiance Memorial is at the end of Washington Avenue in Defiance. It is open daylight hours, and no admission is charged.

East of Defiance in nearby Independence is another historic site. *Independence Dam State Park* is a long, narrow green space between the swift Maumee River and a now-idle section of the old Miami and Erie Canal. This canal, which was built between the 1820s and the 1840s, connected Toledo (and Lake Erie) with Cincinnati (and the Ohio River). As part of the canal construction boom in Ohio early in the nineteenth century, the Miami and Erie provided cheap transportation for goods and new settlers, stimulating the economic development of the region. Nevertheless, by as early as the 1850s, the speed and flexibility of the railroad signaled the beginning of the end of the canal era.

Independence Dam was built to divert water from the river to the canal, and this section of the Miami and Erie holds water to this day. The massive wooden gates of Lock 13 at the entrance to the park are the only such gates still in existence on this canal. In sharp contrast to the boom years, today the banks are overgrown, and the former towpaths have been erased by time.

Visitors to the park can take advantage of the hiking trails, picnic areas, and primitive campsites. Fishing and boating are popular on the wide Maumee River, and the park has boat-launching ramps.

Independence Dam State Park is at 27722 Route 424, 3 miles east of Defiance; (419) 237–1503; www.dnr.state.oh.us/parks/parks/indpndam.htm. Open year-round, no admission charge.

Erie J. Sauder always had an interest in the history of northwest Ohio. First he collected antique woodworking tools to display for his customers at the Sauder Woodworking Company. From woodworking equipment, his collection expanded to include farm tools and household items used in this section of the state in the late 1800s. These were the humble beginnings of the *Historic Sauder Village* near Archbold. This part of the state was one of the last to be settled because of the 2,000-square-mile Black Swamp. Only after massive drainage and land reclamation in the 1850s was this unhealthy muck transformed into fertile farmland.

Historic Sauder Village is a well-organized, carefully presented living museum. The village actually consists of three major areas: the restored farmstead, the pioneer craft village, and the museum.

Period pieces furnish the farmhouse, which was built in 1860. Wood cooking and heating stoves, rope-spring beds, and a wooden pump organ are typical of the items found in the two-story home. Costumed guides in each room explain the history and demonstrate the utility of the furnishings and equipment—how to use a hand-crank apple peeler, for instance. The last stop on the farmhouse tour is the root cellar, where the farm family stored its fruits and vegetables during the winter months. Horses, sheep, turkeys, ducks, geese, and chickens roam the farmyard.

The craft village consists of a cluster of rustic buildings set in a circle, each housing an expert in a particular craft. Brooms are made the old-fashioned way in the broom shop and are available for purchase, while the blacksmith busily forges candleholders, ladles, gates, and railings. One of the most popular shops belongs to Mark Matthews, the village glassblower. Taking 2,000° F glass from the bottom of the furnace, Mark adds color chips to the clear glass, then blows and hand shapes the soft, hot glass into beautiful spheres and paperweights. As with the other craftspeople in the village, Mark explains each step of the process. Other craft demonstrations at Sauder include woodworking and pottery. The village also has a copper, a spinner, a weaver, a tinsmith, and a basketmaker who demonstrate their crafts.

The village museum contains an impressive collection of tools, machinery, and household items used by early settlers in this region. A large number of old farm wagons, buggies, and carts are on display, as are farm craft tools, such as woodworking tools, and farm implements, including an 1886 potato digger and an 1860 cultivator. The museum's Conestoga wagon, first designed in 1755 in Conestoga Valley, Pennsylvania, once transported newcomers to the area. Countless meat grinders, butter churns, wood-burning stoves, and foot-powered sewing machines fill this vast exhibit space. A quilting demonstration also takes place there. If you need more time to see it all, spend the night at the thirty-five-room Sauder Heritage Inn, or in the thirty-seven-site campground, and make it a two-day visit.

Historic Sauder Village is located at 22611 Route 2, northeast of Archbold; (419) 446–2541, (800) 590–9755; www.saudervillage.org. Open May through October, Tuesday through Saturday, 10:00 A.M. to 5:00 P.M.; Sunday, noon to 4:00 P.M. Admission: adults $12.00; children (ages 6 to 16) $6.00. MasterCard and Visa are accepted.

If you have worked up an appetite touring the Historic Sauder Village, stop in next door at the ***Barn Restaurant.*** This restaurant is housed in an actual poplar barn, which was originally built 2 miles northeast of its present location in 1861. Sauder saved the barn from being razed and had it moved in 1974.

Country cooking is the order of the day at this restaurant, which serves family-style dinners of chicken, ham, and beef. Menu items include a selection of steaks, shrimp, and perch. The menu also offers a variety of sandwiches and salads. There are always two fresh soups warming in the large pots, including unusual ones such as Kneppley soup—a ham broth with dough drops. A generous salad bar is loaded with just about every type of salad imaginable, plus a myriad of salad fixings.

The exposed rough beams of this structure, the antique farm implements mounted on the walls, and the period costumes worn by the waitresses all enhance the rustic atmosphere of the Barn Restaurant. All breads and pastries at the restaurant are made fresh daily at the Doughbox bakery, which is next door.

The Barn Restaurant is at Sauder Village on Route 2, northeast of Archbold; (419) 445–2231, (800) 590–9755; www.saudervillage.org. Open Monday through Saturday, 11:00 A.M. to 8:00 P.M.; Sunday buffet, 11:00 A.M. to 2:00 P.M. (The Doughbox bakery is open Monday through Saturday, 7:00 A.M. to 5:00 P.M.) MasterCard and Visa are accepted.

A walk along the trails in *Goll Woods State Nature Preserve* takes you through the best living example of the Great Black Swamp forest that covered much of this region of post-glacial lake plains,

florida, in ohio?

The town of Florida may or may not be on the site of a Native American village named Snaketown. The tribe of Shawnee Chief Captain Snake did occupy a village in this part of the state from about 1786 until 1794, when confronted by the army of General "Mad" Anthony Wayne. But was it where Florida stands today? An archaeological dig in 1984 sponsored by the Ohio Humanities Council attempted to answer this question, with mixed results. Although the dig did uncover arrowheads, animal bones, and a 40-foot canalboat, no conclusive evidence of Snaketown was discovered. One thing is certain: jokes about the name Florida, especially during an Ohio winter, are guaranteed.

located to the south and west of Lake Erie. Native American people and settlers tended to avoid this swampy area, as the old-growth forest combined with the swampy floor imbued the area with a certain eerie and foreboding atmosphere. The Great Black Swamp is one of the few remaining virgin, old-growth forests in the state, with some trees estimated to be 400 years old. This area of swamp forest and wetlands was part of the Goll family farm from the early 1800s. The state purchased the land from the family in the 1960s to preserve this rare and well-preserved piece of Ohio's natural history and the preserve was opened to the public in 1975. The pioneer-era cemetery of the Goll family remains as part of the park.

In the approximately forty-acre forest, white oaks, chinquapin oaks, burr oaks, and cottonwoods create a magnificent canopy in the warmer months, and some have trunks more than 4 feet in diameter. Ohio Department of Natural

Resource officials estimated that one crusty burr oak might be 500 years old. You can also find specimens of big tooth aspen, rock elm, black gum, black maple, dogwood, ironwood, bitternut, and pignut hickory trees. Though many of these giant trees remain in this 321-acre preserve, gone are the population of wolves, beaver, bobcats, cougars, black bear, and elk that once found a home in the preserve. Along with the forest, this natural area also has swamp meadows. This forest and wetland provides a refuge for many animals, including deer, red-tailed fox, and squirrels, and many species of birds, including the red-headed woodpecker, barred owl, scarlet tanager, and the rose-breasted grosbeak. Besides being a popular haunt for birders, the preserve attracts wildflower enthusiasts who visit each spring looking for a glimpse of spotted coralroot or three-bird orchids.

The preserve also boasts a wide array of amphibians, such as salamanders, turtles, and frogs, and is a bit too well known for mosquitoes. While summer brings warmer weather and the magnificent tree canopy, it also brings swarms of mosquitoes. If you are interested in hiking and exploring the preserve, consider an early spring visit, before the mosquitoes hatch. If you come later, be warned to slather on a good coating of strong repellent.

There are roughly 3 miles of trails through the preserve. Trailheads can be found off the main parking lot. The Burr Oak trail is the most popular and is about 1 mile long.

Goll Woods State Nature Preserve is north and west of the city of Archbold; www.ohiodnr.com/dnap/location/goll_woods.html. From Archbold, go north on Route 66 for 1.5 miles to Township Road F, go west for 3 miles to the junction with Township Road 26, then go south about one-quarter of a mile to the preserve parking lot located on the east side of the road. Open sunrise to sunset daily.

The Maumee River town of Waterville has a fine restaurant in a historic three-story building—the *Columbian House.* Painted yellow with white trim, the Columbian House was built as a hotel and tavern in 1828 by John Pray, the founder of Waterville. He insisted on black walnut for all the doors and woodwork in his hotel, which served as the center of activity in Waterville for decades. (There was even a jail on the second floor at one time, used to hold prisoners being brought to the courthouse in Maumee.) The third-floor ballroom measures 20 feet by 60 feet and has fourteen carved poplar windows and a 2-inch-thick white ash floor.

The first part of the twentieth century was not kind to the Columbian House, and the inn was even abandoned for a time. In 1927, however, a Toledo antiques dealer bought the building and began restoration. The next owner, the late Ethel Arnold of Findlay, purchased the structure in 1943 and, after further restoration,

Columbian House

opened it as a restaurant in 1948. Tom and Peggy Parker now operate the Columbian House, which is listed on the National Register of Historic Places.

A large fireplace dominates the entry room, which is furnished with comfortable period pieces. This room has the dark hardwood floors found on the entire first floor, and handsome antiques are scattered throughout. Each of the candlelit downstairs dining rooms has its own color scheme—in one, cool greens; in another, pale reds. The second-floor bedrooms of this former inn, while not available for lodging, are handsomely furnished and left open for visitors to admire.

After your favorite cocktail, it's time to choose from the offerings on the dinner menu, which include roast chicken and dressing, roast pork, your choice of steaks, and roast prime rib. Seafood lovers can select shrimp curry over rice, stuffed orange roughy, or Lake Erie walleye (in season), among others. Along with vegetables, potatoes, tossed salad, and fresh bread, a tasty side dish is also available—the Columbian House tomato pudding. This unusual treat is a sweet tomato concoction, served warm.

A dozen different desserts, including brownies a la mode and strawberries with homemade meringue, tempt those still hungry after the generous entrees. Sunday brunch features roast chicken, pork, beef, and quiche.

The Columbian House is at 3 North River Road in Waterville; (419) 878–3006. Open Tuesday through Saturday, 5:00 to 9:00 P.M.; Sunday, 11:30 A.M. to 2:00 P.M. Visa and MasterCard are accepted.

If you are traveling in Northwest Ohio from the spring to early fall, a visit to the ***Butterfly House in Whitehouse*** could provide a colorful addition to

WORTH SEEING

Toledo Zoo

Toledo Museum of Art

COSI, Center of Science and Industry,
Toledo

Maumee Bay State Park,
Oregon

the day's travels. More than 500 butterflies waft around this indoor environment to the delight of the visitor. The broad range of North and South American and Asian butterflies and moths appear like little flying jewels, with colors ranging from a striking cobalt blue to sunny yellows. Generally around fifty different species play hide-and-seek with the visitors to the butterfly house.

The indoor greenhouse provides an enjoyable environment for people as well as these showy insects. Feeders, filled with sugar water, are a popular gathering point for the colorful insects. A variety of plants and an indoor water feature provide a relaxing setting as you try to spot as many of the species as you can.

There are special programs, presentations, and events that highlight the life cycle, migration, and other facets of butterfly life, so you might want to check the Web site below for dates and times. One very special event takes place in September when hundreds of locally raised Monarch butterflies are released into the wild to begin their fall migration to Mexico.

The Butterfly House in Whitehouse is located at 11455 Obee Road, Whitehouse; (419) 877–2733; www.butterfly-house.com. Open May 1 to September 30; Monday through Saturday, 10:00 A.M. to 5:00 P.M.; Sunday, noon to 5:00 P.M. Admission: adults $6.00, children (ages 5 to 12) $4.50.

Before or after your meal at the Columbian House, you may want to take a scenic train ride that rolls along the tracks of the famed "Nickel Plate Road"— tracks of the Toledo, Lake Erie & Western Railway. The ***Bluebird Passenger Train*** meanders through the Ohio countryside and across a magnificent 900-foot bridge over the Maumee River at Grand Rapids. Train cars on display at the Waterville station include a Baldwin 0-6-0 switcher, a 1908 Porter saddletank switcher, a 1946 Pullman sleeper, and a World War II Pullman troop sleeper.

The Bluebird Passenger Train is operated by the Toledo, Lake Erie & Western Railway and Museum, a nonprofit group dedicated to the preservation and operation of railroad equipment. For information, write Box 168, Waterville 43566; (866) 63–TRAIN, (419) 878–2177; www.tlew.org. The train operates weekends, May through October, with some scheduled weekday runs in summer. Group reservations are accepted, and are recommended in October when the leaves are colorful.

One of the finest art museums in the United States is in Toledo—the **Toledo Museum of Art.** Founded in 1901, the museum is a privately endowed nonprofit arts institution with extensive collections of glass, American and European paintings, sculpture, decorative arts, and graphic arts.

In an hour or a day, browse and discover treasures from ancient Egypt, Greece, and Rome; riches within a medieval cloister; and the splendors of a room from a French château. Marvel at great works by such masters as El Greco, Rubens, Rembrandt, Gainsborough, Turner, van Gogh, Degas, Monet, Matisse, Picasso, Remington, Hopper, and Nevelson.

The Toledo Museum of Art is at 2445 Monroe Street, Toledo; (419) 255–8000, (800) 644–6862; www.toledomuseum.org. Open Tuesday through Thursday and Saturday, 10:00 A.M. to 4:00 P.M.; Friday, 10:00 A.M. to 10:00 P.M.; Sunday, 11:00 A.M. to 5:00 P.M. No admission charge.

The first Libbey Glass factory was founded in Cambridge, Massachusetts, in 1818, a long way from Toledo. But abundant natural gas lured the factory to Toledo seventy years later, helping to make Toledo the "glass capital of the world." Long a pioneer in the development of modern glassmaking, Libbey Glass made its mark internationally in 1893, when the company constructed a house completely built of glass for the World's Columbian Exhibition in Chicago. Many of the other pieces created specifically for the exhibition are now displayed at the Toledo Museum of Art.

But it's not art that draws crowds to the **Libbey Glass Outlet,** rather its bargains. Here you will find stemware, fountain ware, tumblers and mugs, plates and bowls, canisters and ashtrays, plus L.E. Smith handcrafted glassware, all at factory outlet prices.

The Libbey Glass Outlet is at 205 South Erie Street, Toledo; (419) 254–5000, 254–5012. Open Monday through Friday, 9:30 A.M. to 5:30 P.M.; Saturday, 8:00 A.M. to 5:00 P.M.; Sunday, 10:00 A.M. to 5:00 P.M.

Tony Packo's Hungarian hot dogs have been scarfed down by Toledoans for more than seventy years. Billing itself as the place "where man bites dog," **Tony Packo's Cafe** was made famous outside Toledo by Jamie Farr, who, as *M*A*S*H*'s Corporal Klinger, yearned for the spicy food of his favorite hometown eatery.

Farr and other celebrity visitors to Tony Packo's engage in a local tradition—signing a hot dog bun, which is then mounted and displayed for all to enjoy. In addition to hot dogs, diners find spicy pickles and peppers, steaming hand-rolled stuffed cabbage, spicy chili, Hungarian hamburgers, and homemade chicken soup with Hungarian dumplings.

Tony Packo's Cafe is at 1902 Front Street, Toledo; (419) 691–6054; www.tonypackos.com. Open Monday through Thursday, 11:00 A.M. to 10:00 P.M.; Friday and Saturday, 11:00 A.M. to 11:00 P.M.; Sunday, noon to 9:00 P.M.

If you have a chance to visit the International Park of Greater Toledo, you can take a boat ride back into history. The **SS Willis B. Boyer** is a lake freighter that has been painstakingly restored after its sixty-nine years of service in the Great Lakes.

The SS *Willis B. Boyer* was built in 1911 and nicknamed the "Queen of the Great Lakes." Since 1987 she has been open to the public as a living museum. On board you will visit the impressive engine room to see how the ship was powered or visit the galley—to see how the sailors were powered. The officers' mess hall gives you a good idea of the finer things afforded to the ranking officers onboard. Additional displays of artifacts, photographs, and memorabilia of the times are provided by the Western Lake Erie Historical Society.

The SS *Willis B. Boyer* is in the International Park of Greater Toledo, 26 Main Street, Toledo; (419) 936–3070; www.willisbboyer.org. Open daily May through October, Monday through Saturday, 10:00 A.M. to 5:00 P.M.; Sunday, noon to 5:00 P.M. (No tickets sold after 4:00 P.M.); November through April open Wednesday through Sunday by appointment only; closed the month of January, holidays, and the last week of December. Admission: adults $6.00; children (under 16) $4.00.

Lucas County also is the location of one of the state's most scenic parks— **Wildwood Preserve Metropark.** These 500-plus acres of lush natural beauty, with hardwood forests, ravines, meadows, and the serene Ottawa River, contain wildlife such as deer, fox, mink, muskrat, opossum, and raccoon. Owls, hawks, and pheasant nest here, and wildflowers such as bittercress, buttercups, and wild hyacinth are abundant.

The five primary hiking trails allow visitors to explore the high ridge and the cottonwood and sycamore trees in the river floodplain. The prairie trail leads hikers through one of the last tallgrass prairie remnants in the state, where some of the grasses reach a height of 10 feet. The newest area features a boardwalk trail, a covered bridge, and a historic one-room schoolhouse.

The elegant Manor House, a Georgian Colonial brick mansion, is nestled in a clearing and surrounded by deep, cool woods. This stately former residence has twenty-two rooms, with tours offered Wednesday through Sunday from noon to 5:00 P.M. Other facilities in the park include picnic tables, barbecue grills, shelter houses, and playground equipment.

Wildwood Preserve Metropark is at 5100 West Central Avenue (Route 120), east of Interstate 475 and west of downtown Toledo 43615; (419) 407–9720,

(419) 407–9701, (419) 407–9700; www.metroparkstoledo.com/metroparks/wild-wood. Open daily, 7:00 A.M. to dark; no admission charge.

The desire to preserve and honor the traditions and memorabilia from a century and a half of service in a proud profession led to the creation of the **Toledo Firefighters Museum.** This museum is only open on Saturday afternoons, so plan ahead if you want to visit the 1920s-vintage firehouse, Old Station Number 18. The impetus for starting this historical center was to have a permanent home for "Neptune." Neptune is the nickname for a wooden hand pumper that was shipped to the city of Toledo via the Erie Canal. The museum also displays a range of historic firefighting equipment from equipment used by the first bucket brigades to an 1895 Ahrens Steamer, a 1929 Pirch Pumper, a 1936 Schecht ladder track, and a 1948 Buffalo Pumper. One particularly striking and romantic vehicle is the horse-drawn steamer, a shiny red, black, and brass wagon. Also red, and quite rare, is the more modern and utilitarian-looking 1969 Willey's Fire Jeep. The story of more than 150 years of Toledo firefighting also is told in timelines, newspaper stories, pictures, toys, vintage uniforms, and historic documents. The center also helps to educate children about fire emergencies. One display replicates a child's bedroom. Fire prevention bureau staff uses this area to help children role play and learn how to react if a fire were to break out.

The Toledo Firefighters Museum is at 918 West Sylvania Avenue, Toledo; (419) 478–3473; www.toledofiremuseum.com. Open Saturday, 1:00 to 4:00 P.M. Admission: free.

Part of the Toledo area Metropark system, **Oak Openings Preserve** encompasses nearly 4,000 acres. The preserve has been hailed by the Nature Conservancy as one of the "200 last great places on earth." Oak Openings is basically a huge beach that once bordered a lake, but a lake that has long since receded into history. As the huge glaciers moved across Ohio, they created these glacial lakes and thick sandy beaches along their shores. This thick sand now creates an unusual natural area that provides a home to many plant and animal species.

The preserve area is so large that it is a good idea to start off your explorations at the Buehner Nature Center, where you can get an overview of the history of the area through interactive displays. After learning about the formation and current importance of this region for wildlife, you can use the center's maps and information to plot your strategy for exploring the preserve. The park offers more than 50 miles of trails ranging in length from about ½ mile to more than 17 miles. Many trailheads are easy to access from the nature center and their names suggest the varied habitats you can experience. Enjoy a hike on the Ridge Trail (2.5 miles), the Horseshoe Lake Trail (1.5 miles), the Sand

Bowling Green Ghost

Those attending a theater production at Bowling Green State University may, according to university legend, meet the theater department's resident ghost—Alice.

This ghost is Ohio's version of *Phantom of the Opera,* for Alice must, according to the superstitious, be invited to every theater performance. This must be a formal invitation issued by the stage manager, who must be alone on stage. If Alice is not consulted or not thanked after the performance, actors report that Alice is given to shows of temper, such as knocking over set pieces.

Just who Alice is—or was—also is a matter of legend. According to one of the most popular stories, Alice was a Bowling Green student and a budding actress. She was on her way to the theater to receive an honor as "Actress of the Year," but was killed in a car crash before collecting her prize. Another tale is that she actually was killed in the theater when a falling object cut short her performance as Desdemona in Shakespeare's *Othello.*

Those students and staff who have communed with Alice say she sometimes appears as a shadowy figure with long, flowing hair. She also has returned in full costume when *Othello* is being performed, perhaps to finish the performance that she began so many years ago. So, if you attend a Bowling Green State University theater production, just be warned—there is always the possibility of a very special guest appearance by the famous Alice!

Dunes Trail (1.7 miles), the Ferns and Lakes Trail (blue) (2.9 miles), the Lake Circuit Trail (0.6 mile), or the Evergreen Trail (1.9 miles). Some trails are designated for bikes, and there are 26 miles of horse trails too. Cross-county skiing is also permitted on all trails in the winter.

Throughout much of the preserve, it is easy to see the sandy beaches and sand dunes. There are also other types of habitats, such as wetland areas, savannahs, and prairie. Between the sand and the wetland conditions, it is difficult for large trees to take root. Settlers nicknamed the region "Oak Openings" because the soil conditions were such that trees grew far apart here so it was easy to find openings through which to drive wagons.

The preserve provides a haven for many rare and endangered species. Moths and butterflies, such as Edward's hairstreak—brown with touches of blue and orange—and the brown Persius dusky wing have been spotted here. Exotic plant species found in the dunes and oak savannah areas include the strange looking and rain-loving earth star (fungi) as well as sand cherry bushes, prickly pear cactus, and goats rue, which was once employed as a medicine to fight the plague. As you walk the dune, you might spot a glimpse of red as a scarlet tanager flies by. Bluebirds, indigo buntings, and whippoorwills make the preserve their home and migrating songbirds use the wetlands as a refueling stop on their annual journeys north and south. In the wetlands and prairie areas, look for spotted turtles as well as a host of interesting plant species. In late summer the yellow sneezeweed, with yellow petals surrounded a huge center, will be in bloom. Always worth the hunt for the enthusiast of the exotic are the bug-digesting sundews. The grass pink orchids and the fringed orchids are delicate additions to this landscape, but the wildflower photographer will find plenty of other subjects with coneflowers, asters, and a host of others dotting the somewhat soggy ground.

Oak Openings Preserve is located at 4139 Girdham Road, Swanton; (419) 407–9747; www.metroparkstoledo.com/metroparks/oakopenings. Open daily 7:00 A.M. to one hour after sunset. Admission: free.

On August 20, 1794, General "Mad" Anthony Wayne's army engaged a Native American war party led by Chief Little Turtle at the battleground known as Fallen Timbers, so called because a tornado felled a grove of trees here. *Fallen Timbers State Memorial* is today, two centuries after the battle, a peaceful reminder of that pivotal conflict—a conflict that shaped the future of Ohio's settlement by whites from the East. Wayne's defeat of the natives here, on a bluff above the north bank of the Maumee River, led to the signing of the Treaty of Greenville in 1795, under which the Native Americans surrendered their claims to most of Ohio.

Turkey Foot Rock, a large boulder at Fallen Timbers, is the subject of native lore. According to legend, Chief Turkey Foot of the Ottawa tribe stood at this rock to rally his warriors against General Wayne's troops. The chief was later killed on this spot, and for years after the battle, Ottawa braves would come to Turkey Foot Rock and offer tobacco to the Great Spirit for their deceased leader.

Fallen Timbers State Memorial is on U.S. Route 24, west of Maumee; (419) 535–3050, (800) 860–0149; www.ohiohistory.org/places/fallen. Open daylight hours; no admission charge.

A friendly rivalry between Gilead (now Grand Rapids) and Providence— just across the Maumee River—lasted for generations. The Howard family settled at the site of Grand Rapids in 1822, attracted to the location by its great natural beauty and the potential for commerce, thanks to the river.

On the other side of the Maumee, Peter Manor constructed a sawmill in 1822, and Providence took an early lead as the center of development for the area. That original sawmill was razed to make room for the Miami and Erie Canal.

In 1865 a much larger mill went up, and 140 years later, the *Isaac Ludwig Mill* still operates, if only for demonstration purposes. Most of the mill's equipment is more than 75 years old, and some dates back to pre–Civil War

TOP ANNUAL EVENTS

Maumee Valley Walleye Weekend,
Perrysburg and Maumee, March;
www.dnr.ohio.gov

Maple Sugaring Festival,
Toledo, April;
(419) 841–1007;
www.toledoohio.com/Events.html

International Migratory Bird Day,
Oak Harbor, May;
(419) 898–4070;
www.ohiodnr.com

Historic Port Clinton Walleye Fest,
Port Clinton, May;
(419) 573–9370;
www.walleyefestival.com

Put-in-Bay Pooch Parade,
Put-in-Bay, June;
http://put-in-bay.com/calendars/
2006calendar.html

Annual Founder's Day Celebration,
Put-in-Bay, June;
www.put-in-bay.com

Crosby Festival of the Arts,
Toledo, June;
(419) 936–2986;
www.toledogarden.org

Lagrange Street Polish Festival,
Toledo, July;
(419) 255–8406;
www.polishfestival.org

Oak Ridge Festival,
Attica, July and October;
www.oakridgefestival.com

Civil War Days,
Defiance, July;
(419) 784–0107, (419) 782–7255;
www.defiance-online.com/auglaize

Celebrate Summer!,
Marblehead, August;
(419) 734–4424, ext. 2;
www.lake-erie.com/2006calendarof
events.shtml

Great Lakes Wooden Sailboat Regatta,
Sandusky, August;
www.geocities.com/glwss/home.html

days. River water diverted to a canal falls through two turbines, creating a combined force of 230 horsepower.

The canal era in this part of Ohio peaked in the 1850s, and when the railroad arrived here, it arrived in Gilead, renamed Grand Rapids, shifting commerce back across the river. An 1848 fire nearly wiped out Providence, and the great cholera epidemic of 1854 took a particularly heavy toll on the town, which today consists of only the mill, a church a building that once served as a hotel for Canal Travelers, and a lone home.

Although the Isaac Ludwig Mill survived the fire of 1848, a blaze a century later, in 1940, destroyed the top floors of this historic structure. The mill bears the name of its second owner, who acquired it in 1865. Isaac Ludwig died in 1906 and is buried in the township cemetery at Mount Pleasant.

Maumee Summer Fair,
Maumee, August;
(419) 794–1090;
www.maumeesummerfair.com

**National Tractor Pulling
Championships,**
Bowling Green, August;
(888) 385–7855;
www.pulltown.com/main.htm

Milan Melon Festival,
Milan, September, Labor Day Weekend;
 (419) 499–2766, (419) 668–5231;
www.accnorwalk.com/MelonFestival

Hancock Heritage Days,
Finley; September;
(419) 423–4433;
www.campvance.com

Annual Flat Rock Creek Fall Festival,
Paulding, September;
(419) 399–4453;
www.pauldingchamber.com/what_to_
see_and_do.htm

**Tiffin Seneca County Living History
Festival,**
Tiffin, September;
(419) 447–5866;
www.tiffinfestival.com

Johnny Appleseed Festival,
Defiance, October;
(419) 784–0107, (419) 782–7255;
www.defiance-online.com/auglaize

Settlers Day,
Milan, October;
(419) 499–9004;
www.milanhistory.org/calendar.html

White Christmas by the River,
Maumee, mid-November to December;
(419) 893–9602;
www.maumee.org/recreation/wolcott
%20calendar%20blk.htm

Carefully restored and listed on the National Register of Historic Places, Isaac Ludwig Mill today offers a glimpse of Ohio's past. The mill produced flour, meal, and livestock feed commercially until the 1940 fire, and it continues to grind corn into cornmeal and wheat into flour as it has for decades. Visitors not only observe the art of water-powered milling, but also may purchase the results. Water power also drives drills and saws and demonstrations of lumber being cut. The canalboat the *Volunteer* transports visitors through a restored 1-mile stretch of the orginal canal, including Lock 44.

Isaac Ludwig Mill is on U.S. Route 24 at Route 578, across the Maumee River from Grand Rapids; (419) 407–9741; www.metroparkstoledo.com/metro parks/providence. Open May through October, Wednesday through Friday, 10:00 A.M. to 2:00 P.M. (4:00 P.M. in the summer); weekends, noon to 4:00 P.M.

No admission charge to the mill. Canalboat rides: adults $6.00; children (ages 2 to 12) $3.00.

After your mill tour, come across the river to charming Grand Rapids, a town that has overcome considerable adversity. Fire has destroyed nearly every building at one time or another during its century-and-a-half history, and spring flooding has done serious damage, especially the floods of 1903 and 1913. As recently as 1957, floodwaters filled downtown in a mere five minutes, sending residents scrambling to rooftops.

blanchardriver inspiration

"Down by the Old Mill Stream," Tell Taylor's famous song, was inspired by the Blanchard River. Taylor was born in nearby Vanlue and grew up in Findlay. He moved to New York City in 1897, opening one of Tin Pan Alley's first music publishing houses. During a visit home in 1908, Taylor spent some time along the Blanchard at the Misamore mill. It was this visit that inspired the song, published in 1910. Taylor returned to Findlay for good in 1922 and is buried along the river he made famous.

Serious restoration of Grand Rapids began in 1975, and what started slowly has picked up momentum, with most structures now in pristine condition. Special events throughout the year, from the spring flood watch, which attracts thousands to view the surging power of the scenic Maumee, to the October Applebutter Fest, add to the town's interest. Intriguing shops line both sides of Front Street.

LaRoe's Restaurant serves hearty food and relaxing drinks in its restaurant and tavern year-round. Housed in a building dating from the 1890s, this eye- and appetite-pleasing establishment is a local favorite. Tiffany lamps, hanging plants, bentwood chairs, and exposed brick walls create a nostalgic atmosphere. The works of artist Bill Kuhlman, who grew up here and now lives in Whitehouse, Ohio, adorn the walls of the restaurant and tavern. Kuhlman uses oil, pencil, chalk, and watercolor to produce his renderings of past and current residents of the area. And in a town so dominated by a river and its many floods, we suppose it's not surprising to find that the tavern features water-level indicators from some of the floods that have filled the place—water was 4 feet deep in here in 1959!

Owner David LaRoe presents casual dining and straightforward recipes at his eatery. A wide selection of soups, sandwiches, and salads awaits hungry explorers, as do dinners ranging from country ribs and steaks to fettucine Alfredo and blackened redfish.

LaRoe's is at 24138 Front Street, Grand Rapids; (419) 832–3082. Open for lunch and dinner seven days a week, plus Sunday brunch.

Standing in the Grand Battery of *Fort Meigs,* with its three twelve-pounder cannons aimed across the Maumee River, you can almost hear the blast of cannon fire and feel the rain of falling earth and timber from shells exploding nearby. The fort was under siege for nine days and nights in May 1813, but the American forces in the fort held off the British attack and repelled them again when the British launched a second invasion three months later.

Ohio's role in the War of 1812 is not given much space in the history books, but the American forces, commanded by General William Henry Harrison, twice turned back British offensives at the fort that Harrison named for Ohio's governor at the time, Return Jonathan Meigs. Harrison's forces constructed the fort in early February 1813, and this fortification became the base for 3,000 troops. On April 28, British forces began to construct a camp and gun batteries opposite Fort Meigs; four batteries across the river and two east of the fort. The British siege began May 1, 1813, and lasted until May 9.

The entire Fort Meigs fortification has been carefully reconstructed, including the seven blockhouses and the 2,000-yard stockade wall. A flat-topped mound of earth built against the inside of the wall forms a banquette (or firing step), where the soldiers stood to fire musket rounds at the invaders attacking the ten-acre fort. Some of the blockhouses contain museums describing the history of the battles here, while others contain twelve-pounder cannons as they did in May 1813. Signs aid visitors taking a self-guided tour of the fort by explaining the significance of various locations inside the stockade. On weekends, costumed soldiers set up camp at Fort Meigs, further enhancing the sensation that one has stepped back in time to the early nineteenth century. Just outside the stockade walls are picnic tables and barbecue grills.

Fort Meigs is at 29100 West River Road, on Route 65 west of the intersection with Route 25, in Perrysburg; (419) 874–4121, (800) 283–8916; www.ohio history.org/places/ftmeigs. Open April through October, Wednesday through

Fort Meigs

Saturday, 9:30 A.M. to 5:00 P.M.; Sunday, noon to 5:00 P.M. Admission: adults $7.00; children (ages 6 to 12) $3.00.

You can step back into the early 1800s as you visit the **Wolcott House Museum Complex.** James Wolcott and his wife, Mary, a Miami Indian, boarded a dugout canoe and followed the Maumee River down to the foot of the rapids at Maumee City. This part of Ohio was becoming an important shipping point and offered entrepreneurs like Wolcott an opportunity to build a business. Wolcott built warehouses and steamships to transport merchandise during an era of bustling lake and canal trade.

James and Mary also purchased 300 acres of land to build their impressive home, which is a blend of classic and Federal architecture. As you stroll through the museum complex, you can visit this home and also a 1840s salt-box-style farmhouse, a log home, a country church, a Greek Revival-style home from the mid-1800s, and a railroad depot complete with caboose and boxcar. If you have a chance to call ahead, ask about special events. Throughout the year the complex plans craft classes for children and festivals to tempt all members of the family out on the lawns for some old-fashioned fun.

The Wolcott House Museum Complex is at 1031 River Road, Maumee; (419) 893–9602; www.maumee.org/recreation/wolcott.htm. Open Thursday through Sunday; guided tours at 12:30 and 2:30 P.M. Admission: adults $5.00; students $2.50.

As you are driving around Wood County, you just might pass part of the **Snook's Dream Cars Automobile Museum** out on the open road. Bill Snook and his son Jeff are the curators of the museum and since they keep all the "exhibits" in working condition, they just can't help occasionally taking one of the vintage cars for a spin.

This is a living museum where vintage cars are not only displayed but also repaired. The Snooks have re-created a 1940s-era Texaco station, complete with service bays and a variety of the pieces and parts you would have seen on display in a pre-war filling station. There is also an interesting collection of promotional items that would have delighted customers asking for a fill-up some sixty years ago. A collection of coin-operated games will please the children (and the adult children as well).

The cars in the collection cover the 1930s to the 1960s. You will see coupes, convertibles, sedans, roadsters and racecars. American carmakers from the past and present are represented, such as Cadillac, Ford, Chevrolet, Buick, Pontiac, Packard, Kaiser, as well as some foreign dream cars, among them models from Jaguar, Triumph, MG, and Lotus.

Snook's Dream Cars Automobile Museum is at 13920 County Home Road, Bowling Green; (419) 353–8338; www.snooksdreamcars.com. Open daily, 11:00 A.M. to 4:00 P.M. Admission: adults $5.00; children $3.00.

Island Adventure

Gardens, especially traditional Japanese gardens, are havens for contemplation and peace. The **Schedel Arboretum and Gardens** welcomes guests into such a quiet place. An extensive seventeen-acre arboretum surrounds a gracious home that was formerly the residence of Joseph and Marie Schedel.

The home, built in 1882, and the gardens were the beneficiary of the Schedels' loving attention and now serve as their living memorial. They created a foundation to support the home and grounds after their deaths in the 1980s. The home features many unusual items purchased by the couple on their world travels. These include Japanese silk embroideries, Persian rugs, and a Hereke silk prayer rug, as well as carved antique jade and bronze pieces that are more than 3,000 years old.

The grounds are home to a wide variety of native and exotic plant life. The Japanese garden tends to draw the visitor's attention to its stone lanterns, bridges, and a stupa—a stone memorial tower shaped like a pagoda. The landscaped grounds also host sixteen different species of pine trees, including the bristlecone pine, which is believed to be the oldest living tree species on earth.

Waterfalls, pools, and two lakes add the relaxing sounds of water to the landscape. They also provide a home for fish, ducks, blue herons, and white egrets. The gardens also host an annual outdoor sculpture exhibit featuring the work of nationally prominent sculptors.

The Schedel Arboretum and Gardens is located at 19255 West Portage River South Road, Elmore; (419) 862–3182; www.schedel-gardens.org. Open May through October, Tuesday through Saturday, 10:00 A.M. to 4:00 P.M.; Sunday, noon to 4:00 P.M. Admission: adults $8.00; children, $6.00.

The **Magee Marsh Wildlife Area,** adjoining Crane Creek State Park, is a 2,000-acre wildlife area. This wetland is both home to a wide variety of birds and animals, and a resting and feeding place for migratory waterfowl, making it a particular favorite with bird watchers. Bring binoculars and look for warblers and waterfowl, and maybe one of Ohio's small but growing number of bald eagles. More than 300 bird species have been sighted at the marsh, and 143 species are known to nest there. Turtles, frogs, and toads are also residents of the marsh, along with muskrats, mink, raccoons, rabbits, and white-tailed deer.

Visitors can enjoy three walking trails, each about a mile long. You can also take a drive down the road to the beach to get a flavor of the marsh environment. The Crane Creek State Park beach is open for swimming and picnicking in the summer months.

The Magee Marsh Wildlife Area is at 13229 West Route 2, Oak Harbor; (419) 836–7758.

A half dozen islands are sprinkled in Lake Erie just north of Catawba and Marblehead peninsulas. Easily accessible by air or ferry, Put-in-Bay is the center of activity on South Bass Island. A large protected harbor attracts boaters, who often dock their vessels overnight.

This safe harbor also attracted Commodore Oliver Hazard Perry in 1813. His fleet lay at anchor here before defeating the British fleet commanded by Captain Robert H. Barclay in the Battle of Lake Erie on September 10, 1813. To commemorate Perry's triumph and pay tribute to the subsequent decades of peaceful relations between the United States and Canada along their lengthy, unfortified border, a monument was constructed at Put-in-Bay. This 352-foot-tall column, built of pink granite from Milford, Massachusetts, has a 45-foot-diameter base. It was built between 1912 and 1915 and is the world's largest Doric column. ***The Perry Victory and International Peace Memorial's*** observation deck is open to the public daily from late April to late October.

First-class nautical memorabilia abound at Robert Stone's and William Timmerman's ***Cargo Net.*** You can find (and purchase) everything from authentic ships' wheels and massive brass bells to pottery and nautical art in this fabulous shop, which does its own antique nautical-item restoration. Many antique pieces are available—a World War II Navy submarine periscope mounted on a custom mahogany base at $19,500 during our last visit. Also displayed was a spectacular 1870s telescope ($6,200), and a 135-pound ship's bell ($950), plus two magnificent original English pub bars. For those who hear the call of the sea, a visit to the Cargo Net is a must!

The Cargo Net is at 1961 Langram Road, Put-in-Bay; (419) 285–4231; www.thecargonet.com. Open weekends noon to 5:00 P.M. in May, daily during the summer.

After a walking tour of the town of Put-in-Bay, it's time to explore other points on this small, wooded island. Bicycles and golf carts are two of the most enjoyable ways to survey South Bass, and rentals are available. Trams, buses, and taxis also transport visitors around the island.

About halfway across the island from Put-in-Bay (ten minutes by bicycle) on Catawba Road is ***Heineman's Winery and Crystal Cave.*** Heineman's offers tours of both a unique geode cave and its winery and sells wine by the glass, bottle, or case. The cave, 40 feet beneath the surface, is actually an unusually large geode. Geodes (stones with a cavity lined with crystal) are relatively common in nature, but they are normally no larger than a baseball or softball. The Crystal Cave geode is large enough to hold thirty people. It was created under pressure over 4.5 million years. The cave remains a cool fifty-two degrees year-round, and guides explain the history and geology of this unique formation.

After the cave tour, join another guide for a tour of the winery. Heineman's grows approximately 40 percent of the grapes they need, purchasing the rest from other island vineyards. From twelve different kinds of grapes, Heineman's produces twenty wines, plus fresh grape juice, with an output of 30,000 gallons of wine and juice annually. The Lake Erie islands are ideally suited for vineyards because of the soil's high limestone content and a relatively late frost, thanks to the warming influence of Lake Erie.

On the winery tour, visitors can see large presses that squeeze 180 gallons of juice from each ton of grapes. The grapes ferment in oak barrels, some holding as much as 1,680 gallons, or in stainless-steel tanks. Other stops on the winery tour include the bottling, labeling, and packing areas.

After your tour, enjoy a glass of Heineman's wine in the wine garden, which has picnic tables and nicely kept gardens. Cheese plates are also served.

Heineman's Winery and Crystal Cave tours are given from mid-May through mid-September, 11:00 A.M. to 5:00 P.M. daily. The winery and cave are at 978 Catawba Avenue, Put-in-Bay; (419) 285–2811; www.ohiowine.com. Admission for the combined tour is $6.00 for adults and $2.00 for children ages 6 to 11, and it includes a complimentary glass of wine or grape juice.

Across the street from Heineman's is another cave—a much larger one— known as **Perry's Cave.** Commodore Oliver Hazard Perry is credited with the discovery of this limestone cavern, which measures 208 feet by 165 feet and is 52 feet below the surface. Perry used water from the cave to fill the water kegs for his ships prior to the Battle of Lake Erie in 1813.

Along the north wall of the cave is a large lake of crystal-clear water, which rises and falls with the level of Lake Erie. The luxurious Victory Hotel, once the largest hotel in the world, pumped water from this lake for its drinking water. The hotel burned down in 1919, and its ruins are on the south side of the island on the grounds of South Bass Island State Park. Also on the park's grounds are gemstone mining areas where you can sift for semiprecious gemstones, an antique car museum, and a miniature golf course.

Perry's Cave is open weekends in spring and fall, daily during summer months, 10:30 A.M. to 6:00 P.M. The cave is located near Put-in-Bay; (419) 285–2405; www.perryscave.com. Admission: adults $7.00; children (ages 6 to 12) $4.50.

The Lake Erie islands bustle with modern-day visitors during the summer season, but the **Stonehenge Estate Tour** on South Bass Island allows you a quiet retreat to life on the island one hundred years ago.

The estate is an example of the type of family farm and winery that was common on the island in the late 1800s. Both the historic stone farmhouse and the winepress cottage are on the National Register of Historic Places. Antiques, photographs, and island memorabilia in the house and the cottage help you catch the spirit of turn-of-the-twentieth-century island life.

Stonehenge Estate

The estate covers seven acres. Visitors tour the landscaped grounds, as well as search for souvenirs in the gift shop. A self-guided audio tour also is available.

Stonehenge Estate Tour is located on South Bass Island, 808 Langram Road, Put-in-Bay; (419) 285–6134; www.stonehenge-put-in-bay.com. Open daily during the summer, 11:00 A.M. to 5:00 P.M. Admission: adults $5.00; children (ages 6 to 15) $2.00.

English Pines Bed and Breakfast provides quality overnight lodging for visitors not ready to ferry back to the mainland. This home, within walking distance of "downtown," dates from the island's early settlement in the mid-1800s and features ornate flourishes. The inn's guest rooms each can accommodate up to four people and have private baths. A continental breakfast is included.

English Pines Bed and Breakfast is at 182 Concord Avenue, Put-in-Bay; (419) 285–2521; www.englishpines.com. Rates: $60 to $165 per night.

Couples only, please, for stays at the romantic ***Wisteria Inn Bed and Breakfast.*** One of Put-In-Bay's lovely old homes can now be home to your special getaway. The brick structure was originally built in the 1860s as a single family home. Guests will enjoy the light and airy interior that captures the charm of a lake home of a century ago. While much of the feel of the property captures a bygone era, the house has been updated with air conditioning, and a hot tub and decks now provide a modern retreat in the home's garden. Continental breakfast is served on weekdays and a full breakfast on weekends. Inn rooms share bathrooms.

Wisteria Inn Bed and Breakfast is located at 1331 Langram Road, Put-in-Bay; (419) 285–2828; www.putinbaywisteriainn.com. Rates: from $125 to $300 per night. Visa and MasterCard are accepted.

Traveling to South Bass Island is relatively easy most of the year, with Miller Boat Line, providing ferry service from the Catawba peninsula to the south end of the island; (800) 500–2421; www.millerferry.com. The company ferries both autos and passengers, though reservations are sometimes required for automobiles. Ferry service to the island is available only from March through December, because the island is iced-in during winter months.

The fastest boats from Port Clinton to downtown Put-in-Bay are Jet Express's hydrojet catamarans, which make the trip in twenty-two minutes. These 3,500-horsepower, super-modern vessels run circles around the older ferry boats as they zip you to and from South Bass Island. For more information call Jet Express at (800) 245–1538; www.jet-express.com.

Are you dreaming of a walk along a beach, away from cars and the bustle of life? Rather than hop a plane to the Caribbean you can hop on a ferry and spend some relaxing days at *St. Hazards on the Beach* on Middle Bass Island. The resort has villas, cabins, and campsites. Cabins sleep up to four people, and the villas can sleep up to six. Both have refrigerators and microwaves; the villas have a full kitchen. You will have to bring your own towels and linens. For water enthusiasts there is a heated pool and Jacuzzi, along with 200 feet of private beach. The complex also features an on-site store, restaurant, and bike rentals. Call in advance for reservations and ferry information.

St. Hazards is on 1223 Fox Road, Middle Bass; (419) 285–6121, (800) 837–5211; www.sthazards.com. Campground rates: $24 to $45 per night; lodging rates: $49 to $385 per night. Visa and MasterCard are accepted.

The Lake Erie islands and nearby coastal towns were once the center of champagne production in the United States, and that tradition continues at the historic *Mon Ami Winery,* which also houses a pleasant restaurant. This winery has been in continuous operation since 1870, producing champagne by the old-fashioned "method champenoise," the French technique of fermenting in the bottle.

Constructed of native stone and walnut, the restaurant and winery are surrounded by tall trees and lovely gardens. Old aging barrels are stacked behind the building and are available for sale. Natural woods, exposed stone, classy murals, and intimate spaces dominate the main dining room.

The dinner menu at Mon Ami presents delights such as slow-roasted garlic prime rib, poultry, veal, and fresh pastas. For seafood lovers, a half dozen entrees are offered, including scampi a la pesto; swordfish, salmon, and halibut with black bean sauce; and fresh Lake Erie walleye and perch. After your dinner, the dessert cart will tempt you with sweets: cheesecake topped with chocolate, Amaretto pie, and fresh fruit, to name a few. For lunch at Mon Ami, your choices include homemade soups, fresh salads, a number of sandwiches, and entrees such as salmon patties, seafood pasta, and chicken Parmesan.

Mon Ami offers a complete selection of wines and champagnes, made from Lake Erie island grapes, and a large wine store sells bottles and cases of these wines, as well as the popular champagne–celery seed salad dressing. Tours of the winery are given daily at 2:00 and 4:00 P.M. (times may change, so call ahead).

Mon Ami Restaurant and Winery is on Catawba Island (which used to be an island but is now a peninsula) at 3845 East Wine Cellar Road, just off Route 53, east of Port Clinton; (419) 797–4445, (800) 777–4266; www.monamiwinery.com. Open Monday through Saturday, 11:30 A.M. to 10:00 P.M.; Sunday, 11:30 A.M. to 8:00 P.M. MasterCard, Visa, and American Express are accepted.

The *Five Bells Inn* is an interesting Dutch Colonial structure built in 1907. Located on two and a half acres, this bed and breakfast offers a grassy lawn that leads down to the beach on Lake Erie. From the back porch guests have a good view of the lake—and you can enjoy that view while soaking in the inn's hot tub. The inn does have beach access as well as porches and decks for relaxing in the great outdoors.

Rooms are decorated in light and airy colors—giving the guest that summer cottage feeling. Each of the rooms has a private bath. Rooms four and seven have a whirlpool tub (but no shower). Rooms one through five are in the main house. Rooms six through eight are in a cottage behind the main house. Breakfast is included with the inn rooms.

Besides the inn rooms, there is also a two-bedroom cottage for rent during the off-season. Breakfast is not included with the cottage rental, but it is equipped with a full kitchen, linens, and tableware. Guests in the cottage also have access to the hot tub and the beach. The cottage rents for $175 per night.

The Five Bells Inn is located at 2766 Sand Road, Port Clinton; (419) 734–1555, (888) 734–1555; www.5bellsinn.com. Rates: May 15 through September 30, from $129 to $139 per night; the rest of the year, from $89 to $99.

The *Scenic Rock Ledge Inn and Cabins* offers two options for the vacationer. You can stay in one of the freestanding cabins or enjoy a bed-and-breakfast experience while staying at the historic inn. The inn was built around 1900 and has lovely views of the lake. Guests in the five rooms and one suite have private baths and queen-size beds and are treated to breakfast in the morning. The suite also has a whirlpool tub, a lake view, and a fireplace.

The cabins afford a different experience. Some have lake views, and all have fully equipped kitchens, including a microwave, coffeemaker, and tableware. For that outdoor cooking experience, cabin guests also have outdoor grills and picnic tables. The cabins are more rustic than the romantic inn rooms. Cabins, like inn rooms, do have air conditioning, and they vary in size and floor plans. Some cabins have one bedroom; others have two. All can sleep four people (but some on a sleeper sofa). Two bathrooms are also available in some units.

Scenic Rock Ledge Inn and Cabins is located at 2772 East Sand Road, Port Clinton; (419) 734–3265, (877) 994–ROCK; www.scenicrockledgeinn.com. Rates: from $79 to $149 for rooms and $99 to $199 for the suite. Cabins run between $89 and $249 per night. Visa, MasterCard, and American Express are accepted.

Not far away is one of the most popular public beaches on Lake Erie—the lengthy stretch of sand at *East Harbor State Park.* Lifeguards watch swimmers during summer months, and there are snack bars and bathhouses (with showers). Unfortunately, a fierce storm in 1972 severely damaged the original beach area, and it is no longer open to swimmers.

In addition to the lakefront beach, the park contains 800 acres of water in three protected harbors. Middle Harbor, with its restriction on motorboats, offers an ideal environment for the thousands of resident and migratory waterfowl attracted to the lush acreage, making bird-watching a favorite pastime. East Harbor State Park is the home of many black-crowned night herons, and a large great blue heron nesting ground is nearby.

Boat launching ramps are in the park, and a park naturalist conducts nature programs during the summer. Winter sports at East Harbor include ice fishing, ice boating, skating, sledding, and snowmobiling.

East Harbor State Park is at 1169 North Buck Road off Route 269, near the junction of Routes 269 and 163, Marblehead; (419) 734–4424; www.dnr.state .oh.us/parks /parks/eastharbor.htm.

The seventy-six-room *Hotel Lakeside,* a large Victorian structure painted off-white, faces Lake Erie on a shady lot at the water's edge. This three-story frame hotel was built in 1875, with additions completed in 1879 and 1890. The hotel is part of the community of Lakeside, a 1-square-mile educational, cultural, recreational, and religious center listed on the National Register of Historic Places. Lakeside consists of hotels, cottages, private homes, shops, restaurants, and recreation facilities, which are used by both guests and residents of this unique village. A modest gate fee is levied during summer months, and with payment of that fee, visitors may use the tennis courts, playgrounds, and volleyball and basketball courts, and may swim and fish off the community's pier. Included in the gate fee are daily seminars and lectures, and nightly entertainment. The Lakeside Summer Symphony performs in August.

At the Hotel Lakeside, a large yet homey structure, guests can enjoy the evening paper on the long screened porch or on the lawn furniture between the hotel and Lake Erie. The spacious lobby is furnished with wicker chairs and couches and a variety of antiques. The guest rooms are gradually being restored with period wallpapers and furnishings such as marble-topped wash-stands. All have the high ceilings of the era and air conditioning, and many come equipped with ceiling fans.

From the pier, visitors and residents of Lakeside enjoy colorful sunsets, and sailing lessons are available. The shuffleboard and miniature golf areas attract crowds on warm summer evenings in this family-oriented community. Lakeside may not be everyone's ideal vacation or getaway choice—those looking for chic nightclubs will surely be disappointed. But for those who seek a serene and peaceful place to enjoy Lake Erie, Lakeside may be the perfect destination.

The Hotel Lakeside is north of Route 163 off North Shore Boulevard in Lakeside; (419) 798–4461, (866) 952–5374; www.lakesideohio.com. The hotel is open Memorial Day to Labor Day. Rates: $60 to $198 per night. MasterCard and Visa are accepted.

Standing guard at what is known as the "roughest point in Lake Erie," the **_Marblehead Lighthouse_** is the oldest continuously operating lighthouse on the Great Lakes. The shallow water in this part of the lake, along with 200 miles of open water between Buffalo and Marblehead, allows howling northeasters to generate waves 10 to 15 feet tall.

The crash of those waves against the rocks around the lighthouse often shoots spray all the way up to the beacon 67 feet above the water. The Marblehead Lighthouse, built of native limestone in 1821, originally used candles for its light. The candles were replaced by oil-burning lamps, which in turn were replaced by an electric light and a 300-millimeter glass lens, which make the beacon visible for 7 miles.

Although rough water often bashes this peninsula in the spring and fall, peaceful days prevail in the summer. Picnic tables near the lighthouse make this an excellent place to stop and relax as you explore the

Marblehead Lighthouse

Lake Erie shoreline. The Keepers House contains displays relating to the lighthouse and the peninsula's history, plus a small gift shop.

The Marblehead Lighthouse is off Route 163 in Marblehead. Open for tours weekdays, 1:00 to 5:00 P.M.; no admission charge.

One man's love of model trains multiplied by more than forty years' work has produced the *Train-O-Rama.* Max Timmons took up model railroading in 1952, and his family carried on his dream of creating a model-train world that would exhilarate model train enthusiasts and charm everyone.

The miniature world created at Train-O-Rama is alive with two dozen operating model trains and some remarkable landscape features—12,000 pieces of train equipment in all. The display features 0, 0-27 gauges, S-gauge, and HO gauge. Within a few feet you can pass by a whole range of mountains, see rivers and waterfalls, drop by a drive-in movie theater, and go to the circus. The display has more than 1,000 light bulbs flickering on miniature street lamps or in windows. Along with the trains there are many moving pieces that help the scenes come alive, whether it is a farm field, a ski lodge, or the airport.

Judging from the visitor map that the Train-O-Rama keeps, people from around the world share Max's fascination for model trains. Guests from all fifty states and seventy-four foreign countries have all documented their visit to the tiny world of Train-O-Rama.

Visitors can begin or add to their own train sets at the gift shop. Model trains, train supplies, and train-related gift items are for sale.

Train-O-Rama is located at 6732 East Harbor Road (Route 163), Marblehead; (419) 734–5856; www.trainorama.com. Open Monday through Saturday, 11:00 A.M. to 5:00 P.M.; Sunday, 1:00 to 5:00 P.M. Extended summer hours: Monday through Saturday, 10:00 A.M. to 5:00 P.M.; Sunday, 1:00 to 5:00 P.M. Admission: adults $6.00; children (ages 4 to 11) $4.00; seniors (60-plus) $5.00.

Four miles north of Marblehead and 9 miles northwest of Sandusky is *Kelleys Island.* It was originally called Cunningham Island, named for the island's first white inhabitant, who lived here from 1800 to 1812. But Native Americans visited the island sometime between A.D. 1200 and 1600 and created the inscriptions (or pictographs) pecked into the 32-by-21-foot flat-topped slab of limestone known as *Inscription Rock.* The rock rests on the water's edge on the south side of the island, and its pictographs have nearly been erased by erosion. Fortunately, a visitor here in 1850, U.S. Army Captain Seth Eastman, made a permanent record of the inscriptions. He carefully measured and drew in detail the pictographs, and, from his drawings, reliefs have been made of the inscriptions. These reliefs, including the one exhibited at Inscription Rock, clearly reveal at least eight human figures wearing headdresses etched in the rock, plus bird and animal figures.

Inscription Rock is near the intersection of Water Street and Addison Road on the south side of Kelleys Island; (419) 797–4530; www.ohiohistory.org/places/inscript. Open daylight hours; no admission charge.

The quarries on 2,800-acre Kelleys Island once supplied 500 one thousand-ton boatloads of limestone annually, and vineyards, wineries, and fruit and vegetable farms flourished. At the turn of the century, the island had a year-round population of 1,700. Today, the quarries have closed and farming activity has declined, but the island, with a year-round population of approximately one hundred, offers restaurants, lodging, bicycle and boat rentals, and tram tours to visitors.

The site of the *Glacial Grooves* is on the north side of Kelleys island. A glacier moving down from Labrador, Canada, scoured these grooves into the limestone bedrock. The grooved limestone is a trough 400 feet long, 25 to 35 feet wide, and 10 to 15 feet deep, and it's one of the most accessible examples of such grooves in the world.

These grooves were formed at a time when this part of the earth was much colder and wetter than today. Snow and ice would not completely melt during the short summers 30,000 years ago, so an ever-deeper mass of frozen snow accumulated. As the weight of this mass increased, the glacier crept southward at the rate of an inch or two per day, taking 5,000 years to arrive at the site of the Glacial Grooves. The pressure of that mass, which was up to a mile deep, carved the grooves still visible in the island's limestone. Even more spectacular grooves once existed in this area, but they were destroyed by a nearby quarrying operation.

The Glacial Grooves are at the north end of Division Street, Kelleys Island; (419) 797–4530; www.ohiohistory.org/places/glacial. Open daylight hours; no admission charge.

Just across the road from the Glacial Grooves is Kelleys Island State Park. The park offers campsites (rented on a first-come, first-served basis), a sandy swimming beach, and boat ramps; (419) 746–2546.

The Kelleys Island Ferry Boat Line provides daily ferry service between Kelleys Island and Marblehead from April through December; (419) 798–9763, (888) 225–4325; www.kelleyislandferry.com. The Griffing Flying Service provides air transport to the island from the Griffing-Sandusky Airport; (419) 626–5161.

If you aren't ready to take the last ferry back to the mainland, stay overnight on Kelleys at the *Eagle's Nest Bed & Breakfast.* Three rooms are available in the guest house, which is separate from the residence of owners Mark and Robin Volz. The upper unit is a one-bedroom apartment with a living room (and queen-size sofa bed), bedroom, small kitchen, private bath, and sundeck. The two downstairs units each have a microwave and refrigerator, a private bath, and plenty of country charm.

Eagle's Nest Bed & Breakfast is at 216 Cameron Road, Kelleys Island; (419) 746–2708 (summer), (419) 625–9635 (winter); www.eaglesnestbnb.com. Rates: $95 to $125 per night. Visa and MasterCard accepted.

Back on the mainland, amusement park aficionados will definitely want to visit one of Ohio's most popular parks, *Cedar Point.* Situated at the tip of a long, narrow peninsula jutting out into Lake Erie, this 364-acre park delights guests with a wide assortment of rides, more than one hundred entertainers performing in live shows, and a huge eighteen-acre water park. However, it is the park's unmatched collection of roller coasters that attracts visitors from all over the country. Sixteen in all, they range from junior coasters to the Millennium Force, which drops 300 feet at 93 miles per hour, and the 420-foot-tall, 120-miles-per-hour Top Thrill Dragster, the tallest and fastest roller coaster in the world.

For those needing accommodations at Cedar Point, the park has its own 650-room lakeside hotel, an all-suites hotel, RV campground, and the new Lighthouse Point upscale camping complex with cabins, cottages, and luxury RV sites. Hotels rooms range from $115 to $600 per night, while standard six-person suites at Sandcastle Suites range from $175 to $400 per night. The cottages and cabins accommodate six people and range from $135 to $275 per night. Only a short drive away is the Breakers Express, a 350-room value-priced hotel, and the Radisson Harbour Inn. Prices at Breakers Express range from $71 to $184 per night, while rates at the Radisson Harbour Inn range from $109 to $305 per night. Accommodations are available early May through the end of October. Two-night packages are available throughout the summer. For reservations, call (419) 627–2106. Cedar Point also has two marinas with slips available for day rental.

Cedar Point is on the Cedar Point Causeway, north of Sandusky; (419) 627–2350; www.cedarpoint.com. Open early May through August plus weekends in September and October.

On the square in the heart of downtown Sandusky, in a magnificent 1920s neoclassical building that once housed the city's post office, is the unique *Merry-Go-Round Museum.* The centerpiece of the museum is a fully restored and operational Allen Herschell carousel; a ride on this indoor gem is an absolute must. But there is much more to discover in this fabulous structure, now listed on the National Register of Historic Places.

Stop by and watch carousel carvers at work. They will explain and show you what it takes to restore neglected pieces, returning them to their full beauty. The museum includes a series of restoration workshops. Also on display are many examples of classic carousel animals, including those of Gustav Dentzel. A replica of his Philadelphia Caroussell Builder shop, which opened in 1867, is authentic down to the sign over the door, the tools on the wall, the workbenches, and the partially carved animals.

The Merry-Go-Round Museum is at the corner of West Washington and Jackson Streets at 301 Jackson, Sandusky; (419) 626–6111; www.merrygoround museum.org. Open March through December, Wednesday through Saturday, 11:00 A.M. to 5:00 P.M.; Sunday, noon to 5:00 P.M.; weekends only in January and February. Admission: adults $5.00; children (ages 4 to 14) $3.00.

For tranquil accommodations in the heart of Lake Erie vacation country, try a comfortable Sandusky bed-and-breakfast, **Wagner's 1844 Inn.** This fine old structure features three guest rooms, each with a private bath, a Victorian parlor with an antique Steinway piano, a living room with a wood-burning fireplace, and a screened porch and enclosed courtyard.

Innkeeper Barbara Wagner decided the time was right for a bed-and-breakfast after her child moved away from home. Barbara gave up her full-time nursing career to operate her own business. As she puts it, "Since I love to cook, entertain, and decorate, a bed-and-breakfast was a logical choice."

Breakfast is served in the formal dining room in the winter and on the porch in summer. A typical morning meal includes fresh fruit and juice, baked rolls or muffins (perhaps the popular pecan rolls), muesli cereal, or a German pancake. Once the home of grocer and dry goods store owner William Simpson, one of the founders of Sandusky, the 1844 Inn is today loaded with antiques. Its style is Italianate, and it is listed on the National Register of Historic Places.

Wagner's 1844 Inn is at 230 East Washington Street, Sandusky; (419) 626–1726; www.bbonline.com/oh/wagners. Rates: $70 to $100 per night, double occupancy, including continental breakfast. Cash, checks, MasterCard, and Visa accepted. Reservations recommended.

A bed-and-breakfast with an in-ground swimming pool is hardly typical; **Captain Montague's** offers that and more. A lakefront park, beach, boat basin, amphitheater, and pier are just 2 blocks away. And visitors enjoy murder mystery weekends throughout the year; this bed-and-breakfast has earned top honors for its creative murder mystery series.

Judy and Mike Tann offer accommodations in their Southern Colonial–style home, which is a generous 6,200 square feet. Built in 1876, the home has four Victorian guest bedrooms, each with a private bath, and one suite.

Captain Montague's is named for ship captain Charles Montague, who made the house famous for its grand parties at the turn of the century. Four of the guest rooms are named in honor of the Captain, his wife Sarah, son Newton, and daughter Edith.

The intricately carved solid black walnut front staircase, and the parlor and dining room mantles, are exquisite. The large gazebo, once a carriage house, offers a relaxing place to enjoy the inviting pool surrounded by begonia-filled hanging baskets and an ivy-covered white lattice fence; the Amish-built, adult-size swing set; and the well-manicured gardens, which have garnered numerous awards.

Captain Montague's is at 229 Center Street, Huron; (419) 433–4756, (800) 276–4756; www.captainmontagues.com. Rates: $110 to $155 per night, double occupancy, including breakfast. Visa and MasterCard accepted. Reservations and a deposit required.

The achievements of Ohio-born Thomas Edison are staggering—he invented the phonograph, the incandescent light, the motion picture camera, the fluoroscope, and the nickel-iron-alkaline battery. In fact, at the time of his death Edison held 1,093 different American patents.

The *Edison Birthplace Museum* in Milan provides an opportunity for visitors to learn more about this prolific inventor. Edison's father, Samuel, was involved in the Papineau-Mackenzie Rebellion, an unsuccessful Canadian counterpart to the American Revolution. Samuel migrated to Milan in 1839, attracted by the boom in shipping created there by the canal linking Milan, an inland community, with Lake Erie. In fact, in the 1840s, Milan was one of the world's major grain ports and shipbuilding centers. For example, in 1847, 918,000 bushels of grain were shipped from Milan, and fourteen warehouses loaded as many as twenty schooners per day—amazing statistics for a town 8 miles from the lakefront! Milan's boom was short-lived, however, for the coming of the railroad and the flood of 1868 ended the town's brief heyday as a port.

The small, redbrick house where Thomas Edison was born on February 11, 1847, is just up the hill from the former location of Milan's warehouses and port. The Edison home and adjacent small museum contain a number of his inventions—an early mimeograph machine (which Edison sold to the A.B. Dick Company in 1887), phonographs, telegraph equipment, dictating machines, motion picture cameras—and a model of Edison's 1893 movie studio, called the "Black Maria," which rotated and had an adjustable opening in the roof to allow sunlight to illuminate the stage.

Pictures of Edison with family and friends like Henry Ford adorn the walls

huron's shipbuilding era

Lake Erie's coastal communities boomed during the early nineteenth century as trade along the lake expanded. Villages located at the mouths of rivers feeding the lake often had natural harbors, and Huron was no exception. Here shipbuilding flourished, including the construction of the mighty steamships—the royalty of lake vessels. The steamer *Walk-in-the-Water* kicked off the steamship era on Lake Erie in 1818, but met a tragic end when it went down off Buffalo. Huron's shipbuilding dominance ended with the construction of the canal at nearby Milan.

of the home, and Edison's hat, cape, cane, and slippers are displayed, as is an unusual pig-shaped footstool. Edison bought his birthplace from his sister's family in 1906 and was shocked to find on a visit here in 1923 that this house did not yet have electric lights, a situation he quickly remedied.

The Edison Birthplace Museum is north of Route 113 at 9 North Edison Drive, Milan; (419) 499–2135; www.tomedison.org. Open February, March, November, and December, Wednesday through Sunday, 1:00 to 4:00 P.M.; April, May, September, and October, Tuesday through Sunday, 1:00 to 5:00 P.M.; June, July, and August, Tuesday through Saturday, 10:00 A.M. to 5:00 P.M., Sunday, 1:00 to 5:00 P.M. Admission: adults $5.00; children (ages 6 to 12) $2.00.

Two blocks from Edison's birthplace is Milan's central business district, which was built around a 1-square-block park. One-hundred-year-old buildings house many of the town's shops, and the shady park makes Milan a pleasant stop.

Vermilion is perhaps Ohio's most picturesque Lake Erie coastal town, with quaint homes set on meandering lagoons, sumptuous sail and power pleasure craft, and fine dining. Vermilion exudes an atmosphere of peacefulness and prosperity, and attracts visitors with sun, seafood, and recreation.

One Vermilion restaurant warrants special attention—***Old Prague Restaurant.*** Set in a delightful cedar structure in the center of Vermilion's shopping district, this distinctive establishment serves both Old World recipes and American favorites. The large, open dining area offers a homey, comfortable setting, and the friendly people at Old Prague make guests feel almost like family.

The specialties at Old Prague are "Nationality Favorites," which include Bohemian goulash, chicken paprikash (farm-fresh chicken in zesty sour cream sauce) and Wiener schnitzel. Two other popular entrees are roast duck and roast pork, which are served with sauerkraut. All meals come with traditional egg dumplings or spaetzles.

American dinner entrees include Boston strip steak, ham steak, grilled chicken breast, and roast chicken with stuffing. Those who favor fish can choose from a half dozen dinners such as fresh Lake Erie perch, scallops, broiled salmon, or a fisherman's platter. Lighter fare includes sandwiches, vegetarian risotto, cabbage rolls, salads, and appetizers. Two homemade soups are served daily.

The Old Prague Restaurant is at 5586 Liberty Avenue (U.S. Route 6), Vermilion; (440) 967–7182; www.oldprague.com. Open daily June through October, Friday through Sunday, November through February; and Wednesday through Sunday, March through May. Weekday hours are 4:00 to 10:00 P.M.; Saturday and Sunday, noon to 10:00 P.M. MasterCard and Visa are accepted.

The ***Inland Seas Maritime Museum,*** appropriately located on the Lake Erie shore in picturesque Vermilion, has two floors of marine exhibits, photos, and paintings dedicated to the history and lore of the Great Lakes. Navigation equipment such as ships' telegraphs, compasses, barographs, and a pelorus (bearing finder) are displayed, as are ships' bells, foghorns, and a collection of old nameboards from Great Lakes schooners, freighters, and steamers. The museum also contains the figurehead (or busthead) from an unidentified schooner, ca. 1855, that was part of the Cheseborough Lumber Company fleet.

Dozens of old life rings are scattered throughout the museum, including one from the ill-fated *Edmund Fitzgerald,* which went down in Lake Superior on November 10, 1975. The lower level houses a prize-winning wooden 18-foot double-ender, built in 1937, and the complete steam engine from the tug *Roger,* built in 1913. The museum has also acquired several artifacts from the 1813 Battle of Lake Erie, including some old timbers from Commodore Perry's flagship, *Niagara,* plus a grapnel and spike from that vessel, and the telescope used by Perry's staff during the battle.

The pilot house of the 1905 steamer *Canopus* is open to visitors. Next to the museum is a full-size replica of the 1877 Vermilion lighthouse.

The Inland Seas Maritime Museum is at 480 Main Street, Vermilion; (440) 967–3467, (800) 893–1485; www.inlandseas.org. Open daily 10:00 A.M. to 5:00 P.M. (longer hours weekends and summer). Admission: adults $6.00; children (under age 16) $5.00.

Presidential Path

Rutherford B. Hayes (or "Ruddy," as he was known to his friends) was president of the United States exactly one hundred years before Jimmy Carter. For a glimpse at the politics and lifestyle of that era, visit the **Rutherford B. Hayes Presidential Center** in Fremont. The center, on a lush twenty-five acres known as Spiegel Grove, consists of a stately Victorian mansion, the expansive Hayes museum, and a presidential library with more than 70,000 volumes.

The museum contains exhibits from Hayes's early career as a lawyer, first in Fremont (which was then known as Lower Sandusky) and later in Cincinnati. Hayes, in fact, was instrumental in having the name of Lower Sandusky changed to Fremont. With nearby towns named Sandusky, and Upper Sandusky, the residents of Fremont gratefully accepted the change, as did the United States Post Office.

It was in Cincinnati that Hayes became involved in politics, and old party tickets indicate his first race was in 1859 for city solicitor. At the outbreak of the Civil War, Hayes enlisted in the Union army, and a letter from his wife, Lucy Webb Hayes, written to him while he was in the army, is on display. Hayes was wounded several times during the war, seriously at the Battle of South Mountain.

Nominated for a seat in Congress before the war's conclusion, Hayes refused to leave active duty to campaign. After his four years in Congress, he was elected governor of Ohio in 1867 and 1869, and again in 1875. The museum's campaign relics include political cartoons, newspaper clippings, hats, and banners. Hayes's favorite chair, which he used while governor, is also there.

Hayes's election to the presidency took place in 1876, but a dispute over twenty electoral votes was not resolved until March 2, 1877—three days before the inauguration! By an electoral vote count of 185 to 184, Hayes became the nineteenth president of the United States, defeating New York governor Samuel Tilden. Photographs of the inauguration of Hayes are in the museum, as is the Haviland china used by the Hayes White House. A magnificent sideboard carved by Cincinnatian Henry L. Fry for use in the private White House dining room, and the presidential glassware used by presidents from Andrew Jackson through Hayes, are also displayed.

A short walk from the museum across the shady lawn brings you to the elegant Hayes Mansion. This enormous home has thirty-one rooms, and a large front porch faces the towering trees of Spiegel Grove. Members of the Hayes family lived in the mansion until 1965, when it was opened to the public for guided tours.

President and Mrs. Hayes used many of the furnishings now in the home when they returned to Fremont from Washington in 1881. Many of the pieces were gifts from around the world that they received while in the White House. Although each room has lavish appointments, the dining room, with its massive table for twenty-four guests, is exceptional. Fourteen fireplaces warmed the spacious residence, some with mantels of Italian marble, others of hand-carved hardwoods with tile insets. The 13-foot ceilings in the drawing room are just tall enough to accommodate the life-sized portrait of Hayes and its ornate frame. Throughout the home are the original gas lighting fixtures, which have been converted to electricity.

The Rutherford B. Hayes Presidential Center is at the corner of Buckland and Hayes Avenues in Fremont; (419) 332–2081; www.rbhayes.org. The museum and residence are open Monday through Saturday, 9:00 A.M. to 5:00 P.M.; Sunday and holidays, noon to 5:00 P.M. Admission: adults $6.00 for museum or residence; children (ages 7 to 12) $2.00 for museum or residence. The library is open Monday through Saturday, 9:00 A.M. to 5:00 P.M.; no admission charge.

For collectors, the city of Tiffin is well known for its distinctive glass. That legacy continues at *Crystal Traditions of Tiffin.* This glass manufacturing company welcomes visitors to observe glassblowing and handwheel engraving. Sand carving and crystal repair are other services offered. The showroom sells both the company's best and crystal giftware and quality art glass from throughout the world. The outlet offers seconds, closeouts, and discontinued items.

Crystal Traditions of Tiffin is at 145 Madison Street, Tiffin; (419) 448–4286,

(888) 298–7236; www.crystaltraditions.com. Open Monday through Friday, 10:00 A.M. to 5:00 P.M.; Saturday, 10:00 A.M. to 2:00 P.M. No admission charge.

Fort Ball Bed & Breakfast is a fine example of a Queen Anne Revival–style home built at the turn of the century. John King, who also built College Hall at Heidelberg College and the courthouse in Tiffin, built this home. Guests are intrigued by the turret at the front of the home, its wraparound porch, and the lovely details uncovered and refinished during a recent renovation.

It took the innkeeper a year's worth of work to restore the elaborate woodworking in the parlor, the hardwood floors, and the elegant wood paneling to their former elegance. The house now boasts a variety of guest rooms. Some have private baths; others share a bath. Some even come equipped with an in-room whirlpool tub for two. In the mornings, guests enjoy breakfast in the dining room and can then set off on a short walk to nearby antiques shops and museums.

Fort Ball Bed & Breakfast is located at 25 Adams Street, Tiffin; (419) 447–0776, (888) 447–0776; www.fortball.com. Rates: $65 to $95 per night.

The Firelands region of Ohio takes its name from the Revolutionary War period. While the British held New York City, they made frequent raids against the coastal towns in Connecticut, burning homes, barns, and stores. After the conflict, the citizens petitioned the new state of Connecticut for compensation for their losses, and, in 1792, the "fire-sufferers" were awarded land on the western edge of Connecticut's Western Reserve lands in Ohio—the Firelands.

The **Firelands Museum** is operated by the Firelands Historical Society, the second-oldest such society in the state. The museum was described by the society's first members as merely a "cabinet of curios," but today hundreds of items are on display in the two-story Preston-Wickham House, which local newspaper editor Samuel Preston built in 1835 as a wedding present for his daughter, Lucy, and her husband, Frederick Wickham. The extensive gun collection includes dozens of weapons: pistols, rifles, and muskets, some made before the American Revolution, plus military swords and knives. In the Native American exhibit, moccasins, beads, baskets, and tomahawks, as well as ancient points, gouges, and hatchets are displayed.

The basement is filled with an impressive group of pioneer tools, such as a 6-foot blacksmith's bellows, a yarn winder and spinning wheel, butter churns, farm implements, and game traps. On the second floor is a marvelous wooden Indian (ca. 1860) that once stood in front of a local tobacco shop, and the bell clapper from the old Norwalk courthouse that burned down in 1913 (the bell melted in the heat). Period clothing and personal items from early residents of the region are exhibited, as is the first organ manufactured by Norwalk's A.B. Chase Company in the 1870s.

The Firelands Museum is at 4 Case Avenue, Norwalk; (419) 668–6038.

Open weekends in April, May, September, October, and November, noon to 4:00 P.M. From June through August, the museum is open Tuesday through Sunday, noon to 5:00 P.M. Admission: adults $3.00; children (ages 12 to 18) $2.00.

The elegant exterior of the ***Georgian Manor Inn*** reflects the civility and elegance of another era. The Georgian Revival Home, built in 1906 by a local dentist, is now an elegant bed-and-breakfast nicely located on 1.4 acres and surrounded by a number of large historic homes and estates. Each of the four guest rooms in the twenty-seven-room mansion is decorated with antiques and reproductions. The sunroom, the library, the living room with its oak-mantled fireplace, and the parlor offer comfortable indoor surroundings, but guests are often drawn to the tranquility of the gardens and two porches. A patio looks out over a three-foot waterfall and small stream that flows into a lovely pond. In spring and summer, the gardens are filled with the color and scent of a variety of herbs and flowers.

The Georgian Manor Inn is at 123 West Main Street, Norwalk; (419) 663–8132, (800) 668–1644; www.georgianmanorinn.com. Lodging rates: $95 to $180 per night. American Express, Visa, and MasterCard are accepted.

When John Wright arrived in America in 1843, a young man of twenty, he dreamed of one day building a vast estate similar to those in his native England. Forty years later, after acquiring 2,400 acres, he established a sawmill and kiln to prepare lumber and brick for what is today known as ***Wright Mansion.***

When listed on the National Register of Historic Places in 1974, the Wright family home was declared significant as "an unusually substantial and stately example of the Second Empire–style mansion found as a relatively isolated farmhouse rather than an urban residence." But for a "farmhouse," Wright's

Georgian Manor Inn

Wright Mansion

home was constructed with many surprisingly modern conveniences, thanks to his ingenuity. For example, he installed two bathrooms with running water and flush toilets that were supplied with water pumped by a windmill to a large tank on the third floor. This at a time—the 1880s—when most rural residences still used water pitchers and chamber pots.

Piped natural gas was unheard of in this country setting before 1900, but Wright developed his own gas system, making acetylene in a small brick building at a corner of his front yard and routing it to chandeliers on all three floors of his home. And a central heating plant in the basement sent hot steam to radiators throughout the house.

The Wright Mansion is the centerpiece of *Historic Lyme Village,* a sixteen-structure collection of historic buildings. Tours of Wright Mansion take visitors past magnificent woodwork used throughout this expansive residence: beams and rafters of oak, and intricate interior trim of walnut, curly maple, and cherry. After walking past the huge parlor doors, visitors find room after room of period furnishings, including Wright's piano. A graceful staircase ascends to the second floor, which has eight bedrooms. Most of the third floor is a huge ballroom, with a stage set directly under the central tower at the front of the home.

More rustic structures make up the rest of Lyme Village. Ohio settler pieces, such as a rope bed, spinning wheel, and wood cooking stove furnish Annie Brown's log home, built in 1851 in Seneca County. Ms. Brown occupied this modest house from 1869 to 1951.

Spinning and weaving exhibits (and occasional demonstrations) can be found in the Schriner Log House, an 1870-vintage structure that was used as a residence until 1947. Other occasional Lyme Village demonstrations include blacksmithing and woodworking at the North Adams Barn, built more than a century ago.

Antique farm implements fill the Biebricher Centennial Barn (erected in 1876), a Gothic board-and-batten building with unusual louvered windows. The Seymour House, moved to Lyme Village in 1976 to save it from demolition, is one of the oldest homes in this part of Ohio, and it served as the Seymour family home for more than a century (1836–1948). It likely was a stop on the Underground Railroad. Today it houses country furnishings typical of the early nineteenth century, including a fabulous old pump organ. Other structures of note include the Merry School House, built in the 1860s and used as a school until 1935; the Detterman Church, built in 1848 and believed to be one of only two known remaining original log churches in Ohio; and Schug Hardware, the hardware collection from Bellevue's C.W. Schug Hardware, which was in business from 1927 until the 1980s. Visitors may also explore the Cooper-Fries General Store, filled with displays and merchandise and the Greenslade Cobbler's Shop.

Lyme Village also includes a unique museum—the Postmark Collectors Club Museum. Formerly housed in private homes, a converted school bus, and in a building that twice served as the Lyme, Ohio, post office, the museum has found a permanent home in the Groton Township Hall. Millions of postmarks—the "cancels" used by postal authorities to show where mail originated and to void stamps—fill the museum, the most extensive such collection in the world.

Historic Lyme Village is at 5001 Route 4, just east of Bellevue; (419) 483–4949; www.lymevillage.com. Tours are given daily except Monday, June through August, 11:00 A.M. to 5:00 P.M. Open Sundays only in May and September. Admission: adults $8.00; students $4.00; children (under age 12) free.

Railroad buffs, youngsters, and anyone who has ever dreamed of being the engineer on a fast-moving freight train as it streaks across the countryside will want to climb aboard the many trains displayed at the ***Mad River & NKP Railroad Society Museum.*** On self-guided tours of the rail yard, you'll discover a number of intriguing locomotives, passenger cars, and even cabooses. Many of these are open, permitting you to virtually walk through railroad history.

Those who are knowledgeable about trains especially appreciate some of the Nickel Plate Road additions to the museum's collection, including Alco RSD-12 Diesel and Dynamometer Car X50041. But anyone will enjoy visiting the RPO Post Office Car, complete with mail sacks, sorting bins, and mail crane. Inside the Nickel Plate Box Car and Fruit Growers Refrigerator Car are extensive displays of railroad models, lanterns, locks, timetables, signs, photos, badges, and the like.

And when you climb into the cab of the museum's Wabash F Diesel, you can't help but imagine yourself racing along the main line from New York to Chicago or crossing the Rockies on your way to deliver freight to the West Coast. From the cupola of a caboose, you get a feel for the working environment at the other end of a long freight train, while tours of America's first dome car demonstrate how trains treated their passengers in days gone by.

An old section house serves as the welcome center for the museum. It's staffed by volunteers, many of them current and former railroad workers who enjoy answering questions and explaining life on the rails. Be sure to ask about upcoming railroad excursions on Ohio tracks.

The Mad River & NKP Railroad Society Museum is on Southwest Street, just south of U.S. Route 20, Bellevue; (419) 483–2222; www.madrivermuseum.org. Open daily, noon to 4:00 P.M., Memorial Day to Labor Day; weekends only in May, September, and October. Admission: adults $7.00; children (ages 3 to 12) $4.00.

Widely known as the "Earth Crack," **Seneca Caverns** was designated a Registered Natural Landmark in 1997. Discovered in 1872, the cave was opened to the public by the Bell family in 1933.

A one-hour tour takes visitors through seven rooms or levels, the deepest 110 feet below the surface to the Ole Mist'ry River. Fossilized fish, shells, and corals are visible throughout the limestone cavern, which remains a cool fifty-four degrees year-round. Comfortable walking shoes are a must! Visitors also may pan for gemstones and minerals at the cavern or browse the gift shop.

Seneca Caverns is off Route 269, 4 miles south of Bellevue; (419) 483–6711; www.senecacavernsohio.com. Open daily Memorial Day to Labor Day, 9:00 A.M. to 7:00 P.M.; weekends only in May and from September to mid-October, 10:00 A.M. to 5:00 P.M. Rates: adults $11.00; children $5.50.

Places to Stay in Northwest Ohio

HURON

Captain Montague's
229 Center Street
(419) 433–4756,
(800) 276–4756

KELLEYS ISLAND

Eagle's Nest Bed & Breakfast
216 Cameron Road
(419) 746–2708 (summer),
(419) 625–9635 (winter)

LAKESIDE

Hotel Lakeside
North of Route 163 on
North Shore Boulevard
(419) 798–4461

MIDDLE BASS ISLAND

St. Hazards on the Beach
(419) 285–6121,
(800) 837–5211

NORWALK

Georgian Manor Inn
123 West Main Street
(419) 663–8132,
(800) 668–1644

PORT CLINTON

Five Bells Inn
2766 Sand Road
(888) 734-1555

Scenic Rock Ledge
Inn and Cabins
2772 East Sand Road
(419) 734-3265

PUT-IN-BAY

English Pines Bed and
Breakfast
182 Concord Avenue
(419) 285-2521

Wisteria Inn Bed
and Breakfast
1331 Langram Road
(419) 285-2828

SANDUSKY

Wagner's 1844 Inn
230 East Washington Street
(419) 626-1726

TIFFIN

Fort Ball Bed & Breakfast
25 Adams Street
(419) 447-0776,
(888) 447-0776

Places to Eat in Northwest Ohio

ARCHBOLD

Barn Restaurant
North of Archbold, ¼ mile
east of State Route 66
(419) 445-2231,
(800) 590-9755

CATAWBA ISLAND

Mon Ami Restaurant
and Winery
3845 East Wine Cellar Road
(800) 777-4266

GRAND RAPIDS

LaRoe's Restaurant
Front Street
(419) 832-3082

TOLEDO

Tony Packo's Cafe
1902 Front Street
(419) 691-6054

VERMILION

Old Prague Restaurant
5586 Liberty Avenue
(440) 967-7182

WATERVILLE

The Columbian House
3 North River Road
(419) 876-3006

HELPFUL WEB SITES

Ohio Division of Travel and Tourism:
www.ohiotourism.com

Toledo Convention and
Visitors Bureau:
www.toledocvb.com

Toledo Blade:
www.toledoblade.com

Ottawa County Visitors Bureau:
www.lake-erie.com

Erie County Visitors Bureau:
www.buckeyenorth.com

Cedar Point:
www.cedarpoint.com

Indexes

Entries for museums and accommodations appear in the special indexes on pages 235–37.

GENERAL INDEX

MUSEUMS

About the Authors

George Zimmermann is a vice president for travel marketing at the Michigan Economic Development Corporation. Having lived in Ohio for more than twenty years, he served as the chairman of the Ohio Bicentennial Commission. For seven years, George was the tourism director for the state of Ohio. Prior to his appointment in October of 1991, he was bureau chief for the Ohio Public Radio/Public Television Statehouse Bureau. He worked in broadcasting for twenty years, primarily for public television stations in Texas and Ohio. He spent two years in Los Angeles editing situation comedies, including *The Jeffersons*.

Carol and George met when she, too, worked as a statehouse reporter. After producing public television programs and producing, reporting, and anchoring in commercial television, Carol Rapp Zimmermann was appointed to the post of assistant director of the Ohio Department of Youth Services in 1992. Carol earned her Ph.D. in 2006 at Michigan State University, where she is a visiting professor. She and George married in 1989.

An inveterate traveler, George Zimmermann has authored two other travel guidebooks: *The Complete Guide to Cabins and Lodges in America's State and National Parks* and *Travel Writers Recommend America's Best Resorts*. He was prompted to write this guide when he moved to Ohio in 1979 and wanted information about Ohio's attractions. He roamed Ohio's back roads for two years researching the points of interest included in the first edition. Together George and Carol add their latest discoveries in subsequent editions. The Zimmermanns live in Lansing with their border collie, Boots.